ALSO BY ANNE TYLER

If Morning Ever Comes

The Tin Can Tree

A Slipping-Down Life

The Clock Winder

Celestial Navigation

Searching for Caleb

Earthly Possessions

Morgan's Passing

Dinner at the Homesick Restaurant

The Accidental Tourist

Breathing Lessons

Saint Maybe

Ladder of Years

A Patchwork Planet

Back When We Were Grownups

The Amateur Marriage

DIGGING TO AMERICA

DIGGING TO AMERICA

a novel by Anne Tyler

Alfred A. Knopf New York 2006

THIS IS A BORZOI BOOK
PUBLISHED BY ALFRED A. KNOPF

ISBN-13: 978-0-7394-7533-1

Manufactured in the United States of America

DIGGING TO AMERICA

1

At eight o'clock in the evening, the Baltimore airport was nearly deserted. The wide gray corridors were empty, and the newsstands were dark, and the coffee shops were closed. Most of the gates had admitted their last flights. Their signboards were blank and their rows of vinyl chairs unoccupied and ghostly.

But you could hear a distant hum, a murmur of anticipation, at the far end of Pier D. You could see an overexcited child spinning herself into dizziness in the center of the corridor, and then a grownup popping forth to scoop her up and carry her, giggling and squirming, back into the waiting area. And a latecomer, a woman in a yellow dress, was rushing toward the gate with an armful of long-stemmed roses.

Step around the bend, then, and you'd come upon what looked like a gigantic baby shower. The entire waiting area for the flight from San Francisco was packed with people bearing pink- and blue-wrapped gifts, or hanging on to flotillas of silvery balloons printed with IT'S A GIRL! and trailing spirals of pink ribbon. A man gripped the wicker handle of a wheeled and skirted bassinet as if he planned to roll it onto the plane, and a woman stood ready with a stroller so chrome-trimmed and bristling with levers that it seemed capable of entering the Indy 500. At least half a dozen people held video cameras, and many more had regular cameras slung around their necks. A woman spoke into a tape recorder in an urgent, secretive way. The man next to her clasped an infant's velour-upholstered car seat close to his chest.

MOM, the button on the woman's shoulder read—one of those laminated buttons such as you might see in an election year. And the 3 man's read DAD. A nice-looking couple, not as young as you might expect—the woman in wide black pants and an arty black-and-white top of a geometric design, her short hair streaked with gray; the man a big, beaming, jovial type with a stubbly blond buzz cut, his bald knees poking bashfully from voluminous khaki Bermudas.

And not only were there MOM and DAD; there were GRANDMA and GRANDPA, twice over—two complete sets. One grandma was a rumpled, comfortable woman in a denim sundress and bandanna-print baseball cap; the other was thin and gilded and expertly made up, wearing an ecru linen pantsuit and dyed-to-match pumps. The grandpas were dyed to match as well—the rumpled woman's husband equally rumpled, his iron-gray curls overdue for a cutting, while the gilded woman's husband wore linen trousers and some sort of gauzy tropical shirt, and part of his bright yellow hair was possibly not his own.

It's true there were other people waiting, people clearly not included in the celebration. A weary-eyed woman in curlers; an older woman with a younger one who might have been her daughter; a father with two small children already dressed in pajamas. These outsiders stood around the edges, quiet and somehow dimmed, from time to time sneaking glances in the direction of MOM and DAD.

The plane was late. People grew restless. A child pointed out accusingly that the arrivals board still read ON TIME—a plain old lie. Several teenagers wandered off to the unlit waiting area just across the corridor. A little girl in pigtails fell asleep on a vinyl chair, the button on her green plaid blouse proclaiming COUSIN.

Then something changed. There wasn't any announcement—the PA system had been silent for some time—but people gradually stopped talking and pressed toward the jetway, craning their necks, standing on tiptoe. A woman in a uniform punched in a code and swung open the jetway door. A skycap arrived with a wheelchair. The teenagers reappeared. MOM and DAD, till now in the very center of the crowd, were nudged forward with encouraging pats, a path magically widening to let them approach the door.

First off was a very tall young man in jeans, wearing the confused look of someone who'd been flying too long. He spotted the mother and daughter and went over to them and bent to kiss the daughter, but only on the cheek because she was too busy peering past him, just briefly returning his hug while she kept her eyes on the new arrivals.

Two businessmen with briefcases, striding purposefully toward the terminal. A teenage boy with a backpack so huge that he resembled an ant with an oversized breadcrumb. Another businessman. Another teenage boy, this one claimed by the woman in curlers. A smiling, rosy-cheeked redhead instantly engulfed by the two children in pajamas.

Now a pause. A sort of gathering of focus.

A crisply dressed Asian woman stepped through the door with a baby. This baby was perhaps five or six months old—able to hold herself confidently upright. She had a cushiony face and a head of amazingly thick black hair, cut straight across her forehead and straight across the tops of her ears, and she wore a footed pink sleeper. "Ah!" everyone breathed—even the outsiders, even the mother and the grown daughter. (Although the daughter's young man still appeared confused.) The mother-to-be stretched out both arms, letting her tape recorder bounce at the end of its strap. But the Asian woman stopped short in an authoritative manner that warded off any approach. She drew herself up and said, "Donaldson?"

"Donaldson. That's us," the father-to-be said. His voice was shaking. He had somehow got rid of the car seat, passed it blindly to someone or other, but he stayed slightly to the rear of his wife and kept one hand on her back as if in need of support.

"Congratulations," the Asian woman said. "This is Jin-Ho." She transferred the baby to the mother's waiting arms, and then she unhitched a pink diaper bag from her shoulder and handed it to the father. The mother buried her face in the crook of the baby's neck. The baby stayed upright, gazing calmly out at the crowd. "Ah," people kept saying, and "Isn't she a cutie!" and "Did you ever see such a doll?"

Flashbulbs, insistent video cameras, everyone pressing too close. The father's eyes were wet. Lots of people's were; there were sniffing sounds all through the waiting area and noses being blown. And when the mother raised her face, finally, her cheeks were sheeted with tears. "Here," she told the father. "You hold her."

"Aw, no, I'm scared I might . . . You do it, honey. I'll watch."

The Asian woman started riffling through a sheaf of papers. People still disembarking had to step around her, step around the little family and the well-wishers and the tangle of baby equipment. Luckily, the flight hadn't been a full one. The passengers arrived in spurts: man with a cane, pause; retired couple, pause . . .

And then another Asian woman, younger than the first and plainer, with a tucked, apologetic way of looking about. She was lugging a bucket-shaped infant carrier by the handle, and you could tell that the baby inside must not weigh all that much. This baby, too, was a girl, if you could judge by the pink T-shirt, but she was smaller than the first one, sallow and pinched, with fragile wisps of black hair trailing down her forehead. Like the young woman transporting her, she showed a sort of anxious interest in the crowd. Her watchful black eyes moved too quickly from face to face.

The young woman said something that sounded like "Yaz-dun?"

"Yaz-*dan*," a woman called from the rear. It sounded like a correction. The crowd parted again, not certain which way to move but eager to be of help, and three people no one had noticed before approached in single file: a youngish couple, foreign-looking, olive-skinned and attractive, followed by a slim older woman with a chignon of sleek black hair knotted low on the nape of her neck. It must have been she who had called out their name, because now she called it again in the same clear, carrying voice. "Here we are. Yazdan." There was just the trace of an accent evident in the ruffled *r*'s.

The young woman turned to face them, holding the carrier awkwardly in front of her. "Congratulations, this is Sooki," she said, but so softly and so breathlessly that people had to ask each other, "What?" "Who did she say?" "Sooki, I believe it was." "Sooki! Isn't that sweet!"

There was a problem unfastening the straps that held the baby in her carrier. The new parents had to do it because the Asian woman's hands were full, and the parents were flustered and unskilled—the mother laughing slightly and tossing back her explosive waterfall of hennaed curls, the father biting his lip and looking vexed with himself. He wore tiny, very clean rimless glasses that glittered as he angled first this way and then that, struggling with a plastic clasp. The grandmother, if that was who she was, made sympathetic tsk-tsking sounds.

But at last the baby was free. Such a little bit of a thing! The father plucked her out in a gingerly, arm's-length manner and handed her to the mother, who gathered her in and rocked her and pressed her cheek against the top of the baby's feathery black head. The baby quirked her eyebrows but offered no resistance. Onlookers were blowing their noses again, and the father had to take off his glasses and wipe the lenses, but the mother and the grandmother stayed dry-eyed, smiling and softly murmuring. They paid no attention to the crowd. When someone asked, "Is yours from Korea too?" neither woman answered, and it was the father, finally, who said, "Hmm? Oh. Yes, she is."

"Hear that, Bitsy and Brad? Here's another Korean baby!"

The first mother glanced around—she was allowing the two grandmas a closer inspection—and said, "Really?" Her husband echoed her: "Really!" He stepped over to the other parents and held out his hand. "Brad Donaldson. That's my wife, Bitsy, over there."

"How do you do," the second father said. "Sami Yazdan." He shook Brad's hand, but his lack of interest was almost comical; he couldn't keep his eyes off his baby. "Uh, my wife, Ziba," he added after a moment. "My mother, Maryam." He had a normal Baltimore accent, although he pronounced the two women's names as no American would have—Zee-*bah* and Mar-*yam*. His wife didn't even look up. She was cradling the baby and saying what sounded like "Soo-soo-soo." Brad Donaldson flapped a hand genially in her direction and returned to his own family.

By the time the transfers had been made official—both Asian women proving to be sticklers for detail—the Donaldson crowd had started to thin. Evidently some sort of gathering was planned for later, though, because people kept calling, "See you back at the house!" as they moved toward the terminal. And then the parents themselves were free to go, Bitsy leading the way while the woman with the stroller wheeled it just behind her like a lady-in-waiting. (Clearly nothing would persuade Bitsy to give up her hold on that baby.) Brad lumbered after her, followed by a few stragglers and, at the very tail end, the Yazdans. One of the Donaldson grandpas, the rumpled one, dropped back to ask the Yazdans, "So. Did *you* have a long wait for *your* baby? Lots of paperwork and cross-examinations?"

"Yes," Sami said, "a very long wait. A very long-drawn-out process." And he glanced toward his wife. "At times we thought it never would happen," he said.

The grandpa clucked and said, "Don't I know it! Lord, what Bitsy and Brad had to put themselves through!"

They passed to one side of Security, which was staffed by a lone employee sitting on a stool, and started down the escalator—all but the man with the bassinet. He had to take the elevator. The woman with the stroller, however, seemed undaunted. She tipped the front end of the stroller back smartly and stepped on without hesitation.

"Listen," Brad called up to the Yazdans from the lower level. "You-all feel like coming to our house? Joining the celebration?"

But Sami was absorbed in guiding his wife onto the escalator, and when he didn't answer, Brad flapped a hand again in that oh-well, affable way of his. "Maybe another time," he said to no one in particular. And he turned to catch up with the others.

The exit doors slid open and the Donaldsons streamed out. They headed toward the parking garage in twos and threes and fours, and shortly after that the Yazdans emerged to stand on the curb a moment, motionless, as if they needed time to adjust to the hot, humid, dimly lit, gasoline-smelling night.

Friday, August 15, 1997. The night the girls arrived.

2

Sometimes when Maryam Yazdan looked at her new little granddaughter she had an eerie, lightheaded feeling, as if she had stepped into some sort of alternate universe. Everything about the child was impossibly perfect. Her skin was a flawless ivory, and her hair was almost too soft to register on Maryam's fingertips. Her eyes were the shape of watermelon seeds, very black and cut very precisely into her small, solemn face. She weighed so little that Maryam often lifted her too high by mistake when she picked her up. And her hands! Tiny hands, with curling fingers. The wrinkles on her knuckles were halvah-colored (so amusing, that a baby had wrinkles!), and her nails were no bigger than dots.

Susan, they called her. They chose a name that resembled the name she had come with, Sooki, and also it was a comfortable sound for Iranians to pronounce.

"Su-san!" Maryam would sing when she went in to get her from her nap. "Su-Su-Su!" Susan would gaze out from behind the bars of her crib, sitting beautifully erect with one hand cupping each knee in a poised and self-possessed manner.

Maryam took care of her Tuesdays and Thursdays—the days her daughter-in-law worked and Maryam did not. She arrived at the house around eight-thirty, slightly later if the traffic was bad. (Sami and Ziba lived out in Hunt Valley, as much as a half-hour drive from the city during rush hour.) By that time Susan would be having breakfast in her high chair. She would light up and make a welcoming sound when Maryam walked into the kitchen. "Ah!" was what she most often said—nothing to do with "Mari-june," which was what they had decided she should call Maryam. "Ah!" she would say, and she would give her distinctive smile, with her lips pursed together demurely, and tilt her cheek for a kiss.

Well, not in the first few weeks, of course. Oh, those first weeks had been agony, the two parents trying their best, shrilling "Susie-june!" and shaking toys in her face and waltzing her about in their arms. All she did was stare at them, or—worse yet—stare away from them, twisting to get free, fixing her eyes stubbornly anywhere else. She wouldn't take more than a sip or two from her bottle, and when she woke crying in the night, as she did every few hours, her parents' attempts to comfort her only made her cry harder. Maryam told them that was natural. In truth she had no idea, but she told them, "She came from a foster home! What do you expect? She's not used to so much attention."

"Jin-Ho came from a foster home too. *She's* not acting like this," Ziba said.

They knew all about Jin-Ho because Jin-Ho's mother had telephoned two weeks after the babies' arrival. "I hope you don't mind my tracking you down," she'd said. "You're the only Yazdans in the book and I just couldn't resist calling you to find out how things were going." Jin-Ho, it seemed, was doing marvelously. She was sleeping straight through till morning, and she laughed out loud when they played "This Is the Way the Lady Rides," and already she had learned to stop clamoring for her bottle once she heard the microwave starting. And Jin-Ho was younger than Susan! She was five months to Susan's seven, even if Susan was smaller. Were the Yazdans doing something wrong?

"No, no, no," Maryam told them. Slightly altering her story, she said, "It's *better* that Susan's sad. It means the foster family took good care of her and now she's homesick for them. You wouldn't want a heartless, heedless baby, would you? She's showing she has a warm nature."

Maryam hoped that this was true.

And it was, thank heaven. One morning Ziba walked into the nursery and Susan gave her a smile. Ziba was so excited that she telephoned Maryam at once, although it was a Tuesday and Maryam was due to come over very shortly; and she phoned her mother in Washington and later her sisters-in-law in L.A. It seemed that some switch had clicked in Susan's head, for she smiled at Maryam as well when she arrived—her smile already that charming, pursed V that made you feel the two of you shared some merry little secret. And within the week she was chortling at Sami's antics, and sleeping through the night, and showing a fondness for Cheerios, which she pursued single-mindedly around her high-chair tray with her dainty, pincer fingers.

"Didn't I tell you?" Maryam said.

She was an optimist, Maryam was. Or on second thought, not an optimist: a pessimist. But her life had been rocky enough that she faced possible disasters more philosophically than most. She had had to forsake her family before she was twenty; she'd been widowed before she was forty; she had raised her son by herself in a country where she would never feel like anything but a foreigner. Basically, though, she believed that she was a happy person. She was confident that if things went wrong—as they very well might—she could manage.

Now she saw the same quality in Susan. Call her fanciful, but she had felt a deep connection to Susan the moment they met in the airport. Sometimes she imagined that Susan resembled her physically, even, but then she had to laugh at herself. Still, something around the eyes, some way of looking at things, some *onlooker's* look: that was what they shared. Neither one of them quite belonged.

Her son belonged. Her son didn't even have an accent; he had refused to speak Farsi from the time he was four years old, although he could understand it. Her daughter-in-law had a noticeable accent, having immigrated with her whole family when she was already in high school, but she had so immediately and enthusiastically adapted—listening nonstop to 98 Rock, hanging out at the mall, draping her small, bony, un-American frame in blue jeans and baggy T-shirts with writing printed across them—that now she seemed native-born, almost.

Ziba left for work when it suited her; she was an interior decorator and arranged her own appointments. Often she'd be loitering around the house a full hour after Maryam's arrival. She was already dressed for the office, not that you would guess it (she still wore jeans, although she'd graduated to blazers and high heels), but it seemed she couldn't quite tear herself away from Susan. "What do you think?" she would ask Maryam. "Is another tooth coming in, or is it not? A thin white line is on her gum; do you see?" Or she would collect her pocketbook, unplug her cell phone from its charger, but then: "Oh! Maryam! I nearly forgot! Watch how she's learned to play peekaboo!"

Maryam would inwardly chafe, longing to have this child to herself. "Go! Go!" she wanted to say. But she smiled and kept quiet.

Then at last Ziba would be on her way, and Maryam could sweep

Susan into her arms and carry her off to the playroom. "All mine!" she crowed, and Susan giggled as if she understood. Left in charge, Maryam was more sure of herself. Child-rearing had changed so since her day—the endless new lists of forbidden foods (peanuts a toxic substance, you'd think); the regulation car seats; the ban on talcum powder and baby oil and pillows and crib bumper pads—that Maryam often felt incompetent in Ziba's presence. With Ziba there, she walked on tiptoe—the way her own mother had tiptoed, she realized, the one time she had come to visit. Her mother had arrived with a holy medal to hang around Sami's neck, a little gold dime-sized Allah that a two-year-old would have swallowed in a blink, if Maryam had not insisted in putting it aside for later; and her mother had plied Sami with gummy white rosewater candies that would have ruined his teeth and stuck in his throat if Maryam had not clamped the box firmly shut and carried it off to the pantry. By the end of the visit, her mother had retreated to the television set, even though she couldn't understand a word of what was said. Now Maryam recalled with a pang her mother's stoical posture, her hands folded in her lap, her eyes fixed steadily upon a commercial for Kent cigarettes. She batted the image away. She said, "Bunny rabbit, Susie-june! Look!" and held up a little stuffed animal that jingled when she wagged it.

Susan wore blue jeans also. (Who knew they made jeans so tiny?) She wore a red-and-white-striped long-sleeved T-shirt that could just as well have been a boy's, and little red socks with nonskid soles. The socks were a new addition—till the weather turned cold she'd gone barefoot—and she didn't like them. She kept tugging them off her feet with a triumphant squawk, and then Maryam hoisted her into her lap and put them on again. "Wicked girl!" she scolded. Susan laughed. As soon as she was set back down on the rug she would fling herself on her favorite toy, a xylophone that she banged energetically with any object at hand. She didn't crawl yet—she was a bit behind in her physical skills, which Maryam blamed on life in the foster home—but clearly she was working on it.

If it were up to her, Maryam would have dressed this child differently. She'd have chosen more feminine clothes, little white tights and A-line jumpers and blouses with ruffles. Wasn't that part of the fun of having a girl? (Oh, how she used to hope for a girl after Sami was born!) She herself dressed with the utmost care even just to babysit. She wore trousers, yes, but slim, tailored trousers, with a fitted sweater in some jewel color and good shoes. She regularly had the gray tinted from her hair, although she preferred that this not be known, and she secured her chignon with tortoiseshell combs or brightly patterned scarves. It was important to keep up appearances. She believed that. Let the Americans lounge about in their sweatsuits! She was not American.

"Not American! Check your passport," Sami always told her.

She said, "You understand what I mean."

She was a guest, was what she meant. Still and forever a guest, on her very best behavior.

Perhaps if she lived in Iran, she would have been more casual. Oh, not that she would have let herself go, nothing so extreme as all that, but she might have worn a housecoat at home the way her mother and aunts used to do. Or would she? She couldn't even imagine now what her life would be like if she had not moved to Baltimore.

Susan was in the process of giving up her morning nap. She might fall asleep when she was put down or she might not; so while Maryam was waiting to find out which, she read the paper or flipped through a magazine, something that didn't require an uninterrupted block of time. If so much as half an hour passed and Susan was still chirping, Maryam would get her up again. Once more they would go through their reunion scene—Susan's "Ah!"

and Maryam's "Su-Su-Su!" Maryam would change her diaper and put her in a sweater and take her out in the stroller.

There were no sidewalks here. Maryam found that amazing. How could they have constructed an entire neighborhood—long curving roads of gigantic, raw new houses with two-story arched windows and double-wide front doors and three-car garages—and failed to realize that people might want to walk around it? There weren't any trees either, unless you counted the twiglike saplings staked in all the front yards. (*Tiny* yards. The houses had devoured most of the available space.) In weeks past, when it was still hot, Maryam had often kept Susan inside, knowing they'd find not a chip of shade anywhere and the pavements would be radiating heat. But now that fall had arrived the sun felt good. She would stretch their walk till lunchtime, covering every smooth, blank, uncannily deserted street in Foxfoot Acres and commenting as she went. "Car, Susan! See the car? Mailbox! See the mailbox?"

In her own neighborhood there were squirrels, and dogs on leashes, and other children in carriages and strollers. She would have had many more sights to point out.

Lunch was strained baby foods for Susan and a salad for Maryam. Then Susan had a little playpen time in the family room extending from the kitchen while Maryam did the dishes, and after that a bottle and another nap—this one long enough that Maryam was free to fix something for Sami and Ziba's supper. Not that they expected it, but she had always enjoyed cooking and Ziba, it turned out, did not. Left to their own devices, they tended to eat Lean Cuisines.

While the rice was boiling, she straightened the house. She put Susan's toys in the toy chest and carried a bagful of wet diapers out to the garbage can. She stacked and aligned various reading materials but did not throw away so much as a scrap of paper, not a subscription card or a pizza flyer, for fear of overstepping.

Again she had an image of her mother, this time stooping painfully to retrieve a chewing-gum wrapper and placing it silently, almost reverently, in an ashtray on the coffee table.

This house was as big as the neighboring houses, with a room for every purpose. It had not only a family room but an exercise room and a computer room, each one carpeted wall to wall in solid off-white. There wasn't a Persian rug anywhere, although you might guess that the occupants were Iranian from the wedding gifts in the dining-room cabinet—the Isfahani coffee sets and the tea glasses caged in silver. The playroom had been fully stocked with toys as soon as the agency sent Susan's photograph. And the nursery was ready long before that, the crib and bureau and changing table purchased back when Ziba was first trying to get pregnant. (Maryam's mother would have said that preparing so far ahead was what had doomed them. "Didn't I warn you?" she would have asked, each month when Ziba once again reported failure.)

Maryam had told Ziba to trust in the power of time. "You'll have your baby! You'll have a houseful of babies," she'd said. And she had confided her own long wait. "Five years we tried, before Sami was born. I was in despair." This was a great concession on her part. To speak openly of "trying" was so indiscreet. (She had been stunned when Ziba first spoke of it. Not a comfortable thought at all, one's son having a sex life, even though of course Maryam assumed that he did.) Besides which, she had always told her relatives that that five-year wait was deliberate. Visiting back home three years after her wedding, she had parried their sly questions with boasts about her independence, her relief that she was not burdened yet with children. "I take courses at the university; I'm active in the wives' group at the hospital . . ." While in fact, she had wanted a baby right away—something to anchor her, she had envisioned, to her new country.

She saw herself now on that first visit home: her clothes chosen carefully for their Westernness, stylish sheaths in electric prints of hot pink and lime green and purple; her hair lacquered into a towering beehive; her feet encased in needle-toed, stiletto-heeled pumps. She winced.

She winced too at recalling her automatic assumption that Ziba's failure to get pregnant was exactly that—*Ziba's* failure. When they discovered that it was, instead, Sami's failure, Maryam had been shocked. Mumps, perhaps, the doctors said. Mumps? Sami had never had mumps! Or had he? Wouldn't she have known? Did he have them while he was away in college, and he had felt too embarrassed to mention such things to a woman?

He'd been fourteen years old when his father died—just beginning to turn adolescent, with a fuzzy dark upper lip and a grainy voice. She had wondered how she could possibly see him through this stage on her own. She knew so little about the opposite sex; she'd lost her father when she was a child and had never been close to her brothers, who were nearly grown before she was born. If only Kiyan could have stayed alive just a little while longer, just four or five years longer, till Sami had become a man!

Although now she wasn't so sure that Kiyan would have known much, either, about the process of becoming an American man.

And if Kiyan could have shared grandparenthood with her! That was a major sorrow, now that Susan was here. She imagined how it would be if the two of them were babysitting together. They would send each other smiles over Susan's head, marveling at her puckery frown and her threadlike eyebrows and her studious examination of a stray bit of lint from the carpet. Kiyan would have retired by now. (He'd been nine years Maryam's senior.) They would have had all the time in the world to enjoy this part of their lives.

She went out to the kitchen and took the rice off the stove and dumped it briskly into a colander.

By the time Ziba had returned from work, Susan would be

awake again and drinking her post-nap sippy cup of apple juice, or she'd have moved on to haul forth from the toy chest everything that Maryam had put away. Ziba would scoop her up even before she'd taken her blazer off. "Did you have fun with your Mari-june, Su-Su? Did you miss your mommy?" They would delicately touch noses—Ziba's profile beaky and sharp, Susan's as flat as a cookie. "Did you think your mommy would stay away forever?" Always she spoke English to Susan; she said she didn't want to confuse her. Maryam had expected her to lapse into Farsi from time to time, but Ziba plowed heroically through the most difficult words—"think," with its sticky *th* sound, and "stay," which came out "es-stay." (To her own puzzlement, Maryam found Ziba's broken rhythms much easier to understand than Sami's smooth, easy flow.)

Maryam located her purse and put on her suede jacket. "Don't go!" Ziba would say. "What's your hurry? Let me make tea." Most days, Maryam declined. Issuing farewell remarks—instructions for heating dinner, message from the dentist's office—she would blow a kiss toward Susan and let herself out the front door. She was trying to be the perfect mother-in-law. She didn't want Ziba to consider her a nuisance.

Often when she reached home she would just vegetate awhile, slumped in her favorite armchair, free at last to relax and let herself be herself.

ǂ

Jin-Ho's mother phoned in October to invite them all to supper. This was while Maryam was babysitting, and so she was the one who answered. "You come too," Bitsy told her. "It's going to be just us, our two families, because I believe the girls should get to know each other, don't you? So as to maintain their cultural heritage. I meant to ask you before this but what with one thing and another . . . An early, early supper, I thought, on Sunday afternoon. We'll rake leaves beforehand."

Maryam said, "Rake . . . ?"

She wondered if this was some idiomatic expression having to do with socializing. Break the ice, mend fences, chew the fat, rake leaves . . . But Bitsy was saying, "We still have elms, believe it or not, and they're always the first trees to shed. We thought we'd throw a big jolly leaf-raking party and let the girls roll around in the piles."

"Oh. All right. You're very kind," Maryam said.

She liked the way Bitsy called the babies "the girls." It made her visualize a Susan of the future, wearing knee socks and a pleated skirt, with her arm linked through her best friend's arm.

Logically, they should have taken separate cars to the leaf-raking party. The Donaldsons lived in Mount Washington and Maryam a short distance south of them, in Roland Park. (The "wrong side" of Roland Park, so called, although even the wrong side was very nice, the houses just a bit smaller and closer together.) Sami and Ziba, coming from the north, would have to drive right past the Donaldsons' neighborhood to get to Maryam's; but even so, they insisted on giving her a ride. Maryam suspected that this was because Ziba felt the need of moral support. Ziba was subject to fits of insecurity every now and then. And sure enough, when they arrived at Maryam's—where Maryam was already waiting out front, so as not to hold them up—Ziba popped from the car to announce that they were going to come in for a moment because she worried they were too early. Maryam said, "Early?" She checked her watch. It was 3:55. They'd been invited for four o'clock, and the drive would take roughly five minutes. "We're not early!" she said. But Ziba was already extricating Susan from her car seat. Sami, stepping out from behind the wheel, said, "Ziba claims that four o'clock means ten past four, in Baltimore."

"Not when only one set of guests has been invited," Maryam told him. (She had studied these customs at some length herself.) But Ziba had Susan in her arms by now and was coming up the front walk. She wore the offhand kind of clothes appropriate for leaf-raking—jeans and a bulky rose turtleneck—but had obviously spent some time on her hair and makeup. A huge, horizontal pony-tail jutted from the back of her head, so frizzy that it defied gravity, and her lips were two different colors, shiny pink outlined in a red that was almost black. "You look very nice," Maryam told her. She meant this sincerely. Ziba was a strikingly pretty young woman. And Sami was so handsome! He had his father's chiseled mouth and thick eyebrows. His rimless, old-man spectacles somehow made him seem younger, and the collar of his plaid flannel shirt stood up boyishly at the back. "Ten minutes early, ten minutes late, what difference does it make?" he asked his mother. He kissed her on both cheeks. "Check out Susan's work clothes."

Susan wore blue denim overalls, faded convincingly at the knees, and a chambray shirt. Her jacket, also blue denim, had a tractor appliquéd on one pocket. "You're all ready to help us rake!" Maryam told her, and she lifted her from Ziba's arms.

"We're bringing a bottle of wine," Ziba said. "What do you think? Is that wrong? I know it's still daylight, but we're staying for supper, after all."

"Wine is perfect," Maryam said, jouncing Susan on her hip. "We should certainly bring wine. Isn't that so, Susie-june."

Susan gave her a secretive smile.

"Shall we go in and sit down?" Ziba asked.

"What for? We'll just have to get up again," Sami said. "She acts like it's some big deal," he told his mother, and then to Ziba he said, "We visit people all the time. Why is this any different?"

"But these people are older than our other friends," Ziba said. "Bitsy is forty," she told Maryam. "She mentioned it on the phone.

She's a weaver and she used to teach yoga and she writes poetry and . . . oh, what will we *talk* about?" she ended on a wailing note.

"Babies," Maryam said.

"Ah," Ziba said, brightening. "Babies."

"What else do we talk about, these days?" Sami asked the sky.

"The Donaldsons' baby is keeping her Korean name for good," Ziba told Maryam.

"Jin-Ho Donaldson," Maryam tried out. It had a peculiar ring. "Donaldson" seemed so ultra-American, or was that because she was reminded of McDonald's hamburgers?

"Jin-Ho Dickinson-Donaldson, actually," Ziba said.

Maryam's jaw dropped. Sami laughed. Then he said, "Okay, folks, it's four o'clock. Time to hit the road."

Ziba turned to follow him back to the car, but she seemed to be lagging a bit, Maryam noticed.

As always, the two women had their ceremonial disagreement about who should sit where. "Please," Ziba said, gesturing toward the front, but Maryam said, "I *like* the back. This way I sit next to Susan." She handed Susan to Ziba, who would make quicker work of buckling her in, and walked around the rear of the car to slip in on the other side. Sami had his seat adjusted far enough back so that it touched her knees, but not uncomfortably. She had spoken the truth when she said she preferred to sit there. How awkward if she had assumed the seat of honor, as her own mother-in-law used to do! Although she had an odd sense of being a child again, Susan's sibling, as the two of them swayed from side to side when Sami turned a corner.

The Donaldsons' house was a worn white clapboard Colonial on one of the narrower streets in Mount Washington. The sprawling, woodsy yard was ankle-deep in yellow leaves that clattered as the Yazdans waded up the front walk, and the porch was strewn with bicycles and boots and garden tools. It was Brad who opened the door, wearing corduroys and a woolen shirt stretched taut across his belly. "Well, hey!" he said. "Welcome! Great to see you!" and he chucked Susan under the chin. "This kid has plumped up some. She was looking a bit peaked at the airport."

"Fifteen pounds, three ounces, at her last doctor visit," Ziba told him.

"Fifteen?" He frowned.

"And three ounces."

"I guess she's going to be one of those *petite* little people," he said.

Jin-Ho was going to be an Amazon, Maryam thought when she saw her straddling Bitsy's waist. She was stocky and bloomingly healthy-looking, with fat cheeks and bright, laughing eyes. She still wore that squared-off hairstyle she had arrived with, seemingly all of a piece, and although she too was in corduroys, her top was a multicolored, quilted affair with striped sleeves and a black silk sash—the kind of thing Maryam recalled from the days when Sami and Ziba were researching Korea. "Hasn't she grown?" Bitsy asked, shifting Jin-Ho slightly to give everyone a good view. "These pants are size eighteen months! We had to switch her to a full crib the second week she was here."

Bitsy herself wore a black-and-white-striped jersey and black slacks and fluorescent jogging shoes. There was something aggressive about her plainness, Maryam thought—her blatant lack of makeup, her chopped hair and angular, rawboned body. She might almost be making a statement. Next to her, Ziba looked very glamorous but also a little bit flashy.

First they sat a few minutes in the living room, waiting for Jin-Ho's grandparents. Both couples were coming, Bitsy said, but none of the aunts or uncles or cousins because too large a crowd might overwhelm the girls. In fact, the girls seemed fairly impervious. They sat on a braided rug and pursued their separate activities—

Jin-Ho piling alphabet blocks into a dump truck, Susan trying to maneuver a jingle-bell out of a wooden rattle. Susan was so sweet and intent, and her fingers worked so cleverly, that Maryam wondered if the Donaldsons might feel slightly envious.

Bitsy and Ziba were discussing lactose intolerance. Bitsy blamed it on a clash of cultures. It wasn't in the Asian tradition to slug down gallons of milk, after all. No wonder Jin-Ho had tummy trouble! Did Susan? Or . . . Bitsy grew unaccountably flustered. "Or maybe your people don't drink milk either," she said.

"Well, Susan does," Ziba said, "but so far she's been fine."

"You might want to give her soy milk. Soy is more culturally appropriate."

"Oh, maybe I will," Ziba said obligingly.

Though Maryam, in her place, would have asked why. Hadn't Ziba just now said that Susan was fine?

The Donaldsons' living room was attractive without trying too hard. Sunlight poured through the uncurtained windows, and the furniture was old but well made, perhaps handed down from previous generations. Brad was slouched in a leather armchair that creaked each time he moved. Sami sat in an antique rocker a good six inches lower. He was nodding at Brad's description of the joys of fatherhood. "Sunday mornings, Jin-Ho and I go out for croissants and the *New York Times*," Brad said. "It's my favorite thing of the week. I love it! Just me and my kid together. You ever do that with Susan? Go off on your own for a jaunt?"

So far Sami lacked the confidence to do that, Maryam knew. But he didn't admit it. Gazing up at Brad from his lowered position, which made him seem touchingly humble, he said, "Well, I've been thinking of buying a jogging stroller."

"Jogging stroller! Great invention. Fellow up the street has one. I'll find out the brand. Be good for your wife, too; good for Ziba. Get her out of the house."

"*Zee*-buh," he said, almost "zebra," and he slid her a look. American men always found Ziba mesmerizing. Maryam was amused to see that Brad—despite choosing such a homespun wife himself—was no exception.

The two sets of grandparents arrived at nearly the same time, Bitsy's parents first and Brad's close on their heels. Bitsy's parents were big and gray and friendly, Dave in coveralls like some ordinary yardman and Connie in sweatpants and the same bandanna-print cap she'd had on at the airport. Brad's parents, with their glittery blond hair and matching velour warm-up suits, seemed a little more formal. Pat and Lou, their names were. The man was Pat and the woman was Lou, or was it the other way around? Maryam knew she was going to have trouble with that.

For a few minutes the four of them performed their grandparent dance around the babies. They exclaimed at Jin-Ho's quilted top, which Connie called by a foreign name, and made a nice to-do over Susan. "Isn't she just like a *miniature*!" Brad's mother caroled, and Dave scooped her right up. Luckily, Susan took this in stride. She reached for one of his curly gray sideburns and gave it a tug, dead serious, knitting her brow when he chuckled.

"See how Jin-Ho looks so tan-skinned next to Susan," Ziba pointed out. "We think Susan's father maybe was white."

"Yes, you're just a little white tooth of a thing," Dave told Susan, but Bitsy jumped in with, "Oh! Well! But actually that's not something we would *notice,* really!"

There was a silence. Ziba rounded her eyes at Maryam—*Why not?*—and Maryam gave the tiniest shrug. Then Brad said, "So anyways. You guys ready to tackle those leaves?"

Judging by the number of rakes propped out on the porch, Maryam guessed the Donaldsons had held these gatherings before. She would never have done that herself (she kept after her own leaves singlehandedly from the day they began to fall), but that was

Americans for you. And it did turn out to be a real social event. For one thing, they were all put to work on the same section of yard, so that conversation could flow. And then there was no sense of pressure. Brad's mother didn't even make a pretense of raking, but appointed herself the baby-watcher and stood over Jin-Ho and Susan where they sat among the leaves. Bitsy's mother sank immediately into a canvas chair that her husband brought down from the porch, and she tipped her face up to the sunlight and closed her eyes. That cap made sense, all at once. She was ill, Maryam realized; she must have lost her hair. Even though Dave raked with the others, he stopped frequently to go over to her and ask if she was all right. "Yes, fine," Connie said each time, and she would smile and pat his hand. Clearly it was from her that Bitsy got her no-nonsense looks, although Connie seemed softer than Bitsy and more retiring.

Maryam herself worked diligently. She took a position between Bitsy and Lou (it was Lou who was the man of the couple; she believed she had that straight now) and raked in long, steady sweeps toward the pile that had started rising next to the driveway. She and Bitsy got a sort of rhythm going, like a chorus line. Lou was too busy talking to keep up with them. First he talked to Sami, on his other side—boring man-talk about jobs, followed by the high price of housing once he learned that Sami sold real estate. Then it was Maryam's turn: how long had she been in this country? and did she like it?

Maryam hated being asked such questions, partly because she had answered them so many times before but also because she preferred to imagine (unreasonable though it was) that maybe she didn't always, instantly, come across as a foreigner. "Where are you from?" someone might ask just when she was priding herself on having navigated some particularly intricate and illogical piece of English. She longed to say, "From Baltimore. Why?" but lacked the nerve. Now she spoke so courteously that Lou could have had no inkling how she felt. "I've been here thirty-nine years," she said, and, "Yes, of course. I love it."

Lou gave a satisfied nod and turned back to his raking. Then Bitsy poked Maryam in the ribs with her elbow. "Lou thinks the universe ends just east of Ocean City," she said with a roll of her eyes. Maryam laughed. Bitsy was all right, she decided. And the colorful swath of workers stretching across the yard, creating a busy roaring of leaves and stirring up the dusty smell of autumn, made her feel happy and accepted. Even if she didn't have the slightest illusion that she could live this kind of life herself, she enjoyed getting a peek at it now and then.

Jin-Ho plunged forward to hug a whole armful of leaves and bury her face in them. One leaf fluttered over to land on the front of Susan's jacket, and Susan plucked it off fastidiously and held it up to inspect it.

The front yard was finished in a little more than an hour, a beautiful clean sweep of green, and the men moved on to the back. By then, though, both babies were beginning to fuss; so the women took them inside. In the Donaldsons' big old-fashioned kitchen, Bitsy settled Jin-Ho in her high chair and sliced a banana for her while Ziba fed Susan a bottle. Maryam loved the little sounds that Susan made when she swallowed. "Um, um," she said, with her eyes fixed on Ziba's face and one hand rhythmically clutching and releasing Ziba's sweater sleeve. Brad's mother and Maryam sat at the kitchen table with glasses of white wine, but Bitsy's mother went upstairs to lie down awhile. As soon as she'd left the room, Brad's mother said, "How is she *really*, Bitsy?"

Bitsy waited so long to answer that Brad's mother said again, "Bitsy?" But then they all saw that Bitsy's eyes were swimming with tears. She leaned closer to Jin-Ho's high chair and painstakingly aligned several banana slices before she said, in a tight voice, "Not so good, I think."

"Oh, my. Oh, my, my," Pat said. "Well, thank the Lord she's lived to see you get your baby. That means a lot to her, I know."

Bitsy nodded speechlessly, and Maryam, hoping to rescue her, turned to Pat and asked, "Did it take a very long time, getting their baby?"

"Did it ever! It took ages! And then there was that business last year, *you* remember; the Korean officials were talking about letting fewer children out of the country."

"Yes, that was terrible!" Ziba said. "Sami and I were so worried! Almost we thought we'd have to start over again and adopt from China."

Bitsy said, "We thought the same thing," in a voice that was perfectly normal, and nothing more was said about her mother.

A large covered pot was simmering on the stove, and once Jin-Ho had been fed, Bitsy set about stirring and tasting, adjusting seasonings, raising the flame beneath another pot on a back burner. She gave Maryam two avocados to peel and she sent her mother-in-law to the dining room with stacks of plates. "I hope no one minds a meatless meal," she said. "We're not complete vegetarians, but we try to avoid red meat."

"Meatless will be fine. Very healthy," Ziba told her. She had put Susan down on the floor, where Jin-Ho already sat banging pot lids together, and she was watching over both of them.

Bitsy said, "We certainly love *your* cuisine," and she started telling Ziba about something she'd had in a restaurant, a dish whose name she couldn't recall except it had been delicious, while Maryam sliced a peeled avocado into a bowl. Then Pat wanted to know if the Yazdans had run into any unpleasantness during the Iranian hostage crisis, and Ziba said, "Well, I had just barely arrived here then; I wasn't very aware. But Maryam, I believe, *she* had some trouble . . ." and everyone looked expectantly toward Maryam. She said, "Oh, perhaps a little," and cut into the second avocado. Pat and Bitsy tut-tutted and waited to hear more, but she remained silent. She was tired to death of the subject, frankly.

Brad poked his head in the back door and asked, "How are things going here? Do we have time to bag the leaves before we eat?"

"You do not," Bitsy said. "I'm just about to start serving."

"Okay, I'll go call the others." And he shut the door again.

The main dish was a black-bean concoction served over rice. Maryam actually liked American rice if she thought of it as a completely different substance. She helped Bitsy set out the food while Pat filled the water glasses. All around the table were bowls of chopped green onions and tomatoes, shredded cheese, the sliced avocados, a number of other items that Bitsy said should be scattered on top. She showed Ziba and Maryam where to sit and then called up the stairs, "Mom? You feel like coming down?"

"I'll get her," her father said. He gave off the smell of dry leaves as he passed through the dining room; his large, rough-skinned face was ruddy from the fresh air. And Sami had worked up a sweat. He blotted his forehead with his sleeve and sank into a chair next to Ziba. "Everything's raked except for one little patch beside the garage," he told her, and he reached for Susan, who was sitting on Ziba's lap. "Did you miss me, Susie-june?"

"Ah. Hippie food," Brad's father said, peering down at the beans.

His wife reached over to slap his wrist. "Sit," she told him.

"Granola au gratin."

"There's not one speck of granola anywhere in sight; so sit."

He sat. Bitsy sent Brad a resigned look and then plucked Jin-Ho from the floor and settled in the chair at the head of the table. "Now, everybody dig in," she said. "Don't wait for Mom and Dad."

Brad was offering beer or red wine, whichever people preferred. "These days, we don't even get a cocktail hour," he said as he uncorked the wine. "By the time the sun's over the yardarm we're already eating dinner. Nursery hours, that's what we keep. Bitsy goes to bed not much later than Jin-Ho."

"I'm always exhausted," Bitsy told Ziba. "Are you? I used to be such a night owl! Now I can hardly wait to hit the pillow."

"Oh, me too," Ziba said. "And Susan gets up so early. Seven."

"Seven! Count your blessings. Jin-Ho is up at five-thirty or six. But here's what you do, Ziba: nap. Take a nap when your baby does."

"Nap?"

"I put on some classical music; I lie down on the couch; I'm out like a light until she wakes up."

"Oh! I wish!" Ziba said. She ladled rice onto her plate. "But two days a week I'm at work, and the other days I'm trying to catch up with the laundry and the cleaning and such."

"You work?" Bitsy asked her.

"I'm an interior decorator."

"I couldn't bear to work! How could you leave your baby?"

Ziba stopped dishing out rice and sent Maryam an uncertain glance.

It was Lou who broke the silence. "Well, Pat here left *her* baby from the time he was six weeks old, and see how well he turned out?"

Brad took a deep bow before he resumed pouring wine.

"But it's the most formative time of their lives," Bitsy said. "You'll never get those days back again."

Maryam said, "It's very lucky for *me* that she works. I have Susan all to myself, Tuesdays and Thursdays. It gives us a chance to . . ." She tried to think of the word, the most up-to-date and scientific word that would make her point. "Bond," she said finally. "It lets us bond."

Bitsy said, "I see." But she didn't seem convinced. She hugged Jin-Ho tighter against her and rested her chin on the child's gleaming head. And Ziba still wore her uncertain look. Now that her lipstick had worn away the blackish outline seemed accidental, as if she'd been eating dirt.

From the doorway, Bitsy's mother said, "Isn't this lovely!" She made her way into the room, reaching out for the back of her chair. Her husband followed a step or two behind. "I could smell those wonderful spice smells all the way upstairs," she said as she settled herself. She unfolded her napkin and smiled around the table. "Is there a name for this dish?"

"*Habichuelas negras,*" Bitsy said. "It's Cuban."

"Cuban! How exciting!"

Bitsy sat up straighter, as if she'd just had a thought. "You notice I'm wearing black and white," she told Ziba.

Ziba nodded, wide-eyed.

"That's because babies don't see colors. Only black and white. I've worn nothing but black and white from the day that Jin-Ho arrived."

"Really!" Ziba said, and she looked down at her rose turtleneck.

"*You* might want to do that," Bitsy told her.

"Oh, yes, maybe I should."

Bitsy relaxed and set her chin on Jin-Ho's head again.

"But then how is it that Susan is able to pick up her blocks?" Maryam asked Bitsy.

"Her blocks?"

"Her pink and blue blocks on a yellow playpen pad. I say, 'Pick up your blocks, Susan,' and she reaches right over for them."

"She does?" Bitsy asked. She looked at Susan. "She picks up her blocks when you tell her to?"

"From a yellow background," Maryam said. She dished herself some rice and turned to Connie. "May I serve you?" she asked.

"Oh, no, thank you, not just yet," Connie said, although her plate was empty except for a slice of bread.

Bitsy was still studying Susan. For a moment it seemed she

couldn't think of anything more to say, but then she turned to Ziba. "You put your daughter in a *playpen*?" she asked.

Ziba's uncertain expression returned. Before she could answer, though, Maryam said, "And the beans and rice? How about those?"

"Excuse me?" Bitsy said.

"The black beans and the white rice. Are they for the sake of the babies' eyesight also?"

Bitsy looked startled, but when her father-in-law laughed she did manage to smile, a little.

After that the two families got together fairly often, although Maryam politely declined whenever she was invited along. Why would she want to share a young couple's social life? She had friends of her own, mostly women, mostly her own age and nearly always foreigners, although no Iranians, as it happened. They would eat together at restaurants or at one another's houses. They would go to movies or concerts. And then there was her job, of course. Three days a week she worked in the office of Sami's old preschool. No one could say that time hung heavy on her hands.

She did hear about the Donaldsons almost daily, through Ziba. She heard how Bitsy believed in cloth diapers, how Brad worried vaccinations were dangerous, how both of them read Korean folktales to Jin-Ho. Ziba switched to cloth diapers too (though in a week or so she switched back). She telephoned her pediatrician about the vaccinations. She plowed dutifully through *The Wormwood Rice Cake* while Susan, who had not yet got the hang of books, tried her best to crumple the pages. And after the Donaldsons' Christmas party, Ziba bought a forty-cup percolator so that she too could brew hot cider. "You put cinnamon sticks and cloves in the basket where the coffee grounds go. Isn't that clever?" she asked Maryam.

Ziba had a little crush on the Donaldsons, it seemed to Maryam.

Maryam herself didn't see them again till January, when they came to Susan's first birthday party. They brought Jin-Ho in full Korean costume—a brilliant kimono-like affair and a pointed hat with a chin strap and little embroidered cloth shoes—and they stood around looking interested but slightly lost in the sea of Iranian relatives. Maryam stepped forward to take them under her wing. She complimented Jin-Ho's hat and she showed them where to put their coats and she explained just who was who. "Those are Ziba's parents; they live in Washington. And there is her brother Hassan from Los Angeles; her brother Ali, also from Los Angeles . . . Ziba has seven brothers, can you imagine? Four of them are here today."

"And which are from your side, Maryam?" Bitsy asked.

"Oh, well, none. Most of my family is still in Tehran. They don't visit very often."

She poured them each a cup of hot cider and then led them through the crowd, pausing here and there to introduce them. Whenever possible she singled out non-Iranians—a next-door neighbor and a woman from Sami's office—because Brad was carrying Jin-Ho on one arm and you never knew what Ziba's relations might take it into their heads to say. ("In L.A. we have plastic surgeons who make Chinese people's eyes look just as good as Western," she'd heard Ali's wife tell Ziba that morning. "I can get you some names, if you like.")

To be honest, the Hakimis were only one generation removed from the bazaar. Maryam's family would never even have met them, if they were back home.

It was the food that put the Donaldsons at ease, finally. They gasped when they saw the buffet table, with its multiple main dishes and its array of side dishes and salads. They wanted to know the names of everything, and when Bitsy learned that Maryam had cooked it all she inquired almost shyly if she might have some of the recipes. "Well, of course," Maryam said. "They're in any Iranian cookbook." By now she was aware that Americans thought recipes were a matter of creative invention. They could serve a different meal every day for a year without repeating themselves—Italian-American one day and Tex-Mex the next and Asian fusion the next—and it always surprised them that other countries ate such a predictable menu.

"Maryam," Bitsy said, "was Ziba's family very upset when they heard that she and Sami were adopting?"

"Not at all; why do you ask?" Maryam said crisply. (Astonishing, what people asked!) "Now, this is a dish customarily served at weddings," she said. "Chicken with almonds and orange peel. You must be sure to try some."

Bitsy was filling a single plate with double portions, since Brad was carrying Jin-Ho. She took a spoonful of the wedding dish and said, "Brad's parents had a little trouble with it. Not mine; mine were all for it. But Brad was an only child and his folks were more, I don't know; maybe they were worried about passing on the bloodline or something." She tucked a piece of flatbread matter-of-factly into her pocket. (She was wearing a handwoven sort of peasant smock in shades of blue. No more black and white, Maryam noticed.) "Of course, now they just adore Jin-Ho," she said. "They're just as sweet as they could be with her." She paused to look at Maryam. "And you're very close to Susan, I know from Ziba."

"Yes," was all Maryam said, but she couldn't resist sending Susan a glance across the room. Susan wore a rosebud-print dress her other grandma had bought at a fancy shop in Georgetown, and the pale pink made her black hair and black eyes even more startlingly beautiful.

All the American guests were carrying their plates into the living room, while all the Iranian guests remained standing around the buffet table. Every time she saw this, Maryam tried to decide: were the Americans more greedy for rushing off into private corners and huddling possessively over their food, or were the Iranians more greedy for staying close to the source as they ate while other guests, not yet served, did their best to reach in between them? In any case, she knew enough to lead the Donaldsons into the living room. She saw to it that they were seated on the floor around the coffee table, since all of the chairs were taken, and then she went to the kitchen to fetch a bib for Jin-Ho. When she came back, Brad and Bitsy had struck up a conversation with the next-door neighbor, who was sitting on the couch breast-feeding her baby. "You can never begin too young," Bitsy was saying. "I'm talking about the mother-infant exercise program," she told Maryam. "It's not only good for their muscles but it also develops the brain. Something about hand-eye coordination, I believe."

Obviously, she had settled in. Maryam tied the bib around Jin-Ho's neck and went off to see who else needed tending.

It was an excess of politeness that led Maryam to invite the Donaldsons to an Iranian New Year's dinner that spring. In fact, she had more or less stopped celebrating the New Year. Sami and Ziba always went over to Washington, where Ziba's parents gave a gigantic party attended by throngs of bejeweled and perfumed guests—people much more newly arrived than Maryam and really not her type. This year was no exception, but Ziba told Maryam that at some point after the actual New Year's, she would love to serve the Donaldsons a few of the traditional dishes. "They so much enjoyed what they ate at Susan's birthday party," she said. "I was thinking we could ask Brad and Bitsy's parents, too, and my parents if they're free. We could set up a *Haftseen* table and make perhaps a *morgh polo* . . . well, you would make it, but I would help as much as possible. Would you be willing?"

Maryam would have been more than willing, ordinarily, but now she felt an inner pinch of resistance. Why should they have to put on these ethnic demonstrations? Let the Donaldsons go to the Smithsonian for that! she thought peevishly. Let them read *National Geographic*! All she said to Ziba, though, was, "Won't it be too much for you, on top of your weekend in Washington?"

"Too much? Why, no," Ziba said. "Or . . . are you saying it's too much for *you*?"

"Certainly not. I'm not the one going to Washington! But the *Haftseen* table, for instance. It would need to be set up ahead of time, and you will both be away."

There was no reason whatsoever that the table should be set up ahead of time. And anyhow, they were free to schedule this for any date they liked. Surely Ziba must have realized that Maryam was just inventing excuses, but she drew the wrong conclusion. She said, "Oh! You prefer to give the dinner at your house?"

"My house? Well, but—"

"Of course! I should have thought! It's just that our house has more room. If you prefer your house, though . . ."

"Well, it's true that my house is quite small," Maryam said.

"But you're the one who's cooking. You should get to choose."

"You'll be doing the rest of it, though—the decorating, the cleaning up afterward. Your house makes more sense."

"No, that's okay," Ziba said. "We'll use your house. That will be just fine."

So Maryam invited the Donaldsons to her house.

Ten days before the party, Sami took her to Rockville for some of the more exotic ingredients. (It was a longer trip than she felt comfortable driving alone.) Traffic on I-95 was bumper to bumper, and Sami muttered under his breath whenever the stream of red taillights lit up in front of them. "We should just be glad this place is as close as it is," Maryam told him. "When I first came to this country, your grandmother had to mail most of my spices from Iran."

She could see those parcels still, clumsily stitched-together cloth bundles bulging with sumac and dried fenugreek leaves and tiny, blackened dried limes, the homemade cardboard address tags hand-lettered in her mother's shaky English. "What we couldn't get shipped, we cheated on," she said. "We traded around our secret tricks, the other wives and I. Pomegranate sauce made with frozen concentrated Welch's grape juice and tinned pumpkin-pie filling; I remember that one. Yogurt curd made with skim milk and goat cheese whirled in the blender."

In those days, all of their friends had been Iranian, all more or less in the same situation as Maryam and Kiyan. (At one of their big poker parties a wife could call, "Agha doctor!" and every man in the room could answer, "Yes?") Where were those people now? Well, many had gone back home, of course. Others had moved on to other American cities. But some, she knew, remained right here in Baltimore; only she had lost touch with them. Politics had increasingly complicated matters, for one thing. Who supported the Shah? Who did not? Then after the Revolution you could be sure that most of the new arrivals had definitely supported the Shah, had perhaps even held high positions with the secret police, and it was wiser to avoid them altogether. Besides, Kiyan was dead by then and she no longer felt comfortable in that two-by-two social circle.

"If only your father had lived to see the Shah overthrown!" she said to Sami. "He would have been so happy."

"For about three and a half minutes," Sami said.

"Well, yes."

"He would hate to hear what's going on there now."

"Yes, of course."

She'd been listening to music from home one day on Kiyan's old shortwave radio while she ironed. Already there'd been public demonstrations and rumors of unrest, but even the experts had been unable to predict the outcome. And then in midnote the music had stopped and there was a long silence, broken at last by a man announcing, quietly and levelly, "This is the voice of the Revolution." A thrill had run up her spine and tears had filled her eyes, and she had set down her iron and said, out loud, "Oh, Kiyan! Do you hear that?"

"What's going on there now would break his heart," she told Sami. "Sometimes, you know what? I think the people who are dead are lucky."

"Whoa!" Sami said. Maryam glanced reflexively toward the traffic ahead, expecting some emergency. But no, this seemed to be one of those exaggerated reactions you saw so often in young people. "No way, Mom! Hold on there!"

"Oh, I don't mean that literally. But what would he say, Sami? He *loved* his country! He always meant for us to go back there someday."

"Thank God we didn't," Sami said, and he flicked his turn signal on and swung sharply into the fast lane as if the very thought made him angry.

He had never been to Iran himself. The one time since his birth that Maryam had gone back, Sami was already grown and married and working for Peacock Homes, and he had claimed he couldn't get away. He had no interest, was the real reason. She looked over at him sadly, at his large, curved nose so like Kiyan's and his endearing little spectacles. Now he would probably never go, and certainly not with her, because she had resolved not to return after that last visit. It wasn't the restrictions, so much—the funereal long black coat she'd had to wear and the unbecoming headscarf—but the absence of so many of the people she had loved. Of course she had been told about their deaths as they occurred (her mother, her great-aunts, her aunts and some of her uncles, each loss reported one by one in roundabout, tactful terms on thin blue aerogram paper or, in later years, over the telephone). But underneath, it seemed, she had managed not to realize fully until there she was, back in the family compound, and where was her mother? Where was her cluster of aunts clucking and bustling and chortling like a flock of little gray hens? And then at the airport when she was leaving there'd been a problem with her exit visa, something inconsequential that was settled fairly easily by a cousin with connections, but she had felt a sense of panic that was almost suffocating. She had felt like a bird beating its wings inside its cage. *Let me out, let me out, let me out!* And she'd never been back.

In the grocery store, where she and Sami had to struggle through a crowd of other Iranians shopping for their New Year's parties, she couldn't help asking, "Who *are* these people?" The children were using the familiar "you" when speaking to their parents; they were loud and unruly and disrespectful. The teenage girls were showing bare midriffs. The customers nearest the counter were pushing and shoving. "This is just . . . distressing!" she told Sami, but he surprised her by snapping, "Oh, Mom, get off your high horse!"

"Excuse me?" she said, truly not sure she had heard right.

"Why should they act any better than Americans?" he demanded. "They're only behaving like everyone else, Mom; so quit *judging*."

Her first impulse was to snap back. Was it so wrong to expect her countrymen to set a good example? But she counted to ten before she spoke (a tactic she had learned during his adolescence) and then decided not to speak at all. Instead she proceeded down the aisle in silence, dropping cellophane packets of herbs and dried fruits into the basket he was carrying for her. She paused before a bin of wheat kernels, and Sami said, "Will there be time enough to sprout them?" There was plenty of time, as he knew full well. He must be asking only to make amends. So she said, "Well, I *think* there will be. What's your opinion?" and after that they were all right again.

She did judge. She knew that. Over the years she had become more and more critical, perhaps because of living alone for so long. She would have to watch herself. She made a point of smiling at the next person who jostled her, a woman with short hair dyed the color of a copper skillet, and when the woman smiled back it turned out she had a single, deep groove at the outer corner of each eye just like Aunt Minou's, and Maryam felt a rush of affection for her.

The Donaldsons had been invited for lunch on a Sunday that fell a full eight days after Ziba's parents' party; so there was less reason than ever for Maryam to host the event at her house. By now, though, she was resigned. She cooked the whole week before, a dish or two a day. She set up the *Haftseen* table in the living room—the seven traditional objects, including a vibrant little putting green of sprouted wheat kernels, artfully arranged on her best embroidered cloth. And Sunday morning she rose before dawn to make the final preparations. The only other windows alight were in houses where there were small babies. The only sounds were the birds, a clamor of new and different songs now that spring was here. She padded around the kitchen barefoot, wearing muslin pants and a long-tailed shirt that used to belong to Sami. Her tea cooled on the counter as she rinsed the rice and set it to soak, and climbed on a stool to fetch down her trays, and snipped the stems of the yellow tulips that had been waiting overnight in buckets on the back porch. By now the sun was rising, and through the open window she heard the newspaper carrier's squeaky-braked van and then the slap of the *Baltimore Sun* against her front step. She brought the paper into the kitchen to read with her second cup of tea. From where she sat she could see into the dining room, where the silver gleamed on the table and the stemware sparkled and the tulips marched down the center in a row of slim glass vases. She loved this time before a party when the napkins had not yet been crumpled or the quiet shattered.

At twelve-thirty, freshly bathed and dressed in narrow black trousers and a white silk tunic, she was standing at her front door to welcome Sami and Ziba. They came early to help with last-minute preparations, although, as Sami pointed out, she had left them nothing to do. "No, but this way I get to have a little visit with Susan," she said. Susan was a very competent walker by now, and the minute Sami set her down she made a beeline for the basket where Maryam kept her toys. Her hair had grown long enough that it fell in her eyes if they didn't tie it up into a sort of vertical sprout on top of her head. It wisped around her little shell ears and trailed in thin strands down the back of her flower-stem neck. "Susie-june," Ziba told her, "say, 'Hi, Mari-june!' Say, 'Hello, Mari-june!'"

"Mari-june," Susan said obligingly, only it came out more like "Mudge." She gave Maryam one of her tucked smiles, as if she knew exactly how clever she'd been.

Ziba wanted to fiddle and fidget—"Is there anything we can do? Should Sami open the wine? Which tablecloth did you use?"—but Maryam told her it was all taken care of. "Have a seat," she said. "Tell me what you'd like to drink."

Ziba didn't answer because she was pummeling cushions, even nudging Sami aside so she could get to the one he was sitting against. She was nervous, Maryam supposed. She had dressed up a little too much for daytime, in the same shiny turquoise mini-dress she'd worn to her parents' party, and two circles of rouge on her cheeks made her seem feverish. Probably she was comparing Maryam's house to her own—Maryam's too-small living room and traditional, rather dowdy furniture overlaid with paisley scarves and little Iranian trinkets—and finding it lacking. "Susan, put that back!" she said when Susan hauled out a plush dog. "We can't have toys scattered all over the place when guests are coming!"

"Oh, why not? Jin-Ho will want to play too," Maryam told her; and Sami, lazily twirling a string of clay prayer beads he'd picked up from the coffee table, said, "Relax, Zee. Settle down."

She made a cross little puffing sound and flung herself into a chair.

It didn't help that the next arrivals were Ziba's parents. They were a bit early, having misjudged the travel time from Washington, and when Mrs. Hakimi apologized to Maryam in Farsi ("I'm very sorry; I ask your forgiveness; I told Mustafa we should just drive around a bit but he said—"), Ziba cried, "Mummy, *please;* you promised you'd speak English for this!"

Mrs. Hakimi sent Maryam a rueful glance. She was a pleasant-looking woman with a plump, tired face, and she let her family walk all over her, Maryam had noticed—especially her husband, who maintained the rigid posture of a military man although he'd made his money in business. He imported things. (Maryam wasn't sure what.) He had a bald yellow head and an enormous stomach that strained the vest of his gray sharkskin suit. "Susie-june!" he roared, and he pounced on Susan, who smiled shyly but curled over till she was practically a shrimp shape, and no wonder; Mr. Hakimi was a cheek-pincher. *Pinch-pinch!* with his big yellow fingers while Susan squirmed and looked around for Ziba.

"I understand your party last week was a great success," Maryam told Mrs. Hakimi.

"Oh, no, it was nothing. A very plain affair," Mrs. Hakimi said, and then she took a sudden swerve back into Farsi. "I'm sure our meal today will be much more elegant, since you were the one who prepared it and no one else I know makes such delicious—" Her words came all in a rush, as if she hoped to get as much said as possible before she was apprehended; but Ziba said, "Mummy!" and Mrs. Hakimi broke off and looked at Maryam helplessly.

In Maryam's experience, it used to be the wives who adapted more quickly. Almost overnight they had decoded the native customs, mastered the ins and outs of supermarkets and car pools, grown confident and assertive while their husbands, buried in work, confined their new English to medical terms or the vocabulary of seminar rooms. The men had depended on the women, back then, to negotiate the practical world for them; but in the case of the Hakimis the situation seemed to be reversed. When Brad's parents arrived in their spring outfits the colors of Easter eggs, proclaiming their names vivaciously before Maryam could introduce them, Mrs. Hakimi only smiled at her lap and shrank lower in her chair. It was Mr. Hakimi who assumed command of the conversation. "So you are the paternal grandparents! May I say how pleased we are to meet you! And what do you do for a living, Lou?"

"Why, I'm an attorney, retired!" Lou said, nearly matching Mr. Hakimi's hearty tone. "The wife and I are leisure folk now. We take a lot of cruises, golfing trips; I'm sure you've heard of Elderhostel . . ."

Maryam excused herself and went off to check on dinner. She lowered one flame, raised another, and then allowed herself a little spell of gazing out the kitchen window before the sound of the doorbell pulled her away. When she returned to the living room Brad and Bitsy were just coming in, Brad carrying Jin-Ho, while Bitsy's parents followed at some distance. Connie was having a little trouble with the steps. Dave cupped a palm beneath her elbow as she struggled to lift one foot to meet the other. "Oh, I'm sorry," Maryam said, crossing the porch to greet her. "I should have told you to come in the back."

But Connie said, "Nonsense, I need the exercise," and she squeezed both of Maryam's hands in hers. "I can't tell you how I've been looking forward to this," she said. At long last she had given up her baseball cap. Her scalp was thinly furred with a half inch of gray hair, very fine and soft-looking, and she wore a navy cotton dress that seemed too big for her. When she reached the door, she paused and took a deep breath as if she were bracing herself. Then she plunged into the living room. "You must be Ziba's parents!" she cried. "Hello! I'm Connie Dickinson, and this is my husband, Dave! Hi, Pat! Hi, Lou!"

There was a flurry of greetings and compliments (Pat's new hair color, Bitsy's drawstring trousers), and then Dave asked about the *Haftseen* table, which gave Mr. Hakimi the chance to deliver a lecture. "*Haftseen* means 'seven *s*'s,'" he began in a public sort of voice. "We have here seven objects that start with the letter *s*." Dave and Connie nodded solemnly, while Bitsy prevented Jin-Ho from snatching the embroidered cloth off the table.

"Now, hold on there!" Lou said. "Those hyacinths don't start with *s*!"

Brad said, "Dad—"

"That plate of grass doesn't start with *s*!"

"*S* in *our* language," Mr. Hakimi told him.

"Oh. Aha. Very interesting."

"Your house is charming, Maryam," Bitsy said. "I love the mixture of textiles. I'm a weaver, you know, so of course I notice such things." She made another grab for Jin-Ho, this time picking her up. "Did you bring all these rugs with you when you first came?"

"Oh, no," Maryam said. She laughed. "When I first came, I brought a single carpetbag."

"But a *Persian* carpetbag, I'll bet, in some fascinating pattern."

"Well, yes . . ."

She had given away the carpetbag a month after she arrived, ashamed it wasn't Samsonite. Oh, in those days she wouldn't have brought rugs from home even if she'd had the space. She'd wanted everything sleek and modern, solid-colored, preferably beige—American-American, as Kiyan used to say. Both of them had so admired the Western style of decorating. Only later did she understand that they had embraced the worst of the style—the cheap beige plastic dinnerware, the wasteland of bland beige carpeting, the chairs upholstered in beige synthetics shot through with metallic threads.

Now it was Dave carrying on the what-do-you-do conversation. He had just informed Mr. Hakimi that he was a physics teacher, and while Maryam circled the room with soft drinks and wine and (for Mr. Hakimi) whisky on the rocks, she learned that Connie taught high school English and Brad taught biology. So perhaps it was only natural that this family felt entitled to tell other people how to do things. Could genes determine occupations, even? she wondered as she returned to the kitchen.

The rice was beginning to send out its browned-butter, popcorn smell. She moved the pot to the sink and switched off the burner. From the living room she heard Mr. Hakimi introducing the next topic: politics, specifically Iranian politics—the long, noble history of Iran and its bitter end in the Revolution. Just as well she was out of sight; she avoided discussing such matters with any of Ziba's relatives. She ran cold water into the sink and waited for the pot to stop steaming, although she could easily have left it unattended. When she heard small, uneven footsteps behind her, she was delighted. "Susie-june!" she cried, turning, and Susan smiled and raised both arms and said, "Up?" She enunciated very carefully, as if she were aware that she was working to learn a language. Maryam picked her up and laid her face against Susan's soft cheek. Then Jin-Ho toddled in with a toy truck clasped to her chest and said, "Kack? Kack?" and Maryam took a guess and went to the cupboard for Triscuits. "Cracker," she said, handing one to each child. "Thank you, Mari-june!" and she set Susan down. Susan and Jin-Ho started rolling the truck between them, each clutching a Triscuit in one hand and squatting in that boneless way that only small children can manage, feet set flat and wide apart and bottoms an inch from the floor. They were such a pleasure to watch. Maryam could have stood there all afternoon just drinking in the sight of them.

As it turned out, that was the high point of the party. By the time the guests were seated at the table, both little girls had gone past their nap times. Susan was carried wailing to the crib Maryam kept for her upstairs, while Jin-Ho stuck it out in her mother's lap, growing steadily crankier and squirmier and violently averting her face from the morsels of food Bitsy offered.

And it wasn't only the children who were fractious. First Pat took it upon herself to suggest that Connie might like to try wrapping her head in a pretty silk scarf (did even the in-laws in this family feel free to give advice to each other?), and Connie flushed and looked unhappy, and Dave said, "Thank you, Pat, but I think Connie's beautiful just the way she is," and Pat said, "Oh! Why! Of course! I never meant—!" Then Bitsy, apparently hoping to smooth things over, said, "While we're speaking of fashions, Ziba, Susan's little topknot was darling," and Ziba said, "Yes, I'm trying to get her hair out of her eyes," and Bitsy said, "Ah, well, Jin-Ho doesn't have that problem because we're keeping the style she came with. I guess we just don't feel we should Americanize her."

"Americanize!" Ziba said. "We're not Americanizing!" (As if anything really could Americanize a person, Maryam thought, having watched too many foreigners try to look natural in blue jeans.) It must be that Ziba still felt insecure around the Donaldsons, because ordinarily she would not have bristled like that.

And when Mr. Hakimi took his own stab at peacemaking, he just made the situation worse. "But! We're neglecting our hostess!" he bellowed. "This is such excellent food, my dear madam, and you were so kind to relieve Ziba of the burden of entertaining!"

Ziba said, "It wasn't a burden! What are you talking about? We could have had it at our house! I was longing to have it at our house!"

Maryam said, "You were?"

"We have more room at our house! I told you that! We wouldn't need to squeeze around the table on desk chairs and porch chairs and kitchen chairs!"

Maryam said, "But I thought you said—"

Now she couldn't remember what either one of them had said. She had trouble reconstructing the whole conversation. All she knew was that once again, they must both have been too polite, too please-I-insist and whichever-you-prefer. "Well," she said finally. "I wish I had known."

Connie set down her fork and leaned across the table to touch Maryam's hand. "In any case, it's a lovely party," she said.

"Thank you," Maryam told her.

"And besides," Bitsy chimed in, "this way we get to see your house, and all your beautiful things! Tell me, Maryam; I'm dying to know: what was in that one carpetbag you brought? What does a person choose to take with her, when she's leaving her country for good?"

Gratefully, Maryam turned her thoughts to the carpetbag. A silk peignoir set, she remembered. And two sets of lacy lingerie hand-sewn by Aunt Eshi's seamstress . . . She smiled and shook her head. "It wasn't how you imagine," she told Bitsy. "I was a brand-new bride. I was thinking about how *I* looked, not my house."

"A bride! You came over as a bride?"

"I had been married just one day when I boarded the airplane," Maryam said.

"So the trip to America was your honeymoon! How romantic!"

From his place at the head of the table, Sami said, "Now, Mom. Tell the whole story."

"Oh, tell!" Bitsy said, and Lou tapped his water glass with his knife. Jin-Ho, who was just nodding off, started a bit and then resettled her head against her mother's shoulder.

Maryam said, "There is no story."

"Yes, there is," Sami said. He turned to the others. "She made that so-called honeymoon trip alone," he said. "My dad was already over here. She had a proxy wedding all by herself and joined him afterward."

"Is that true?" Pat asked her. "You had a wedding without the groom? But how did that work?"

"Show them the photo," Sami told Maryam.

"Oh, Sami, they don't want to see the photo," she said, and she ignored their protests ("Yes, we do! Show us, Maryam!") and rose to pick up the platter of stuffed grape leaves. "Would anyone care for seconds?" she asked.

"A photo of Mom in her wedding dress," Sami said, "standing alone beside a long table you can hardly see for the presents. It looks as if she's marrying the presents."

Maryam said, "Well, I wouldn't say . . ." There was something in his tone that hurt her feelings. Something amused; that was it. And perhaps Mr. Hakimi felt it too, because he cleared his throat and said, "In fact many, many girls married that way at the time. All those young men who went to America, don't you know, or Germany or France . . . Of course they needed wives, by and by. It was a reasonable solution."

"But how did you court at such long distance?" Pat asked Maryam.

"Court!" Sami said. He laughed. "They didn't. The marriage was arranged."

Maryam sensed a new alertness around the table, but she didn't look up from the platter she stood holding in both hands. No one had taken seconds. Maybe they had disliked the grape leaves. Maybe they had disliked the whole meal.

"So you see," Sami told Bitsy, "it wasn't as romantic as you think."

Maryam said, "Oh, Sami." She spoke very gently, to hide the outrage in her voice. "You can't know everything about it," she said. And then she turned away, with as much dignity as possible, and carried the grape leaves out of the room and shut the swinging door behind her.

In the kitchen, she filled the kettle with water for tea. Obviously she should clear the table before she served the pastries and fruit, but she wasn't quite ready yet to go back and face the others. She lit the burner beneath the kettle and then remained at the stove, her arms folded tightly across her chest, her eyes stinging with tears.

When Kiyan had told her, for instance, that her hair smelled like an Armenian church: what could Sami know about that?

The swinging door opened slowly and Connie walked through, carrying two plates. Maryam said, "Please, you mustn't," and took the plates from her. "You'll tire yourself," she said.

Connie said, "That's okay; I wanted to stretch my legs." Instead of going back to the dining room, she settled on the stool and watched Maryam scrape the plates. "Aren't family gatherings wearing?" she said. "All those people who know you so well, they think they can say just anything."

"It's true," Maryam said. She began fussing with the stacks of soiled cookware that cluttered her one small counter. While she was facing away from Connie, she dabbed hurriedly at the tip of her nose. "And really they *don't* know you so well," she said.

"You're right; they don't know the half of it," Connie agreed. She turned toward the swinging door, where her husband was just entering with two more plates. "We're commiserating about family gatherings," she told him.

"Ah, yes, dreadful affairs," Dave said, and he went straight to the garbage bin in a familiar way and started scraping the plates. Maryam never could get used to men helping out in the kitchen. Where was Ziba? Wasn't it Ziba who should be doing this? "Families in general," Dave was saying. "They're vastly overrated."

Connie tsked and gave him a friendly swat.

"And holding this dinner at my house," Maryam went on (reminded by thoughts of Ziba). "I never asked to do that! I mean . . . forgive me; of course I'm pleased to have you, but—"

"We understand," Dave told her. Probably he didn't understand, but he was nice enough to nod his woolly gray head in a sympathetic manner, and Connie nodded too and said, "It's funny how we get maneuvered into these things."

"We're too careful with each other, Ziba and I," Maryam said. She turned toward the stove and uncovered the kettle to see if the water was boiling. "Our family is not very good at saying what we want. Sometimes we end up doing what *none* of us wants, I suspect, just because we think it would satisfy the others."

"Be rude, like us," Dave suggested, and he draped an arm around Connie's shoulders and winked at Maryam. She had to laugh.

Then Connie and Dave returned to the dining room for more plates, and Maryam spooned tea leaves into her best china teapot. She did feel better now. There was something consoling about those two. She poured boiling water into the teapot and replaced the lid and then balanced the teapot on top of the kettle.

Maybe the hiss of the simmering water was what brought back, all at once, a scene from the earliest days of her marriage. Whenever she had felt particularly lonesome, she remembered, she used to set a tumbler of club soda on her nightstand. She used to go to sleep listening to the bubbles bounce against the glass with a faint, steady, peaceful whispering sound that had reminded her of the fountain in her family's courtyard back home.

3

It was Bitsy who thought up the idea of an Arrival Party. That was what she called it, right off, so that Brad had to ask, "A what, hon? Come again?"

"A party to commemorate the date the girls arrived," she told him. "In two weeks it will be a year; can you believe it? Saturday, August fifteenth. We ought to mark the occasion."

"Would you be up to it, with your mother?"

Bitsy's mother had suffered a setback—a whole new tumor, this time involving her liver. They'd had a hard couple of months. But Bitsy said, "It would do me good. It would do us all good! Get our minds off our troubles. And we'd confine it to the two families; no nonrelatives. Make it kind of like a birthday party. A daytime event, right after the girls' naps when they're at their best, and I wouldn't serve a full meal, only dessert."

"Maybe a Korean dessert!" Brad said.

"Oh. Well."

"Wouldn't that be neat?"

"I checked Korean desserts on the Internet," Bitsy told him. "Spinach cookies, fried glutinous rice . . ."

Brad started looking worried.

She said, "I was thinking maybe a sheet cake frosted like an American flag."

"That's a great idea!"

"With candles? Or one candle, for one year. But absolutely no presents; remind me to tell the Yazdans that. They're always bringing presents. And we might sing some sort of song together. There must be a suitable song about waiting for someone's arrival."

"There's 'She'll Be Coming Round the Mountain,'" Brad said.

"Well . . . and the girls can wear Korean outfits. Shall we offer to lend Susan a *sagusam*? You can be sure she doesn't own one."

"That would be good."

"We could have a ceremony, sort of. The girls would be in another room; we'd light the cake and start singing; they would walk through the door hand in hand . . . just like arriving all over again. Don't you think?"

"And, hey!" Brad said. "We could show the video!"

"Perfect! The video," Bitsy said.

Her brother Mac had taken all the different airport videos to be edited into a single tape. Since then the tape had sat on a shelf—there never seemed to be time to watch even the news, anymore—but this was their chance to view it. "Maybe at the end of the party, to wind things up," Bitsy said. "Is this all too hokey, maybe?"

"Not a bit."

"You're sure, now. You would tell me if it was."

"You couldn't be hokey if you tried," Brad said.

The nice thing was, he meant it. She knew that. He had this notion that she could do no wrong. It was "Bitsy says this" and "Bitsy says that" and "Let's ask Bitsy, shall we?" She took his face between her hands and leaned forward to give him a kiss.

≠

Bitsy never liked for this to get around, but Brad was not her first husband. Her first husband had been Stephen Bartholomew, the only son of her parents' oldest friends. Bitsy's parents and Stephen's parents had double-dated all the way through Swarthmore and kept devotedly in touch ever since, even though the Bartholomews lived clear across the country in Portland, Oregon. Bitsy had seen Stephen precisely twice in her life—both times when she was too young to remember—before they entered Swarthmore themselves; but the idea was, they were bound to be instant soulmates. The first letter her mother wrote her, the first week of Bitsy's freshman year, began with "Have you met Stephen yet?" And no doubt Stephen's mother was asking him the same thing.

Of course they did meet, by and by, and to nobody's surprise they promptly fell in love. He was an ethereally beautiful boy with a narrow, calm face and sea-gray eyes. She was plainer but a born leader, the campus star, outspoken and impassioned. They went through four years of college as an established, recognized couple, although they had such different interests (chemistry for him and English for her, not to mention her various political activities) that it was a struggle to find the time to be together. Christmas of their senior year they became engaged, and they married the next June, the day after graduation, and moved to Baltimore, where Stephen had a fellowship at Hopkins and Bitsy went to work on her education credits at College Park.

Then she met Brad.

Or no, first she started noticing Stephen's flaws. Actually, which *did* come first? Now she couldn't say. But she remembered realizing one day that Stephen's most consistent emotion was disapproval. Oh, that narrow face of his was more significant than she'd guessed! This was a man who could get all worked up about the phrase "too simplistic," for Lord's sake; a man who refused to be moved by a haunting rendition of "I Wonder As I Wander" because he was offended by the ungrammatical construction of "people like you and like I." "I mean, where will it all *end*?" was his favorite question, and more and more he seemed to ask it about Bitsy herself—her tendency to procrastinate, her offhand housekeeping methods, her increasingly lackadaisical attitude toward her studies. He saw the rest of the world as a sliding heap of ever-sinking standards, and it made him frown and fidget; it made him clear his throat in an edgy, portentous manner that drove her to distraction.

Well, certainly a person could have worse faults than that. It was not enough to justify divorcing him. But the fact was, they had married without much more than an acquaintanceship beforehand. She saw that belatedly. They had been smitten with the mere idea of each other—two obedient children trying too hard to please their parents—and had spent four years keeping to opposite sides of the campus just so they wouldn't have to find out how very ill-suited they were. (Wasn't their marriage almost arranged, really? Was it so different from Maryam Yazdan's? Maryam's might have been happier, even. Bitsy would have loved to ask about that.)

So anyway, along came genial, contented, easygoing Brad with his fuzzy haircut and his loopy smile and his absolute faith that she was the most wonderful person in the world. They met at a campus rally for John Anderson; Bitsy was very gung-ho for Anderson but Brad thought he might stick with Carter. He just wasn't sure. She reasoned with him, and went out for coffee with him later to reason some more. He hung on her every word. They invented further excuses to meet. (Wouldn't voting Independent mean throwing his vote in the garbage? Hmm? What was her honest opinion?) She had never known anybody so trustful. Even what others might disparage—his gee-whiz style of speech, his beginnings of a beer belly—warmed her heart.

Every time they were out in public she worried he would find some other woman more attractive. How could he not? She knew she was no beauty. That girl behind the counter at their favorite coffeehouse, for instance: she was so much bustier than Bitsy, but it wasn't only that; she was so much *softer,* more yielding somehow. And furthermore, she was single! Then the girl said, as she refilled their cups, "I am completely and totally bushed," and Bitsy felt a vindictive thrill because that was such a redundant, ignorant-sounding phrase—"completely and totally," good grief!—until she realized that Brad hadn't even noticed it. He wouldn't notice; he lacked that critical quality. But never mind: he was looking only at Bitsy anyhow. His eyes were the same shade of blue as a baby's receiving blanket, just that pure and mild.

She told him her marriage had been over for months, and he shouldn't give it a thought. She was shameless, ruthless, single-minded, without a shred of conscience. She spent the night in his sweatsock-smelling bachelor apartment and didn't even bother offering Stephen an alibi. And when Brad accepted a teaching job in Baltimore she dropped her education courses flat and never set foot in College Park again.

Of course, both her parents and Stephen's were shocked when they heard the news. Not so much Stephen himself; he seemed more relieved than anything else. But their parents couldn't believe that such a perfect match had not worked out. They blamed it on "adjustment problems" (a full year after the wedding). Her mother asked her, privately, whether she'd given any thought to the great, great importance of intellectual compatibility in a marriage. And Brad's parents, well. The less said about them, the better. You could tell they thought their son had lost his mind. Such a gangling, graceless girl, not to mention already married and one year older than he and politically ridiculous! The Donaldsons voted Republican. They lived in Guilford. When they got together with Bitsy's parents, even now, you could see them open their mouths and draw in their breath and then fail to find a single subject they could imagine discussing with such people.

Bitsy had assumed that as soon as Brad's parents became grandparents, things would ease up. But then they didn't become grandparents. (One more strike against Bitsy.) She spent fifteen years trying to get pregnant while other women, heedlessly lucky women, cruised blithely past her in the supermarket with grocery carts full of children. She endured every possible test and grueling medical procedure, and more than once it was on the tip of her tongue to ask her doctors, "Could this be *my* doing? I don't mean just my body's doing; I mean, is it my nature? Am I not soft enough, not receptive enough—a woman who ditched her first husband without the least little twinge?"

Absurd, of course. And see how well it had all turned out! They had their precious Jin-Ho, the most perfect daughter imaginable. And a child in need, besides—an opportunity to do good in this world.

When Bitsy looked back on Jin-Ho's arrival, it didn't seem like a first meeting. It seemed that Jin-Ho had been traveling toward them all along and Bitsy's barrenness had been part of the plan, foreordained so that they could have their true daughter. *Oh, it's you! Welcome home!* Bitsy had thought when she first saw that robust little face, and she had held out her arms.

But she supposed no one would understand if she called this a Reunion Party.

Bitsy's two brothers were younger than she, but their children were half-grown. (That used to rankle, a bit.) Mac and Laura had a teenage son—a certified genius, antisocial and geeky—and a disturbingly sexy blond ten-year-old daughter. Abe and Jeannine had three girls, ages eight, nine, and eleven but alike enough, in looks and in temperament, that they could have been triplets. Poor Brad was forever mixing up their names.

On the afternoon of the party, these two families arrived before anyone else and even before the specified time by a good half hour or so, pulling up in front of the house one after the other as if they had traveled in tandem, although they lived in opposite directions. At first Bitsy felt annoyed; she was still trying to stuff Jin-Ho into her costume, and the coffee urn had not been started yet or the cake set out on the table. Then she wondered if they had come with some agenda in mind. The wives seemed uncharacteristically eager to steer the children toward the TV room, and once the grownups were settled in the living room, Abe (the younger one) kept looking expectantly at Mac. For some reason, Bitsy felt no particular need to help them out. In fact, at the very moment that Mac said, "So! Well, ah. Since we're all here—," she was seized by the urge to head him off. She said, "You know what I did this morning?"

Everyone looked at her.

"I listened to the audiotape we made at the airport that night. Goodness, it seems long ago! I'm talking into the mike; I'm saying, 'Everybody's gathered around; everybody's brought presents. Mac and Laura are here, and Abe and Jeannine.'" Although actually, she had not referred to them by name. She was just trying to make it more interesting. "I sounded so shaky and scared! Well, face it: I was scared to death. I thought, What if it turns out that I can't warm to this child? What if—well, we'd seen that one photo and we already knew she was beautiful, but what if in person she was somehow off-putting or unappealing? These things can happen, you know! Although no one likes to admit it. And look at Susan. Of course she's a darling, but I've always wondered, didn't the Yazdans feel maybe the faintest bit disappointed when they saw how homely she was? With that sallow skin and bald forehead? And then *later* come to love her; I don't mean we wouldn't have loved her, but still . . . Oh, I was a nervous wreck that day! And you can hear it in my voice. Then I say, 'Oh! She's here! Oh, she's lovely!' and there's this clattering sound; that would be me letting go of the tape recorder—"

"Say, maybe we should play that tape today at the party!" Brad said.

"Well, I don't know; I think I'd feel sort of stupid if other people heard it."

"Aw, hon, it wouldn't be stupid. It would be sweet."

"Bitsy," Laura said in a declarative tone. (She was a grade-school principal; she was accustomed to taking charge.) "We need to have a talk about your parents."

"My parents?"

Laura looked at Mac. He straightened and said, "Right. Mom and Dad. I guess we don't have to tell you that Mom seems to be sinking."

"*I'll* say you don't have to tell me!"

Her brothers and their wives had not been as attentive as they might have been, in Bitsy's opinion. She directed a special glare toward Jeannine, who had once declined to drive Connie to a chemo appointment because her youngest had a playdate.

"And you can see that it's wearing on Dad," Mac went on. "This summer's been bad enough, but with classes starting in September, well, I'm not sure how he's going to manage. He's talking about taking early retirement. But you know how much he loves teaching. I'd hate to see him give that up just when . . . just before he's going to need something to do with his days, you know? We think he ought to hire some kind of nursing help for Mom."

"Oh," Bitsy said. She was relieved. She had worried they

might ask *her* to be the nurse, or even to take her mother into her house.

"But for sure they're both going to argue. Dad will say he wants to care for Mom on his own. Mom will say she doesn't need any care."

"She's so *obstinate*!" Laura burst out. "Doesn't she realize how difficult she makes things? People who refuse to accept their limitations: oh, it's all very admirable, all very brave and heroic, but in practical terms it's infuriating! Getting into fixes she can't get out of, refusing canes and walkers, insisting on going to places where the restroom's a hundred miles away and up three flights of stairs—"

Bitsy knew exactly what she meant, but to hear it from a mere sister-in-law—someone not even related, so efficient and professional in her cat's-eye glasses and square-cut pantsuit—seemed an insult. She said, "Oh, Laura, who knows what we'd do ourselves in her situation?"

"We'd bow gracefully to circumstance, I would hope," Laura snapped. Her husband sent her a warning glance and Abe started looking anxious, but she ignored them both. "So," she said to Bitsy. "Are we agreed? We offer to hire caretakers?"

"Givers," Bitsy said automatically.

"Pardon?"

"Care*givers*, is what they're called these days."

"And around the clock, don't you agree? So your dad won't have to get up nights."

"How much would that cost, exactly?" Brad asked. "I mean, of course we do agree—don't we, Bitsy?—but wouldn't this cost an arm and a leg?"

"Not if we all chip in," Laura said.

Everyone looked at Bitsy.

She said, "Well, of course we would chip in. But I don't think they'll accept it. And the issue isn't money, anyhow. I'm sure Dad makes enough money."

"Yes, but offering to pay is a way of bringing up the subject," Laura told her. "Here's what you do: say it's for your sake. Say you're losing sleep over this and it would make you feel better if you and your brothers could pay for some help."

"Me?" Bitsy asked. "*I'm* supposed to say? What about the rest of you?"

"Well, naturally we'll back you up—"

"Back *me* up?"

But then the doorbell rang and she sprang to her feet, glad for the interruption. This was supposed to be a party! A celebration for Jin-Ho! (Who had been hustled off to the TV room with the most minimal of greetings, just so the grownups could conspire together.)

On the porch she found Ziba's parents—Mr. and Mrs. Hakimi, beaming, in stiff dark clothes. Mrs. Hakimi mutely held out a huge, extravagantly wrapped gift, contrary to all instructions, while Mr. Hakimi cried, "Felicitations, Mrs. Donaldson!" They were so exotic, so blessedly distant from the scritch-scratching irritation of the scene back in the living room. Bitsy said, "Oh, what a pleasure to see you!" and then she said, "Please, it's Bitsy," and took the gift from Mrs. Hakimi and kissed her on the cheek. Mrs. Hakimi's cheek was as soft as an old velvet purse. Mr. Hakimi's parchment-colored head resembled an antique globe. They entered the house in a hesitant, respectful manner, even though the front hall was littered with toys and yesterday's Dyper Delyte delivery sat by the umbrella stand.

"Such an occasion! Such a joyous occasion!" Mr. Hakimi announced in the living-room doorway. It was like a stage direction. Immediately the men stood up and put on welcoming faces, and the sisters-in-law began stirring and bustling, and the children streamed in from the TV room clamoring for something to eat. The doorbell rang again, and again, and then again—the Yazdans with

Maryam, then Brad's parents, and last of all Bitsy's parents, her mother quite alert today and steady on her feet—and it really did start to feel like a joyous occasion.

Why was it that Bitsy loved Sami and Ziba so? The two couples had little in common, other than their daughters. And the Yazdans were so much younger. Too much younger, it seemed at times. Sami had that very young habit of taking himself too seriously, although that could have been just his foreignness showing. (Even though his accent was dyed-in-the-wool Baltimore, something studiously, effortfully casual in his manner marked him as non-American.) And Ziba, with her noticeably manicured, dark red nails and her hennaed hair and two-tone lipstick: why, Bitsy herself had not bothered with such concerns in years! Or ever, as a matter of fact.

Even on issues pertaining to their daughter, the Yazdans took a very different approach. Imagine changing that charming name, Sooki, part of her native heritage, to plain old Susan! "Su-zun Yazdun": it didn't even sound right. ("Yaz-*dan,*" Ziba had corrected her, when Bitsy once wondered aloud how well that really worked. Okay, but still . . .) Not to mention the outfit Susan was wearing today, a party dress from one of those grandmother stores over in D.C. The *sagusam* Bitsy had lent her was lying now on the couch, shucked off as soon as everyone had had a chance to admire it. And their child-rearing philosophy in general: the working mother, the regimented bedtime, the singsong, fluty-voiced baby talk—"Su-Su-Su! Susie-june!" as if Susan belonged to some whole other, less intelligent species of being.

Still, they were the first ones Bitsy thought of when she was in the mood for company. "Let's call the Yazdans! See what they're up to." And Brad seemed to feel the same way. Maybe it had to do with the Yazdans' gentleness. They were so pliant and accepting; they lacked sharp edges. (Bitsy didn't include Maryam in this. Maryam could act very superior sometimes.) And also . . . well, wasn't it true that those women who'd actually given birth formed a complacent sort of sorority, with their talk of sonograms and labor pains and breast-feeding? None of Bitsy's other friends had adopted, as it happened. They were very supportive and all that, very diplomatic, but she could tell that underneath, they felt that to adopt was to settle for second-best. Oh, so many secret hurts and bruises lay behind this Arrival Party! And Sami and Ziba must have experienced them too.

Ziba had told her once that her parents believed that people who couldn't have children *shouldn't* have children; it wasn't meant to be. "Destiny!" Ziba had said with a laugh, but Bitsy had not laughed with her. Instead she had reached out and covered Ziba's hand with her own, and Ziba's eyes had flooded suddenly with tears.

Now the two little girls were rolling across the dining-room rug and giggling. They had started noticing each other lately. They were beginning to play together instead of back to back. And Sami was asking Brad how he liked his new Honda Civic, and Ziba was helping Bitsy set out the refreshments. It had become the custom for Ziba to be the one to make the tea when she was visiting. Surely the Yazdans could not actually taste the paper on a tea bag, but Ziba maintained that they could and so Bitsy kept a box of loose tea in her cupboard (a box she regularly had to discard because another thing the Yazdans could taste was *old* tea, in theory) and Ziba brewed it herself in a complicated process that involved a precarious tower of teapot on top of kettle and a periodic sniffing for the proper "melting smell" to the leaves. Jeannine and Laura were fascinated. They hovered around the stove, getting in everyone's way and asking questions. "Shouldn't there be some easier method? This seems a little . . . makeshift." "Why not just dump the leaves directly in the kettle? Streamline the operation?" Ziba merely smiled. Bitsy felt secretly proud, as if some of the Yazdans' mystery had transferred itself to her.

The one boy cousin, Linwood, was asked to light the candle on the cake. Bitsy had thought this would make him feel more included. He was such an awkward creature, all Adam's apple and knobby joints, with thick, smudged glasses and too-short hair. But even stepping up to the table turned his face a deep red, and when he finally got a match lit he somehow managed to drop it as he was lurching toward the cake. Bitsy's father, who was closest, snuffed it out easily with one palm and said, "No harm done," which wasn't quite true because a charred spot showed on the tablecloth, not that Bitsy cared about such things; but Abe's three daughters squealed as if he'd set the house on fire. "God, Linwood, you're such a dork," his sister said, tossing her adult-looking mane of blond hair, and Laura said, "That's quite enough out of you, young lady!" and Linwood wheeled blindly and tried to escape through the ring of relatives, leading with his lowered head. It took a while for people to persuade him to try again.

Meanwhile, Brad was waiting out in the kitchen with Jin-Ho and Susan, listening for their entrance cue, but evidently neither child understood the situation. Bitsy could hear Susan asking, "Mama? Mama?" "Just *light* the damn thing, Linwood," Mac said, and Laura said, "Mac!" and Linwood struck another match and lit the candle on his first try. It was fortunate there was just one candle. Bitsy was already calculating that next year, when there were two, the girls might be old enough to do it themselves—with proper supervision, of course.

"All right, everybody," Bitsy said, and she started singing. "They'll be coming round the mountain when they come . . ." She had been searching till the very last minute for a more appropriate selection. There must be a song in grand opera about a long-awaited arrival. Or almost certainly in *The Messiah,* if that wasn't sacrilegious. But nothing had occurred to her, and this at least was a song the children knew. Everyone but the Hakimis (who were gamely smiling) joined her halfway through the first line—even Linwood, in a mumbly undertone—while Brad flung open the kitchen door and called, "Ta-da! They're here!" The two girls—Jin-Ho resplendent in red-and-blue satin, Susan in pink organdy—clung to his trouser legs and looked bewildered.

"Oh, we'll all go out to meet them when they come," Bitsy sang. "Come on, honey!" she called to Jin-Ho. "Come on, Susan! See your cake?"

It was a beautiful cake—a huge Stars and Stripes. "The lady at the bakery counter thought we were just really, really late for the Fourth of July," Brad told Sami. The two of them were hoisting their daughters in their arms now so that they could have a view of the table. Abe stepped forward to aim his camera at them. "You get in this too," he told Bitsy. "You too, Ziba, get into the picture. Okay, all together now! Smile!"

Everybody smiled (well, except for the girls, who still seemed baffled), and the camera flashed.

"We'll let the cousins blow the candle out," Bitsy said. "I'm not sure the girls are up to that yet. And Jeannine, if you would pour the tea, and Laura can serve the coffee, and I'll ask you to cut the cake, Pat . . ." For once, she refused to do everything on her own. She was celebrating the most important anniversary in her life (yes, even more important than the anniversary of her marriage), and she intended to enjoy it.

Predictably, Linwood held back from the candle-blowing, but the four girl cousins fell into the spirit of things, shoving each other and sputtering with laughter until more or less by chance the candle happened to go out. Then Brad's mother cut precise little squares of cake and Bitsy's father handed them around. He started with Bitsy's mother, probably out of solicitude, but she had not been able to eat much lately and she waved the plate aside. She was settled at the table in a ladder-back chair. The others remained on their feet, keeping to the small groups they felt most comfortable with, but Maryam pulled out the chair next to Connie and sat down also. "I imagine tea would go well right now," Bitsy heard her say, and Connie said, "Oh, you know, I believe it might." Maryam placed her own cup in front of Connie and turned to Jeannine for another, and Bitsy sent her a thankful smile even if Maryam didn't notice. Maryam was dressed in one of those super-stylish outfits she favored—cigarette-legged white slacks and a black scoop-necked top that showed off her tanned arms—but all at once she seemed much more likable than usual.

The girl cousins were competing at lugging the little ones here and there, staggering around with them as if Jin-Ho and Susan were giant dolls. Linwood was huddled in a corner glumly wolfing down his cake. The men were discussing baseball, and Pat and the two sisters-in-law were making more of the business of serving than seemed called for. Only Ziba and her parents, standing slightly to one side, appeared at loose ends. Bitsy went over to them. "Did you get tea?" she asked the Hakimis, although both were holding cups and saucers. "Are you not having any cake?"

Mrs. Hakimi smiled even more broadly, and Mr. Hakimi said, "So kind of you, Mrs. Donaldson—"

"Please: it's Bitsy," she told him for the dozenth time. Also, she had kept her maiden name, but no sense getting into that now.

"Mrs. Hakimi and I are watching our waistlines," he said. He patted his stomach, which certainly could have used watching, although his wife had one of those short, cozy figures that made calorie-counting seem beside the point.

Ziba said, "It does look delicious, though. Did you bake it yourself, Bitsy?"

"Oh, my heavens, no! I've never been good at pastry."

"Me neither," Ziba said. "My mother's the pastry expert. She makes delicious baklava."

"Is that right!" Bitsy turned to Mrs. Hakimi. She knew it was laughable to think that a louder tone of voice would make her more easily understood, but somehow she couldn't stop herself. "Isn't that wonderful! Baklava!" she said, with more animation than she'd shown since high school.

Mrs. Hakimi said, "I do not ever buy the . . . ," and then she gazed helplessly at Ziba and dissolved in a stream of Farsi.

"She doesn't buy the filo dough. She makes her dough from scratch," Ziba said. "She rolls it out herself, thin enough to see daylight through."

"Isn't that . . . wonderful!" Bitsy said again.

"My wife is a very talented person," Mr. Hakimi announced.

Mrs. Hakimi made a tsking sound and looked down into her teacup.

"Well, next we're going to show a videotape," Bitsy said. She figured it would count for something if she faced the Hakimis as she spoke, even though her words were meant for Ziba. "My brothers and one of Brad's uncles and, oh, just lots of people, some of our friends too, brought video cameras to the airport when we went to meet Jin-Ho. So we're going to show the tape, but I want to apologize right now for the fact that it's all Jin-Ho and no Susan. We didn't know back then that Susan would be there! Otherwise we'd have filmed her too."

"Oh, that's okay," Ziba said. "I have the memory in my head."

"You do?" Bitsy asked. "Isn't it funny, the whole evening's such a blur to me. I remember when I first saw Jin-Ho's face; I remember reaching out for her. But then what? How did she react? It all seems like a dream now."

Mrs. Hakimi poked Ziba's arm. "Tell about Susan," she ordered.

"What about her, Mummy?"

"Tell about when we first met her."

"Oh," Ziba said. She turned to Bitsy. "My parents didn't come to the airport, remember. They had a prior engagement." She lowered her sweeping lashes a fraction of an inch. (Prior engagement. Right.) "They visited later that week, and when they walked in, Susan was sitting in her high chair and she raised her eyebrows at them and said, 'Ho?' Only babbling, you understand. She didn't mean anything by it. But it sounded like a Farsi word, *khob*. The word for 'well.' 'Well?' she was saying. 'Do I pass inspection, or don't I?'"

Mrs. Hakimi said, *"Khob?"* and doubled over with laughter, covering her mouth with one hand. Her husband said, "Ha. Ha." He looked across the room toward Susan. "A child of spirit," he said. "We Hakimis are known for our spirit. We have, how do you say. We have backbone."

Bitsy smiled and followed his gaze. It was true that Susan generally showed a certain dauntlessness, puny though she was. At the moment she seemed to have decided that she had been toted around long enough, and she had planted herself in Jin-Ho's child-sized rocker and was gripping its arms so stubbornly that when one of the cousins tried to lift her, the rocker came along with her.

Mrs. Hakimi was still saying, *"Khob?"* and laughing behind her cupped palm, and Ziba was watching her fondly. "Now they dote on her," she told Bitsy. "She's their favorite grandchild."

Mr. Hakimi said, "*No,* no, no, no, no. No favorites," and wagged a thick index finger at his daughter, but it didn't seem he really meant it.

"Well, why don't we go watch the video," Bitsy told them. "Everybody!" she called, clapping her hands. "Shall we move into the TV room for the video?"

She threaded through the crowd, rounding up those who hung

back to continue their conversations. “Brad, are you coming? Laura? Jeannine? Somebody bring the girls in; they haven't seen this either.”

She had straightened the TV room earlier that morning, but already the children had managed to wreck it. Various cushions were strewn on the rug, and a *Teen People* magazine lay in the seat of the armchair. (Stefanie's, no doubt—the ten-year-old going on twenty.) Bitsy plucked it up between thumb and forefinger and dropped it on the windowsill. “Sit here,” she told her mother. “Will this be comfortable? Somebody hand me a cushion for Mom.”

Brad, meanwhile, was rummaging through the videotapes heaped on top of the TV. “You kids took my tape out of the machine,” he complained. “I had it all ready to roll! Now, where . . . ? Ah. Got it.”

Some of the older people packed themselves in a row on the sofa—the Hakimis and Brad's parents. Dave settled on one arm of Connie's chair and everyone else sat on the floor—even Maryam, assuming almost a lotus position with her back very straight. Abe offered to bring her a chair from the dining room, but she said, “I prefer this, thank you,” and she drew Susan onto her lap and wrapped her arms around her.

A while ago, Sami and Ziba had gone away for the weekend and left Susan with Maryam. Bitsy was amazed when she heard about it. During her own brief absences—never longer than a couple of hours, and only for unavoidable reasons such as doctor appointments—she used a person from Sitters Central, a woman certified in infant CPR. Anyhow, her mother was too frail to babysit and her in-laws had made it plain that they had their own busy lives. But under no circumstances would she have considered leaving Jin-Ho overnight. She would have been frantic with worry! Children were so fragile. She realized that now. When you thought of all that could happen, the electrical sockets and the Venetian-blind cords and the salmonella chicken and the toxic furniture polish and the windpipe-sized morsels of food and the uncapped medicine bottles and the lethal two inches of bathtub water, it seemed miraculous that any child at all made it through to adulthood.

She reached for Jin-Ho and pulled her closer, even though it meant pulling her cousin Polly along with her.

Brad said, "Here we go!" and stepped back from the TV. On a dated-looking, pale blue watered-silk background, copperplate script spelled out *The Arrival of Jin-Ho.* "Classy," someone murmured, and Mac called, "This was a firm I found in the Yellow Pages. Very reasonably—"

"Ssh!" everyone told him, because now a voice could be heard from the TV set—Mac's own voice, but more public-sounding. "Okay, folks, we're at the Baltimore/Washington Airport. Friday evening, August fifteenth, nineteen ninety-seven. It is seven thirty-nine p.m. The weather is warm and humid. The plane is due to land in, let's see . . ."

Brad closed the curtains, turning the watered silk a deeper blue, and then settled on the floor next to Bitsy. "Watch, sweetheart," he told Jin-Ho. She was sucking her thumb and her eyes were at half-mast. (She hadn't slept during her nap today, perhaps sensing the excitement.)

A jumble of figures appeared: Dickinsons and Donaldsons, intermingled, wearing summer clothes. You could tell it must have been hot because people had a frazzled, sweaty look, even the most attractive of them not quite at their best. Well, except for Pat and Lou, as cool and chalky as two bisque figurines. (Although Pat was heard to say, from her place on the couch, "Good heavens! I'm so old!") A girl cousin scampered across the screen, green plaid shirt-tails flying. "That's me! That's my old shirt!" little Deirdre shouted, and Jeannine said, "Ssh."

"I *loved* that shirt!"

"Straight ahead you see the proud parents," Mac's onscreen

voice was announcing. "Brad and Bitsy, both very happy. Bitsy got up at five this morning. This is an extremely important day in their lives."

Just hearing him say those words made Bitsy a little teary. To herself, though, she looked not so much happy as terrified. And so unformed! So tentative and shy, as if it would take motherhood to turn her into a grownup. She was clutching her tape recorder and speaking into it inaudibly, her chin tucked in an unbecoming way. Beside her, Brad held a car seat level in both arms as if he expected their daughter to drop into it from the heavens.

The scene broke off and then, confusingly, Mac himself appeared, filmed by someone else. He was squinting into his video camera, and just beyond him Uncle Oswald was squinting into *his* camera. Bitsy thought of the childhood Christmas when she and both of her brothers had been given Kodaks, and every photo from that day showed not faces but head-on cameras aimed glaringly at whoever happened to be taking the picture.

The onscreen voice—Abe's voice, now—said, "I started counting up who was here and lost track at thirty-four. So Jin-Ho, honey, if you're watching this from some point in the future, you can see how eager your new family was to meet you."

Everybody glanced at Jin-Ho, but she was sound asleep.

Connie appeared, looking healthier than she had in months, and Dave beside her and then Linwood, propped against a wall intently punching a Game Boy. Abe was introducing people as he filmed them. "Now, here is your Aunt Jeannine. Here's Bridget, your cousin, and here's your cousin Polly." The camera careened past two strangers, rested briefly on Laura, and swooped back to Linwood. You could get carsick watching this. Bitsy closed her eyes for a moment, and when she opened them she found that whoever had spliced the tapes must have felt the same way, because now it was no longer Abe speaking but Mac again. "All right, folks, it's quite a while later. Been a bit of a delay. But the plane has landed, finally, and we're watching the first passengers come in off the jetway. Big moment! Big, big moment."

Bitsy saw a very tall young man and realized that she'd seen him before. She saw two businessmen, a boy with a backpack, a woman dropping her briefcase to hug two children in pajamas. How odd: these people were so familiar, and yet she hadn't given them a thought since that night and had certainly not been aware that they were stored in her brain. It was something like rereading a book and coming across a passage where you can recall every word a split second before you see it, even though you could never have summoned it up on your own.

The woman from the agency, for instance. The Korean woman in the navy suit that resembled an airline uniform, with her broad cheekbones and her stern, official manner. Bitsy had mentally dismissed her the instant she and Brad took possession of their daughter—she'd exorcized her, you could almost say—and yet now the two fine creases below the woman's eyes were so well known to her that she wondered if she had dreamed about her every single night of this past year. And the diaper bag! Oh, look. Pink vinyl, cheap and poorly made, already beginning to peel along the edges of the strap. They had discarded it immediately in favor of the one that Bitsy had sewn from her own handwoven fabric, but here it was, back again, like a statesman's casket reappearing on the evening news after you have spent the day watching it being buried.

And Jin-Ho. Ah, there: the camera zoomed in on her face and held steady. She was so much smaller! Her features were so much closer together! "Look at you, Jin-Ho," Brad murmured, but to Bitsy, the child asleep in Polly's lap bore almost no connection to the baby on the screen. The sudden ache she felt was very like grief, as if that first Jin-Ho had somehow passed out of existence.

The woman from the agency was handing the baby to Bitsy. Bitsy was hugging the baby close and her relatives were smiling and dabbing their eyes with tissues. Everybody, both onscreen and off, was making soft cooing sounds like a barnful of mourning doves.

Oh, wasn't adoption *better* than childbirth? More dramatic, more meaningful. Bitsy felt sorry for those poor women who had merely delivered.

Evidently someone else was filming now, because Mac could be seen making googly eyes at the infant Jin-Ho. Maybe it was Uncle Oswald who was sweeping his camera across the assemblage one last time and then drawing back, back to take in the jetway door and the final trickle of passengers, the man with the cane and the gray-haired couple and—oh!

There was Susan.

"We did get her in! We did!" Bitsy cried. "There she is in her carrier!"

And there were Sami and Ziba, too. There was Maryam following behind with her faultless posture and her imperious, bugle-clear "Here we are. Yazdan." All three were remarkably free of appurtenances. No cameras, video cameras, or tape recorders. They traveled light, these people. ("I have the memory in my head"—wasn't that how Ziba had put it? All at once Bitsy felt envious.) The photographer tracked their progress toward the jetway and then focused again on Susan, or on what little could be seen of her, which was mostly a pink T-shirt and a tuft of scanty black hair. Bitsy leaned past Brad to search out Ziba in the audience. She found her sitting next to Sami on the floor near the bookcase. "Doesn't this bring it all back?" she called, and Ziba said, "But she's tiny!" without taking her eyes from the screen. "She's like a whole other person!" she said.

"I know."

"It makes me sad."

"Oh, I *know*!" Bitsy cried, and if she'd been nearer to Ziba she would have hugged her, and hugged Sami too with his sweet little glasses glittering like tears in the light from the TV.

Then she turned back to the movie and found it had ended without her. Credits were gliding across the watered silk. *Special thanks to the Loving Hearts Korean-American Adoption Center.* Brad clicked the remote control and rose to open the curtains, and light flooded the room. People blinked and stretched. Jin-Ho was still asleep, her head lolling against Polly's chest, but that was all right; she would have many more chances to watch this movie in years to come. Bitsy patted Jin-Ho's satin-draped leg and then struggled to her feet and made her way toward Sami and Ziba. Sami was holding a wide-awake, squirmy Susan and listening to Mac's advice on the best brand of video camera, but Ziba turned to Bitsy and threw her arms around her. "Why do I feel so *sad*?" she asked Bitsy. "Isn't it silly?" She collected herself and wiped her eyes. She'd left a damp spot on Bitsy's shoulder. "It was the happiest day of my life! It's a day I'll never forget."

"Me either, but would you want to go back to it?" Bitsy asked her.

"Never!"

They both laughed.

"Come help me brew another pot of tea," Bitsy told her.

They made their way through the crowd, which wasn't easy. Other people were damp-eyed too; other people wanted to hug them. Bitsy's mother said, "It broke my heart to see our Jin-Ho arriving all alone like that," and Bitsy's father said, "Alone? She had that nice Korean woman."

"Yes, but you know what I mean."

"Maybe that's why we're sad," Bitsy told Ziba as they entered the kitchen. "We're so used to having the girls by now; we forget they haven't always been with us. We see them coming off the plane and we say, 'Oh, no, they made that long trip without us! Where were *we*?' "

"And they lived those first months of their lives without us," Ziba said. "All alone! Coping for themselves!"

They fell into each other's arms again, crying and laughing both.

"Oh, Ziba, who else understands how it feels?" Bitsy asked as she leaned back against the sink and fished in her pocket for a tissue. "I wish you lived closer. I hate that I have to get in my car to go see you. I'd like to have you next door. We could call to each other over the fence, and the girls could play together whenever they wanted without all these formal arrangements."

She could see it in her mind: the casual comings and goings, the screen doors slamming as the girls raced out to meet the first thing after breakfast. Maybe the Sansoms at 2410 could sell to the Yazdans. They were getting on in years, after all, and their Cape Cod was much, much nicer than any McMansion out in Hunt Valley. She blew her nose and said, "We could babysit for each other. Soon the girls would hardly notice if one of us was gone."

"When they got a little older they could have sleepovers," Ziba said.

Maryam had joined them by now. She was gently setting Bitsy to one side so she could fill the kettle. "Being together so much," Bitsy said, "they would think adoption was natural. I mean, they would know it was. They wouldn't have any self-doubts or sense of inferiority."

"Does this stove need a match to light it?" Maryam asked.

"Oh, I'm sorry! No, just that one burner; the others are fine," Bitsy told her. "You know," she said, turning back to Ziba, "when I was in that poetry group, I read about these two women poets who had so much they wanted to share with each other, they installed a separate telephone line and left their receivers off the hook at all times so as to keep in constant contact. Not that I'd want to do that myself, but don't you sympathize with the urge?"

"They left them off night and day?" Ziba asked. "Wouldn't the telephone company send one of those beeping signals?"

"Well, I don't . . . I may have some of the details a little wrong," Bitsy said. "I'm just talking theoretically here. I did wonder how they could hope to catch every last word. What if one of them happened to speak while the other was in a different room? They surely couldn't have heard from everywhere in the house."

From her place at the stove, Maryam said, "How interesting that that's what you would worry about."

"Pardon?" Bitsy said.

"Why wouldn't you worry too *much* would be heard, rather than too little? Private things, that families should keep separate."

"Oh," Bitsy said. "Well, of course." She glanced toward Ziba. "Of course, that would be . . . Well, maybe they didn't have the phones off the hook every single instant."

"Ah," Maryam said. "In that case, then."

"I mean, it isn't something I would want to do myself. I *said* that. I said it was just the general urge that I understood."

Maryam didn't comment. She had a disconcerting way of letting a conversation drop, Bitsy had noticed. All she did was spoon tea leaves into the teapot. It was Ziba who spoke up next. "Another thing about the video," she said. "I kept thinking I could smell the smells. I remembered how Susan smelled when I first held her, like a spicier kind of vanilla, and now she doesn't smell that way at all. She's more like *regular* vanilla. Did you think of the smells, too?"

"Well, no . . . I know what you mean, though," Bitsy said. But her heart was not in it. A sort of dullness fell over her, and all at once she felt out of place in her own kitchen. She was underfoot here. She had nothing to do. In a sense she had nothing to do with her *life,* if you didn't count Jin-Ho. She had never completed her education courses, never held a full-time job. She had busied herself with dribs and drabs like teaching yoga and attending poetry seminars and throwing pottery and weaving—little made-up activities without steady pay or health-care benefits. Brad said her weaving was beautiful, but he would, of course. In fact she hadn't sat at her loom in months, and last week when she was wearing one of her old creations she had happened to notice herself in the full-length mirror upstairs and all at once she saw that she might as well be wearing a rug. The fabric was so coarse and so boldly striped, a board-stiff rectangle from which her bare arms and legs emerged all scraggy and ropy.

"Oh," she said, "I should see to . . . ," and she turned and left the kitchen. She drifted through the dining room, where Laura and her sexy daughter were hissing at each other over the coffee urn. She passed Linwood, slouched in the doorway chewing a thumbnail, and Bridget hauling Susan toward the miniature rocker. In the corner chair in the living room she saw her mother—the person she'd been looking for, she realized. She sidled past Mr. and Mrs. Hakimi, who apparently had no one to talk to just now but what concern was that to her? She settled on the arm of her mother's chair. "Oh, good," her mother said instantly, and Bitsy took comfort from the thought that one person in this room, at least, was pleased to see her. But next her mother said, "Here," and handed her a slip of paper.

"What's this?" Bitsy asked.

"It's the name of a woman."

Bertha MacRae, Bitsy read, and a telephone number, in a careful, rounded hand.

"A woman who comes to the house," her mother said.

"Comes to the house?"

Her mother gazed up at her, unblinking. Lately her eyes had changed shape. The lower lids had dropped and pouched, which somehow gave her an expression of reproach although she was not the kind of woman who had ever reproached anyone. She said, "I don't believe she's a nurse, exactly. She must be some sort of aide, but she's licensed. She's been trained. And she has a couple of sisters who might take the other shifts. Evidently the twenty-four hours are divided into three shifts."

"Where did you get this?" Bitsy asked.

"Maryam gave it to me. This woman nursed Maryam's husband when he was dying."

The word "dying" had a sharp, shocking sound, but Connie seemed not to notice. She passed smoothly on. "Maryam says the woman's still working. They still keep in touch. She's not sure about the sisters, but if they aren't available, Maryam thinks the woman would know other people who are."

She took Bitsy's hand. Connie's skin was so dry these days that her fingertips had a puckered feel, as if she'd just stepped out of a bath. "Will you help me with your father?" she asked.

"Help you how, Mom?"

"You know he's going to object. He's going to tell me he can take care of me himself. But he can't do it all, Bitsy. Not morning, noon, and night. And I want to be able to ask for things. I want to ask and not have to worry that I'm asking for too much."

Bitsy said, "Oh, Mom," and bent to lay her cheek on top of her mother's head. Connie's poor hair was so thin that it felt warm. "Of course I'll help," she said.

"Thank you, dear."

Bitsy knew she should feel grateful to Maryam, but instead a wall of resentment rose up within her. It seemed that some belonging of hers had been taken away from her. Or some plan of hers had been foiled; that would be more accurate. Although in fact she had not had any plan, and it should have been a huge relief that someone else had come forward with one.

The children were laughing and tumbling, and the men were trading technical specifications, and Mr. Hakimi was apparently telling Mrs. Hakimi something instructive, although he was speaking in Farsi and Bitsy couldn't understand his words. She had to guess at his meaning just from his tone, as if she were a foreigner in an unfamiliar country.

4

Sami had a sort of performance piece that he liked to put on for the relatives. He was known for it. They would be sitting around the living room with their afternoon tea—a few of Ziba's brothers and sisters-in-law visiting from L.A., or maybe a couple of aunts or the cousins who'd settled in Texas—and one of them would say, almost slyly, "These Americans: can you figure them out?" Then this person would offer some anecdote to start things rolling. For instance: "Our hostess asked where we were from and I told her Iran. 'Oh!' she said. 'Persia!' 'No,' I said, 'Iran. Persia is only a British invention. From the start, it was always Iran.' 'Well, I prefer Persia,' she told me. 'Persia sounds much more beautiful.'"

People would cluck and nod, having been through such exchanges many times themselves, and then they would gaze expectantly at Sami. Sami would roll his eyes. "Ah, yes," he would say, "the Persia Passion. I know it well." Sometimes that alone was enough to start them grinning; they were so ready for what came next.

"What you should have told her is, 'Oh, then! In that case! Please don't let a mere twenty-five hundred years of history stand in your way, madam.'" (The "madam" came out of nowhere. He tended to slip into a fusty, overstarched style of speech on these occasions.) "You can be certain she'll argue. 'No, no,' she'll insist, 'Iran is a newfangled name. They announced the change in the thirties.' 'They announced what their *real* name was in the thirties,' you tell her, and she'll say, 'Well, anyhow. I myself plan to keep calling it Persia.'"

Or he would get going on the American craze for logic. "Logic's why they're always suing each other. They believe that for every event there has to be a cause. Surely somebody is to blame! they say. Stumble in the street when you're not looking and break your leg? Sue the city! Sue the store where you bought your glasses and the doctor who prescribed them! Fall down the stairs, bang your head on a cabinet, slip on the bathroom tiles? Sue your landlord! And don't just sue for medical bills; sue for pain, emotional trauma, public humiliation, lowered self-esteem!"

"Ooh, low self-esteem," a relative might murmur, and everyone would laugh.

"They feel personally outraged by bad luck," Sami would go on. "They have been lucky all their lives and they can't imagine that any misfortune should have the right to befall them. There must be some mistake! they say. They've always been so careful! They've paid the closest attention to every safety instruction—the *DANGER* tag on the hair dryer saying *Unplug after every use,* and the print on the plastic bag saying *This is not a toy,* and the recycling pamphlet saying *Warning: Before stepping on milk jugs to flatten them, please take firm hold of a reliable source of support.*"

Or he would embark upon a little riff about the Americans' fond belief that they were of breathtaking interest to everyone else in the world. "Imagine this: A friend of my father's, a famous poet, was invited here on some sort of grant. They escorted him to every state in the Union and demonstrated how they fed their livestock. 'Now, here, sir, we use the most modern methods of crop rotation to ensure an adequate supply of . . .' A lyric poet! A city man, born and raised in Tehran!"

Or he would examine their so-called openness. "So instantaneously chummy they are, so 'Hello, I love you,' so 'How do you do, let me tell you my marital problems,' and yet, have any of them ever really, truly let you into their lives? Think about it! Think!"

Or their claim to be so tolerant. "They say they're a culture without restrictions. An unconfined culture, a laissez-faire culture, a do-your-own-thing kind of culture. But all that means is, they keep their restrictions a secret. They wait until you violate one and then they get all faraway and chilly and unreadable, and you have no idea why. My cousin Davood? My mother's nephew? He lived here for six months and then he moved to Japan. He said that in Japan, at least they tell you the rules. At least they admit they *have* rules. He feels much more comfortable there, he said."

Then others would chime in with stories of their own—the friendships unaccountably ended, the stunned silence after innocent questions. "You can't ask how much someone's dress cost. You can't ask the price of their houses. You don't know *what* to ask!"

These conversations were conducted in English, because Sami would not speak Farsi. He had flat-out refused to ever since the day back in preschool when he had discovered that none of his classmates spoke it. And there lay the irony, according to his mother. "You with your Baltimore accent," she said, "American born, American raised, never been anywhere else: how can you say these things? You're American yourself! You're poking fun at your own people!"

"Aw, Mom, it's all in good humor," he said.

"It doesn't sound so good-humored to *me*. And where would you be without this country? I ask you! You take it for granted, is the problem. You have no idea what it feels like to have to watch every word, and keep every opinion to yourself, and look over your shoulder all the time wondering who might be listening. Oh, I never thought you would talk this way! When you were growing up, you were more American than the Americans."

"Well, there you have it," he told her. "Hear what you just said? 'More American than the Americans.' Didn't you think to wonder why?"

"In high school you never dated anyone but blondes. I'd resigned myself to being Sissy Parker's mother-in-law."

"I didn't even come close to marrying Sissy!"

"Well, I certainly never expected that you would pick an Iranian girl."

"I don't know why not," he said.

This wasn't entirely truthful, because in his heart he too had always thought his wife would be American. As a child he had longed for a *Brady Bunch* family—a father who was relaxed and plaid-shirted and buddy-buddy, a mother who was sporty rather than exotic. He had assumed that his schoolmates enjoyed an endless round of weenie roasts and backyard football games and apple-bobbing parties, and his fantasy was that his wife would draw him into the same kind of life. But then his senior year in college, he met Ziba.

Unlike the daughters of his parents' old friends, Ziba had a nonchalant, sauntering style about her. She was confident and plainspoken. She came right up to him after their first class together ("The Industrial Revolution," spring semester) and said, "Iranian, right?" "Right," he said. He braced himself for the usual chitchat about what-part, what-year, whom-do-you-know, all voiced in that combination of flirtatiousness and cloying deference that Iranian women put on with the opposite sex. Instead, she said, "Me too.

Ziba Hakimi," and she breezily trilled her fingers at him and moved off to join her friends—American friends, male and female mixed. She wore jeans and a Tears for Fears T-shirt, and her hair in those days was short enough so that she could gel and spike it into something resembling punk.

As he came to know her, though (as their exchanges grew slightly longer each day, and they fell into the habit of walking out of the classroom together), he noticed how much they understood about each other without discussion. A cloak of shared background surrounded them invisibly. She asked him in mid-March if he planned to go home the next weekend, and she didn't need to explain that she meant for New Year's. He passed her on the library steps where she was eating a snack with a friend, and her snack was not chips or cookies or Ring Dings but a pear, which she was slicing into wedges with a tiny silver knife like the ones his mother set out with the fruit tray after every meal.

That summer after graduation he drove over to Washington often to take her to dinner or a movie, and he met a whole string of her relatives. To him the Hakimis seemed both familiar and alien. He recognized the language they spoke, the foods they served, the music they were listening to, but he was uncomfortable with their lavish parties and their collector's zeal for the most expensive, most ostentatious brand names—Rolex and Prada and Farragamo. He would have been even more uncomfortable with their politics, no doubt, if he had not had the good sense to avoid discussing the subject. (Ziba's parents all but genuflected whenever the Shah was mentioned.)

What would his mother think of these people? He knew what she would think. He brought Ziba home to meet her but he left Ziba's relatives out of it. And his mother, although she welcomed Ziba graciously, never proposed that the two families get together.

But she might not have in any case. She could be very unforthcoming.

In the fall Sami and Ziba went back to the university—Sami to work on his graduate degree in European history and Ziba to start her senior year. They were deeply in love by then. Sami had a shabby apartment off campus and Ziba spent every night with him, although she continued to keep all her clothes in her dorm room so that her family wouldn't suspect. Her family visited constantly. They showed up every weekend with foil-wrapped platters of eggplant and jars of homemade yogurt. They hugged Sami to their chests and kissed him on both cheeks and inquired after his studies. In Mr. Hakimi's opinion, European history was not the best choice of fields. "You propose to do what with this? To teach," he said. "You will become a professor, teaching students who'll become professors in turn and teach other students who will become professors also. It reminds me of those insects who live only a few days, only for the purpose of reproducing their species. Is this a practical plan? I don't think so!"

Sami didn't bother arguing. He would chuckle and say, "Oh, well, to each his own." Somehow, though—how did this happen?—by the time he and Ziba were married, late the following June, he had agreed to work in her uncle's development company. Peacock Homes built and sold houses in the more upscale areas—northern Virginia and Montgomery County—and they were expanding to Baltimore County. At first Sami's job was temporary. Just try it, everyone said, and go back to school in the fall if he didn't like it. He did like it, though. He grew to enjoy the wish-fulfilling aspects of it—the couples confiding their cherished, touchingly specific dreams. ("Got to have an eye-level oven. Got to have a desk nook next to the fridge where the wife can make out the week's menus.") He studied for his real-estate exam and passed it. He and Ziba moved into the company's newest project, and Ziba found work with her cousin Siroos at Siroos Design ("Serious Design," customers tended to call it), decorating the houses that Peacock Homes sold.

If Maryam was disappointed that Sami had given up his studies, she never said so. Well, of course she was disappointed. But she told him it was his decision. She was cordial to the Hakimis and affectionate with Ziba; he knew she liked Ziba, and he didn't think that was only because Ziba was Iranian. For their engagement she had offered them a ring he'd never seen before, an antique ring with a diamond that satisfied even the Hakimis. Or maybe it didn't. It wasn't *huge*. But at least they had professed to be satisfied. Oh, everybody on both sides had been exceedingly well behaved.

Sami didn't exempt the Donaldsons from his tirades about Americans. If anything, he was harder on them. They were such easy targets, after all—especially Bitsy, with her burlap dresses and her more-organic-than-thou airs and her with-it way of phrasing things. "She called her mother's funeral a 'celebration,'" he told the relatives. "She said, 'I hope you two will come to the celebration for my mother.'"

"Did she misspeak, perhaps, out of grief?" Ziba's father asked.

"No, because she repeated it. She said, 'And please will you tell Maryam about the celebration, too.'"

In this case it was Ziba who objected. "What's the matter with that?" she asked Sami. "People say all the time they're gathering to 'celebrate a life.' It's a very common expression."

"My point exactly," he told her. "It's a knee-jerk, trendy, *chic* expression."

"Well, for shame, Sami. The Donaldsons are our best friends! They've been wonderful to us!"

It was true that they had been wonderful. They were so good-natured, so warm, so hospitable. Best friends, though? There Sami had his reservations. It wasn't that he could come up with any better friends, but Bitsy really got on his nerves sometimes. And he couldn't resist poking fun at her. She just invited it! "Listen to this," he told Ziba's sisters-in-law. "A few weeks back, Bitsy decides it's time to toilet-train her daughter. She's going to bring it about by 'positive reinforcement.' Bitsy's very big on positive reinforcement. So what does she do? She throws a Potty Party. She puts Jin-Ho in Wonder Woman underpants and sends off invitations to four other kids the same age, including Susan. I believe the suggested dress code was underpants for the guests as well, but she didn't insist, which was lucky for us since Susan hasn't a clue yet. We brought Susan in her diaper. But Jin-Ho was wearing underpants—she kept lifting her dress to show us—and so were two of the other kids. And someone—I'm not naming names, here—must have had a little misadventure, because gradually all the parents started getting funny looks on their faces and sniffing at the air and sliding their eyes toward each other, and finally one of them said, 'Um, does it seem to you . . . ?' By then it was too late, though. *Way* too late, because evidently this misadventure had happened in the backyard where all the kids were playing, and they must have run through it a dozen times before they came inside for refreshments and tramped across the rugs, climbed up on the dining-room chairs . . ." He was laughing so hard that he had to pause for breath, and the relatives were shaking their heads and trying not to laugh too. "I mean!" he said. "Talk about your theme party!"

Ziba said, "Oh, Sami, show a little mercy."

"And while we're on the subject of parties," he said, "doesn't it strike you all as quintessentially American that the Donaldsons think the day their daughter came to this country was more important than the day she was born? For her birthday they give her a couple of presents, but for the day she came to America it's a full-fledged Arrival Party, a major extravaganza with both extended families and a ceremony of song and a video presentation. Behold! You've reached the Promised Land! The pinnacle of all glories!"

"Ignore him," Ziba told her relatives.

Her relatives, after all, were thrilled to have arrived in America themselves; but even so they couldn't help smiling. Sami told them, "*You* understand. And guess what: this second time around, we're the ones who have to throw the party."

"We don't *have* to throw it; I offered," Ziba said. "It's our turn," she told the relatives. "They threw the party last year. Only they served just cake and beverages, and I always think it's nicer to give people a whole meal."

"Yes! An Iranian meal," one of her sisters-in-law said.

"With kebabs," another said, "and *morgh polo* and *sabzi polo* and perhaps a nice *shirin polo*—"

Sami said, "Whoa," but he was drowned out by Ziba's Aunt Azra. "I've just been given a secret recipe for making real rosewater ice cream," she said, and then she leaned forward and cupped her mouth with one hand, as if she worried about spies, and whispered, "You take a quart of Cool Whip—"

"You've missed my whole point!" Sami told them.

But he could see he had lost his audience.

There happened to be seven relatives visiting at the time of the Arrival Party: two of Ziba's brothers and their wives, two young nieces, and Aunt Azra. And naturally Ziba's parents had to drive over from Washington to share in the excitement; so this meant nine extra people milling around the house preparing for the party. It took them a week. Or it took the women a week. The men steered clear of it all. They sat in the family room attached to the kitchen, out from underfoot but separated only by a counter and close enough, therefore, to eavesdrop on the women's conversation; and they drank their tiny glasses of tea and thumbed their ropes of fat amber prayer beads and gave little grunts of amusement when they overheard something choice.

Aunt Azra, for instance, was leaving her husband. She had traveled alone from Tehran to visit their children in Texas, and now she had made up her mind to stay for good. She had decided she didn't like sex. (The men raised their eyebrows at each other.) It was a lot of mess and effort, she said, and she clapped a lid on a rice pot. The women wanted to know how her husband had reacted when she told him. "Well," she said, "I telephoned on a Friday morning, early. Friday morning was best because at home it would be afternoon, and I knew he'd be going to his brother's house later on for poker. He would have people there to console him. His brother's wife, especially—Ashraf. Do you remember Ashraf? An unfortunate greenish complexion but very kind, very comforting. That time I had that miscarriage she came to my house and she said, 'I'm going to make you a little halvah to build up your strength, Azi-june.' I said, 'Oh, I don't have the appetite,' but she said, 'Trust me.' And then she went into the kitchen, sent Akbar away—this was in the days when people still had servants; remember Akbar? He and his twin brother came to us from some village, hardly old enough to talk and dressed in rags, both of them. The brother walked with a limp but he was very strong, and he took over our garden and he grew the most beautiful roses. Never before or since have our roses bloomed so well. In fact my neighbor, Mrs. Massoud, once said—this is the Mrs. Massoud whose son fell in love with a Baha'i girl—"

"But your husband?" Ziba's father bellowed across the counter. "What about your husband?"

The women exchanged glances, and Azra stepped closer to them and lowered her voice.

"It would make her look very bad if after she bores us with all this trivia, we learn that her husband shot himself," Mr. Hakimi told the other men.

He was speaking in Farsi. All of them spoke in Farsi, unless they were addressing Sami or Susan. Each time Sami walked in upon these gatherings (he, at least, had to go out to work every day), everyone greeted him in English, and his father-in-law would ask him in English, "How many houses you have sold today? Eh?" But before Sami could answer, Mr. Hakimi would revert to Farsi to tell his sons, "Mamal says the real-estate market has been excellent these past months." Just like that, the English was abandoned. Which was fine with Sami. It let him off the hook. It relieved him of the burden of keeping up his end of things. He would lift Susan into his lap and settle down comfortably to listen.

Like these men following the women's gossip—*depending* on their gossip, relying on it for connection—Sami floated on the gentle current of the relatives' Farsi, comprehending some ninety percent and letting the other ten percent wash past him. The men discussed a cousin's investment proposal; the women debated adding an extra pinch of saffron; the nieces quarreled over a Walkman. If Sami stayed silent long enough, people might forget him so completely that they said things he shouldn't hear—mentioned Uncle Ahmad's new tax-evasion scheme, or let slip some sharp-tongued reference to Maryam. ("Well, Khanom would claim it was cheating to put potatoes in the bottom of the rice pan"—the "Khanom" emphasized in an acid and satirical tone.) Their attitude toward his mother didn't offend him as much as it might have, because he figured she deserved it. After all this time, for instance, she still called Ziba's mother "Mrs. Hakimi" and not "Gita-june." He knew that was no mere oversight.

"Where is the cinnamon? Who's taken it?" Ziba asked. Her Farsi was twangier than his mother's, just unfamiliar enough to give her a sheen of added appeal. "I asked him when he was leaving," one sister-in-law told the other, "and he said he wasn't sure; either before the wedding or after. 'Well, what date is the wedding?' I asked, and he said he didn't know because he hadn't found someone to marry yet." Ziba's mother, swathed in a traffic-sign-yellow apron reading CAUTION! GUY AT THE GRILL, hoisted a casserole onto the counter with a little puff of a breath. Iranian women were very hardworking, Sami always noticed. They produced such labor-intensive dishes—hundreds of hand-rolled stuffed grape leaves, dozens of butter-brushed filo sheets—and so many of them for each meal. Aunt Azra was shaping several pounds of ground lamb into a single enormous ball, patting it all over with efficient little slaps. The men were heaving themselves from their chairs and moving out to the backyard for a smoke. Mr. Hakimi favored thick black cigars that smelled like burning tires, and both of Ziba's brothers (middle-aged, and as bald as their father) had nicotine-stained fingers from their two-pack-a-day cigarette habit. They felt it was unreasonable that they couldn't smoke indoors. "Secondhand smoke!" one of them scoffed, spitting the phrase out in English before slipping back into Farsi. "I have smoked around my daughters all their lives, and look at them! They're much healthier than Susan."

They all thought Susan was too small for her age, and too pale. They also thought she looked too Chinese, but a few confrontations with Ziba had taught them not to mention that.

"How would your family feel about a child who was Asian?" Sami had asked Ziba when she first brought up adopting. Ziba's instant answer had been "I don't care what my family feels; I care about having a baby." And because it was Sami's fault that she couldn't have one of her own, he had felt compelled to go along with her plan. He had hidden his doubts from everyone but his mother; to her he had poured them out, stopping by her house several times a week as furtively as if she were the Other Woman and sitting in her kitchen, letting his cup of tea grow cold, clamping his hands between his knees and talking on and on while Maryam listened noncommittally. "I know Ziba believes that we'll be rescuing someone," he said. "Some child who never had a chance, some disadvantaged orphan. But it's not as simple as she thinks, changing a life for the better! It's so easy to do harm in this world but so hard to do good, it seems to me. Easy to bomb a building to smithereens but hard to build one; easy to damage a child but hard to fix one who has problems. I don't think Ziba knows this. I think she just imagines we'll swoop up some lucky baby and give it a perfect life."

He waited for his mother to contradict him (he *wanted* her to contradict him), but she didn't. She took a sip of her tea and set down her cup. He said, "And it's not as if children come with return guarantees. You can't simply hand them back if they don't work out."

"You can't hand a birth child back either," his mother said.

"But it's less likely you would want to. A birth child is blood-related; you recognize certain traits and so you tolerate them better."

"Or worse," his mother said. "Traits in yourself that you've always disliked. That happens too, on occasion."

It did? He decided not to pursue this. He stood up and circled the kitchen, fists thrust deep in his pockets, and when his back was toward her he said, "Also, um, I worry that this child will feel out of place. He or she will always look so unmistakably foreign to other people, so Korean or Chinese. You know?"

He turned back to find his mother regarding him with what seemed to be amusement, but she said nothing.

"I realize that sounds very superficial," he told her.

She waved a hand dismissively and took another sip of tea.

"And then," he said. "Speaking of which. It would be so obvious that we were not the true parents. There wouldn't be even a possibility of any physical resemblance."

His mother said, "Ah, well. When your children resemble you, you tend to forget they're *not* you. Much better to be reminded they're not, every time you set eyes on them."

"I don't think I'd need reminding," he said.

"I remember once when you were in high school, I heard you phoning a girl and you said, 'This is Sami Yaz-dun.' It came as such a shock: my oh-so-American son. Partly I felt pleased and partly I felt sad."

"Well, I wanted to fit in!" he said. "I wasn't so American! Not to them, at least. Not to the kids in my school."

She waved a hand again. She said, "At any rate. You're thinking you might not love this child. You will, though. I promise."

He wasn't sure which claim was more presumptuous: that she knew what he was thinking or that she could predict how he would feel.

But she was right, of course, on both counts. In the last few weeks before Susan arrived he dreamed almost nightly that their baby was some sort of monster, once a lizardy creature and once a normal human but with evil vertical pupils like a goat's; and that Ziba was unsuspecting and angrily turned away when he tried to warn her. Then as soon as he saw Susan's fragile hair and pinched, anxious face, not beautiful at all despite what Ziba believed, he had felt a kind of caving-in sensation and a wave of fierce protectiveness, and if that wasn't love it soon became love. Susan was the greatest joy of his life. She was endlessly charming and funny and fascinating and, yes, eventually beautiful, which in some ways he regretted because her plainness had tugged at his heart so. Her cheeks rounded out but her mouth kept its pursed shape, as if she were forever carrying on some interior deliberation, and her hair grew long enough to be caught up in two paintbrush ponytails, one above each ear. When he sat among the relatives with her, she nestled against him trustfully and from time to time patted his wrist or twisted around to look up at him, her breath smelling sweetly of the trashy grape soft drink she liked.

The women had started discussing Aunt Azra's immigration prospects—had she any hope of a green card?—and Sami had to guess at some of the officialese. "Ali told me I would need a . . ." something, something, something. Then the men returned from the yard, wrapped in an almost visible veil of tobacco and ash, and the women interrupted themselves to announce a shortage of tomato paste. This made the men very happy. "I'll go! I'll go!" the three of them said. They loved American supermarkets. "Sami, are you coming?"—this last in English. He felt that he ought to say yes, although he was sorry to leave the women's talk, which was turning, by the time the car keys had been found, to Ziba's conviction that Bitsy preferred Maryam's house to this one. Atusa, her oldest sister-in-law, told her she must be imagining things. "Prefer Khanom's little unstylish house to this big, fancy, nice, modern one? You're just nervous, Ziba-june. You're just nervous about your party."

Reluctantly, Sami set Susan down next to her cousins and went off to join the men.

"Happy Arrival Day, all!" Bitsy caroled. "Don't we have the perfect weather for it? We've brought the videotape. We've brought a propane lighter for the candles; much safer for the girls than matches. We've brought photographs from last year, so we can set up an exhibit."

She pecked Sami on the cheek and moved forward to hug Ziba,

followed at some distance by Brad with an overstuffed shopping bag. Last of all came Jin-Ho, strolling slowly up the front walk and admiring her own sandals, which had the too-big, too-stiff look of shoes very recently purchased. (So: no Korean costume this year.) It always worried Sami a little that Jin-Ho was taller than Susan, and heavier. He felt a competitive uneasiness every time he saw her.

"Now, I've been thinking some more about the song," Bitsy was telling Ziba. "I've never been really happy with 'She'll Be Coming Round the Mountain.'"

Meanwhile, the curbside rear door of the Donaldsons' car swung open and Bitsy's father inched out, hauling himself forth like a man weary to the bone. He must have had to be coaxed into coming. Since Connie's death Bitsy had dragged him along to every possible social event, but he didn't have much to say anymore and his large gray head had developed a droop.

"Hello there, Dave!" Sami called. Dave lifted an arm and let it flop and proceeded doggedly up the walk.

"Do you know 'Waiting for a Girl Like You'?" Bitsy was asking. "That's one possibility. Unless it's too hard to sing; what do you think? Or then there's the Beatles. 'I Saw Her Standing There'; do you remember that? It occurs to me that if we rehearsed the children ahead of time—oh, hello, Mrs. Hakimi! Happy Arrival Day!"

Mrs. Hakimi wore flowered black silk and her husband was in a suit, but the relatives following them out of the house were dressed more informally—especially Aunt Azra, who could have been heading for aerobics class, in her tank top and tight, knitted capri pants that revealed every bulge and ripple. "How do you do? How do you do?" they all murmured, except it sounded more like "Do . . . do . . ." They arranged themselves two and three deep across the front steps, so that when it came time to go inside there was some difficulty negotiating the doors. While everyone was still trying, another car pulled up—Abe and Jeannine with their three girls. Right behind came Maryam, and as she was unloading a giant cake box from her back seat another car slid in behind hers with a disturbing rasp of sidewall against curb. "Jesus Christ!" they all heard Mac say. He was in the front passenger seat and Linwood was at the wheel. Apparently Linwood had earned his learner's permit since Sami had last seen him. Laura was sitting in the rear, and she climbed out and started up the walk without a backward glance as Mac went into a long harangue about the cost of new tires these days.

"Where's Stefanie?" Bitsy called.

Laura grimaced and said, "Majorette camp."

Sami waited for Bitsy's reaction. The week before, she'd thrown a fit on the phone because Brad's parents were off on a cruise even though they knew full well they'd be missing Arrival Day. "I mean! A cruise!" she'd told Ziba. "When their only grandchild is celebrating her second year in this country!" But all she said now was, "Oh, what a shame," in an offhand, trailing-away voice. Maybe she was relieved. The last time they'd all been together, Stefanie had painted the little ones' toenails a ghoulish electric blue.

Abe's three girls made a beeline for Jin-Ho and Susan, and this freed Ziba's nieces to peel off from the grownups and join them. They headed toward the backyard, where Sami had set up a gym set. By then Bitsy's brothers had spotted Sami's new car in the driveway. "Say!" Abe said. "A Honda Civic!" All the men trooped over to inspect it, including the Hakimi men although of course they had seen it before. Even Dave showed some interest. Before long he was arguing with Linwood's announcement that air bags did more harm than good. Meanwhile the women went into the house, and by the time the men had rejoined them Maryam was offering pistachios to Bitsy and her two sisters-in-law. They were the only ones in the living room. All the Hakimi women were crowded into the kitchen, where they remained, clanking pot lids and clattering dishes, until it was time to call people to the table.

An exhausting amount of discussion had gone into the serving arrangements. Sami had argued for a buffet. "I don't see how there's any choice," he'd told Ziba. "There'll be twenty-some people! Our table doesn't seat that many."

"A buffet's not as intimate, though," Ziba said. "I want this to feel intimate."

"Well, how are you going to manage that with twenty-some people, Zee?"

"I'll seat the children separately, with the older ones in charge of the younger. That's, let's see . . . two, four, seven . . . And then if I put a couple of card tables at one end of the grownups' table . . ."

She prevailed, finally. The children settled themselves at the breakfast nook in the kitchen, while in the dining room the grownups crowded around the single immense, paisley-draped expanse that stretched almost from one wall to the other. You'd have to look closely to see the break where the card tables started. The main dishes were lined up on the sideboard—huge crocks and platters and bowls—and lesser dishes filled a quartet of TV trays in one corner. Bitsy's relatives couldn't get over it. "I've never seen so much food in all my life!" Jeannine said. "This is a banquet!" But Ziba said, "Oh, it's nothing."

"More kebabs are coming," Sami announced. "Finish up what's here, everybody." He headed for the kitchen, edging around Bitsy, who was trying to lead a song rehearsal. He couldn't tell *which* song, though, because a mutiny seemed to be under way. Several of the children were drowning her out with "She'll Be Coming Round the Mountain." "They'll be wearing red pajamas when they come," Bridget sang, and the others, even Ziba's two nieces, shouted, "Scratch! Scratch!" and pounded their silverware on the table. Bitsy said, "Children! Please!" Sami grinned and lifted a platter of skewered meats from the counter. When he stepped out the back door, the quiet came as a jolt. His ears were ringing slightly, and he took his time laying the meat on the grill just to give himself a respite.

≠

It was while they were passing seconds around that Ziba mentioned preschool. "Did I tell you?" Sami heard her ask Bitsy. "Susan's starting Julia Jessup in the fall."

Bitsy was helping herself to another grilled tomato. She paused and looked at Ziba. "What's Julia Jessup?" she asked.

"It's the preschool Sami went to. The one where Maryam works now."

"She's starting there *this* fall?" Bitsy asked.

Ziba nodded, beaming.

"But she's only two years old!" Bitsy said.

"Two and a half," Ziba reminded her. "Julia Jessup accepts them at two."

"That may very well be," Bitsy said. She was sitting indignantly straight, almost swaybacked, the grilled tomato suspended in its serving spoon. "But just because they accept her at that age doesn't mean she should go."

"It doesn't?" Ziba asked.

"Two is *way* too young! She's still a baby!"

Ziba's lips parted and she looked toward the kitchen, although she couldn't have seen Susan from where she was sitting.

"Look," Bitsy said briskly. She dropped the tomato on her plate with a plunk. "I've tried to understand about your working outside the home—"

"Just a couple of days a week!" Ziba broke in. (This was a sore point between them, Sami knew from past discussions.) "And more like half days, really."

"Sometimes, though, you work on Saturdays," Bitsy pointed out.

"But Sami's with her on Saturdays! And Maryam is with her on weekdays, or my family if they're visiting."

"Yes, and so that I can understand," Bitsy went on in her forbearing tone. "But to send a teeny tiny toddler off to preschool, a child still in diapers . . ." She faltered. "Am I right? She *is* still in diapers? She isn't trained yet, is she?"

Ziba shook her head. Bitsy seemed to take heart. "And furthermore a child who had a very rocky beginning," she said. "When you consider the adjustments she has had to make so far—"

"Now, isn't that interesting!" Ziba's brother Ali said suddenly. He leaned toward Maryam, who was seated across the table from him. "I didn't realize you worked in a preschool, Khanom. Nobody ever informed me of that. You teach small children?"

Sami had to admire the man. Evidently life in a large family had honed his peacemaking skills. And Maryam proved equally adept. She sent him the brilliant, purposeful smile of someone being interviewed. "Oh, no, I just help part-time in the office," she told him. "When Sami was a pupil there I used to volunteer, you see. I filed, I typed, I made phone calls . . ." She gazed brightly around at the others. "And then my husband died and I experienced, you might say, a little spell of financial panic. I believe that often happens with widows. They might have a perfectly adequate pension or life insurance or whatnot, but for the first time they're on their own and so they panic."

"Really," Bitsy's father said. "And do widowers suffer a similar panic?"

Sami couldn't tell if Dave honestly wanted to know or was just contributing to the rescue effort. Maryam might have been doubtful herself, from the assessing gaze she sent him. "Ah," she said finally. "Well, widowers, now: I believe their panic relates more to household issues. They worry because now they will have no woman to take care of them. Sometimes they grow quite desperate. They make very sad mistakes."

Dave gave a short laugh. "I'll bear that in mind," he told her.

Sami expected her to protest—to assure him that she hadn't meant anything personal—but she merely nodded. And then Linwood appeared in the kitchen doorway, several grains of rice sticking to one lens of his glasses, and cleared his throat and announced that Jin-Ho had a stomachache. "Oh, dear," Bitsy said. "It must be all the excitement." She rose and laid her napkin aside and went into the kitchen.

Ziba wasn't enjoying herself anymore. Sami could tell that, if no one else could. She was gazing down at her plate, not eating, fiddling with her fork. He was too far away to reach over and stroke her hand. He tried to catch her eye but she wouldn't look up. Instead, by accident, he caught Mrs. Hakimi's eye. Mrs. Hakimi seemed to have been lying in wait for him, because the instant he glanced toward her she put on a toothy smile. He didn't know how much of the conversation she'd understood. He smiled back at her and looked away.

Why couldn't Ziba just shrug Bitsy off? Why was she so susceptible to Bitsy's criticisms? Maybe they should find some Iranian friends. Enough of this struggle to fit in, to keep up!

He heard Brad, at the other end of the table, telling Aunt Azra that he envied her. "Envy," Aunt Azra said slowly. Sami knew she was repeating the word because she wasn't sure of the meaning, but Brad must have thought she was disputing him. He said, "No, I mean it! Absolutely. One day not too far off, immigrants are going to be the new elite in this country. That's because they bear no burden of guilt. Their forefathers didn't steal any Native American land and they never owned slaves. They have perfectly clear consciences."

Aunt Azra was staring at him with a look of blank astonishment. Sami was fairly certain it was the word "consciences" that had stumped her.

If Ziba had not been so downcast, she would have been nagging Sami about the final round of kebabs. He slid back his chair and stood up. "Save some room, folks! There's one last batch coming," he said. He went out to the kitchen, where he found his way blocked by Bitsy. She was kneeling beside Jin-Ho at the children's table. "Sweetie?" she was asking. "You want to go lie down?" Jin-Ho shook her head. Susan, seated next to her, leaned forward to peer into Jin-Ho's face with a comical expression of concern.

Then Bitsy said, "Oh."

She was looking at Jin-Ho's tumbler, which was empty except for the ice cubes. "You had a *soft* drink," she told Jin-Ho.

Jin-Ho stuck out her bottom lip and averted her eyes.

"Well, no wonder!" Bitsy said. "Of course your stomach hurts! My goodness!"

Sami said, "Oh, give her a break, Bitsy."

Bitsy pivoted to look up at him.

He felt a sort of rush to the head, a surge of joyous rage. He said, "Don't you ever quit?"

"Excuse me?"

"You and your little digs about soft drinks, refined sugar, working mothers, preschools—"

"I don't understand," Bitsy told him. She rose, holding on to the back of Jin-Ho's chair. "Did I say something wrong?"

"You've said everything wrong, and you owe my wife an apology."

"I owe . . . Ziba? I don't understand!"

"Figure it out," he said, and then he brushed past her and headed toward the back door.

From behind him, in a very small voice, Susan said, "Papa? Is Bitsy *bad*?"

"Uh," he said. He paused and glanced back at her. She had her eyebrows raised in two worried slants like the two sides of a roof. He said, "No, Susie-june, never mind. I guess I'm just feeling irritable."

It was only when he was searching for the word "irritable"—literally, "quick-tempered"—that he realized that both he and Susan had been speaking Farsi. This was a shock but also a satisfaction, for some reason. He flung a triumphant glance at Bitsy, who was still holding on to Jin-Ho's chair and gaping at him, and then he went on out into the yard.

By now the kebabs were way overdone. The lamb chunks might still be salvaged, but the chicken looked like leather. He used a pot holder to grab the skewers one by one and shift them to the platter, and then he lifted the grate so he could stir the coals apart with the tongs. His heartbeat was gradually slowing. The rage had dimmed and he was left feeling slightly foolish.

When the screen door clicked shut, he turned to see Brad approaching. In his Orioles T-shirt and flapping shorts Brad looked mussed and uncomfortable. He stopped a foot or so away and swatted at some insect buzzing around his head. Then he said, "How you doing there?"

"I'm okay," Sami said. He turned back to the grill. He poked a coal with the tongs.

"Guess we've had a little misunderstanding of some sort," Brad said.

Sami poked another coal. Then he said, "*We* didn't have a misunderstanding."

"All right," Brad said. "Why not tell me what happened."

"*We* were all fine," Sami said. "Then your wife comes along and hurts my wife's feelings."

"Well, how, exactly?"

Sami looked at him. He said, "You have to ask?"

"I'm asking, friend."

"You sat there at the table; you heard her slam our entire approach to child-rearing; you saw how she ruined our party—"

"She ruined . . . ? Aw, gee, Sami," Brad said. "I know Bitsy can be outspoken sometimes, but—"

"'Pushy' is a better word for it," Sami said.

"Now, hold on, here—"

"Pushy, and self-righteous, and overbearing, and . . . pushy," Sami said.

To demonstrate, he stepped forward and pushed against the front of Brad's T-shirt with one palm. Brad's chest felt spongy, almost bosomy. It made Sami want to push him again, harder, and so he did. "Now, hold the *phone*!" Brad said, and he pushed back, but in a halfhearted way. Sami dropped the tongs and grabbed hold of him with both hands and tried to butt him in the stomach with his head, and Brad seized two fistfuls of Sami's hair and lunged against him and knocked him flat on the ground, luckily clear of the grill, and landed panting on top of him. For a moment they both lay there, as if wondering what to do next. Sami had a dizzy feeling and he couldn't get his breath. He heard high, thin sounds from the direction of the back door—the distressed cries of the women, no different in Farsi than in English, as everyone streamed out onto the steps.

Brad rolled off Sami and staggered to his feet and wiped his face with his sleeve. Sami sat up and then stood. He bent forward, wheezing, and shook his head to clear it.

He should have been aghast at himself. He should have been

mortified that anyone had witnessed this. Instead, though, he felt exultant. He couldn't seem to keep a straight face as he raised his eyes to his guests, who were frozen in poses of horror. The children were dumbstruck and the men were openmouthed and the women were pressing their hands to their cheeks. He turned to Brad and found him sheepishly grinning, and they fell on each other and hugged. Clapping Brad's broad, damp back, stumbling around the yard in a clumsy dance, Sami imagined that to the relatives, the two of them must resemble two characters in some sitcom, two wild and crazy Americans, two regular American guys.

5

Brad and Bitsy were talking about adopting a second child. To Dave's mind, this was insane. He didn't say so, of course. He said, "Is that a fact." But Bitsy must have caught something in his tone, because she said, "All right, Dad, out with it. What do you have against it?"

"Nothing!" he told her. "Why do you ask?"

"You think I'm too old, don't you."

"Absolutely not," he told her.

This much was true. He wasn't quite sure of her age, frankly. Thirty-five? Forty? Connie would have known. He did some quick math. Okay, forty-three. But that wasn't his objection. Mainly he just felt that people shouldn't press their luck. He'd been so apprehensive with the first adoption, and so relieved when it worked out. Jin-Ho was his most interesting grandchild. And probably the brightest, or second-brightest next to Linwood. Why not quit while they were ahead? Anyhow, children were a lot of trouble. You would think Brad and Bitsy could content themselves with just one.

He had felt the same about his own children. He had embarked on parenthood reluctantly, sending regretful backward glances at his carefree young-married days, and although the first baby had proved a delight he hadn't hankered for more. If not for Connie's lobbying, Bitsy would have been an only child. Then of course the two boys were delights as well, and he wouldn't have traded them for anything, but still he could remember quite clearly sitting in the melee of tantrums and wet diapers and little sharp-edged building blocks and thinking, Too many children and not enough Connie. He had felt almost childlike himself as he angled for Connie's attention, snatched the smallest stray bits of her, competed for her ear and for her thoughtful, focused gaze.

What would Connie have said to Bitsy's new plan?

Oh, probably "Go ahead, dear. I'm sure it will turn out wonderfully."

He missed Connie more than he could say. He tried *not* to say, in fact. She had died in March of '99, over a year ago. Almost a year and a half. He could see people thinking that he must be past the worst of it. Time to buck up! Time to move on! But the truth was, it was harder now than immediately after her death. Back then he had felt so grateful that she no longer had to suffer. Besides which, he'd been just plain exhausted. He'd just wanted to get some sleep.

But now he was as lonely as God. He was rackingly, achingly lonely, and he rattled around the house with far too much time on his hands and not enough to do. It was summer. School was over not only for the year but forever, in his case, because in June he had retired. Had this been a mistake? He had always had other interests—his hobbies and his volunteer work and community concerns—but now he couldn't get up the energy. He sighed a lot and he spoke aloud to Connie. He said, "Going to fix that door lock, finally," and "Well, drat. I meant to buy eggs." Once or twice he thought he caught a glimpse of her, but in situations so unlikely that he couldn't pretend they were real. (On a hot July afternoon, for instance, she stood by the backyard bird feeder tugging off a snow-flecked mitten with her teeth.) More satisfying were the memories of past events that popped up out of nowhere, as vivid as home movies. The time soon after they married when she drove their VW Beetle into the driveway with smoke pouring from the back seat (something to do with the engine) and flung open the door and jumped out and threw herself into his arms; or the time she sent in his name for a local TV station's Hero of the Day award and he had been so gruff and ungracious when she told him (his heroism had involved carpooling three children at all hours of the day and night, not any rescues from burning buildings), although now his eyes filled with tears at her gesture.

He thought, Why, this is just unbearable.

He thought, I should have been allowed to practice on somebody less important first. I don't know how to do this.

He forgot that he *had* practiced, on four grandparents and two parents. But there was no comparison, really.

He had tended her illness for so long that it had become second nature, and now he couldn't believe that she could manage without him. Was she comfortable where she was? Did she have everything she needed? He couldn't stand to think she might be feeling abandoned.

Yet he was completely unreligious and had never conceived of an afterlife.

He kept her voice on the answering machine because erasing it seemed an act of violence. He knew some people were disquieted when they heard her cheery greeting. "It's the Dickinsons! Leave a message!" He could tell by their initial "Uh . . ." when he played back their calls. Bitsy, though, said she found it a comfort. Once she phoned him and said, in a quavering voice, "Dad? Can I ask you a favor? Can I just dial this number a few times and you not answer?

I'm having a kind of blue day today and I wanted to hear Mom's voice."

It was Bitsy who was his partner in mourning, much more so than her brothers. "Remember your mother's silk pie?" he would ask her, or "Remember that song she used to sing about the widow with her baby?" and he wouldn't have to offer any excuse for bringing it up. Bitsy fell in with him unquestioningly. "Her tomato aspic, too," she would say, and "Yes, of course, and what was that other song? The one about the lumberjack?"

Even with Bitsy, though, he rationed these conversations. He didn't want to worry her. He didn't want her sending him one of her probing glances. "Are you all right, Dad? Are you *really* all right? Would you like to come to dinner this evening? We've invited the next-door neighbors but you're more than welcome, I promise. It would do you good to get out."

It would not do him good to get out. That much he was certain of. In social situations, now, all he could think was, What is the *point*? The chitchat about the weather, politics, property taxes, children—useless, every bit of it. And the neighbors dropping by his house with casseroles and cookies. "Guess what!" Tillie Brown told him from behind a Saran-wrapped platter. "I'm another grandma!"

"Pardon?"

"My daughter just gave birth to her fourth little boy!"

"Good God," he said, and he gazed down at the platter. Salmon loaf, from the looks of it. He was touched by these offerings but puzzled. What did they imagine he could do with it all? There was only one of him! And anyhow, food tasted to him like sawdust these days.

A couple of the unattached women had told him they would love to go out some evening for dinner—although not nearly as many women as the folklore would have you believe. He always put them off. Even if he'd had any interest, which he didn't, the effort of adjusting to a new person was beyond him. It had been hard enough the first time. He said, "Well, now, isn't that nice of you," and never followed up. They didn't pursue it. He suspected they were just as glad not to have to bother. More and more of the world seemed to be barely trudging along, from what he had observed.

Bitsy said they hoped to adopt this second child from China. There was a greater need in China, she said. But applying was more complicated than it had been for Korea, and physically obtaining the child would be more complicated too. They would have to travel there to get her. And it would definitely be a "her," she said. She gazed off at Jin-Ho, who was playing in the sandbox some distance from the patio where they sat. "Two little girls," she told Dave. "Won't that be sweet? Luckily, Brad has never been the type who thought he had to have a son."

"Will you take Jin-Ho with you to China?" Dave asked.

"Oh, my Lord, no! With all those unfamiliar germs? Besides, the trip will be so difficult. It isn't just the flight; we'll have to stay for several weeks while we go through the paperwork." She set her iced-tea glass down with a sudden, decisive motion and looked at him directly. "In fact, I've been meaning to ask you," she said. "Do you think we could leave her with you?"

"With me?"

"Now that you're retired."

"But—"

"You know how she adores you."

"But, honey, it's been a long time since I took care of a three-year-old."

"Unfortunately," Bitsy told him, "she'll be more like four or five. Maybe even in kindergarten. This whole process could take a couple of years, we hear."

"Oh," Dave said. "Well, then."

It crossed his mind that he might very well be dead in a couple of years. He was surprised at how the thought cheered him.

It was the Donaldsons' turn to host the girls' Arrival Party. Bitsy was already debating the best day for it. "The fifteenth falls on a Tuesday this year," she told Dave, "and so Ziba's asking why not have the party the Sunday before. But . . . I don't know. Granted Sunday is more convenient, but I'd prefer to celebrate on the actual date, wouldn't you?"

"Well, either way," Dave said.

"I mean the real, actual date the girls arrived in our lives!"

"Right," he said hastily. "Sure. The actual fifteenth."

He felt he'd been backed into a corner. He often did, with Bitsy. Oh, this daughter of his had always managed to make life harder than it needed to be, for herself and for everyone around her. From earliest childhood she had held fierce, unbending opinions, and even though she tended to be right he could see that there were times when people wished they disagreed with her. Maybe global warming was not so bad after all! he could hear them thinking. Maybe world peace was less desirable than they had imagined!

Connie used to say that Bitsy's problem was, she doubted her own goodness. At heart she was insecure; she worried she was unworthy. Dave found it helpful to remind himself of that, on occasion. (And what would he do without Connie's forgiving slant of vision to guide him in the future?)

Then after the date had been settled—Tuesday, what a shock—

there was the issue of the menu. Apparently Bitsy felt that the Yazdans had "changed the rules," as she put it, when they'd served a full meal the year before. "I mean, look what we did the first year," she told Dave on the phone. "We put out the simplest refreshments, tea and coffee and cake. But last year! Last year we had enough food to feed a homeless shelter for a month. Jin-Ho got a stomachache and slept clear through the movie; never saw a bit of it."

"So?" Dave said. "This year you do it your way again."

"The Yazdans might feel that was inhospitable, though. You know how they focus on food. And then if I do serve a meal, I could never cook so many dishes. I don't have enough pots and pans! I don't have *big* enough pots and pans."

"Make your nice tart lemonade with the little bits of peel," Dave said in his most coaxing voice, "and get a sheet cake from the bakery . . ."

But Bitsy wasn't listening. She said, "My vegetable lasagna, do you think? Or my Pakistani dish? No, wait; nothing with rice. Talk about a big pot! Remember the time I served *habichuelas negras*? The first Yazdan to spoon out some rice took almost the whole platterful!"

Dave laughed. He enjoyed the Yazdans. On the surface they seemed all primary colors, so innocent and impressionable, but he'd had glimpses of more complicated interiors from time to time. Mr. Hakimi, for instance. Now, *there* were some darker hues, for sure. "Will the Hakimis be coming?" he asked Bitsy hopefully.

"Yes, and one of Ziba's brothers but I can't remember which. She's always got so many relatives staying there; wouldn't you think they'd be missed at work? While our own family, on the other hand . . . I'm very distressed about Mac and Laura. They knew it would be Arrival Day; they could have taken Linwood on his college visits any other time this summer or this whole year, for that matter. But oh, no. Oh, no. And then Brad's parents; well, typical, I guess. Them and their never-ending cruises: it's as if they didn't care! I wonder if they'd act differently if Jin-Ho were their biological grandchild."

If Jin-Ho were their biological grandchild this whole damn-fool Arrival Party would not have been cooked up, Dave thought. But what he said was, "Ah, now. They're just scared they won't have enough to do with their time; that's why they overschedule."

Good Lord, he sounded like Connie. Maybe Bitsy thought so too, because instead of arguing she changed the subject. She said, "Do you remember *Guys and Dolls*?"

"What? *Guys and Dolls*?"

"Do you remember a song they sang called 'I'll Know When My Love Comes Along'?"

"Oh. The song."

"I've always felt 'She'll Be Coming Round the Mountain' lacks dignity, somehow," Bitsy said.

If Dave stretched the telephone cord to its very farthest limit, he found he could just reach the remote control for the television set. He switched on the evening news and then hit the mute button so that Bitsy wouldn't suspect.

Arrival Day dawned heavy and humid, with enough clouds building in the west to give hope for a cooling thunderstorm. None arrived, though, and by evening Dave was dreading the thought of putting on decent clothes and venturing forth in the heat. At home he'd taken to going about in just his swim trunks. He lumbered upstairs to his closet, where he stood idly ruffling the gray hairs on his chest as he contemplated his choices. Eventually he settled on a seersucker shirt and khakis. He should shower again, but he wasn't up to it. He went off to the bathroom to splash cold water on his face instead.

One thing he had learned about Bitsy's parties was that it didn't pay to be early. She grew very managerial just before her guests arrived. He would have been put to work folding napkins or re-arranging chairs or something equally unnecessary. So he took his time leaving the house, and when he reached the Donaldsons' place he found several cars already parked at the curb. The girls were out on the sidewalk—Susan industriously pedaling Jin-Ho's tricycle while Jin-Ho stood watching. (Somehow it was always Susan who got first dibs, Dave had noticed. She might be smaller and frailer, but she was laughably determined.)

"Hey, there," he told them. "You two ready for your party?"

Jin-Ho said, "Grandpa!" and came over to give him a hug. Susan gazed up at him with her usual dubious expression. He cupped her head with one hand as he passed her. She wore her hair in two thin braids, nothing like Jin-Ho's thick, bowl-shaped bob, and there was something poignant about the perfect roundness of her little skull inside his palm.

"We're waiting for Polly and them," Jin-Ho told him. Polly was the oldest of Abe's three daughters—thirteen, now; just the right age to fascinate small girls. "Mama said we could, if we didn't go near the street. Mama doesn't know about the hummet."

"Hummet?" Dave asked.

"Susan's not wearing the trike hummet."

"Ah," Dave said. Yes, he could see the helmet now on the top porch step—a sleek black beetle-shaped object with racing stripes on the sides. "Well, I imagine life as we know it will go on," he said.

"Huh?"

He waved at her and continued toward the house. As he reached the porch, the screen door opened and Bitsy said, "Finally!" She came out to kiss his cheek. She was wearing a sundress made from one of her more attractive pieces of weaving—purple bands threaded with blue—although it billowed out from the bodice in a way that he found unfortunate. He liked for women's waists to be evident. (Connie used to claim that this preference revealed a masculine fear of pregnancy.) "Everyone's here now but Abe," Bitsy told him. "All the Iranians . . ." and then she leaned closer to whisper in his ear. "They've brought an extra."

"Pardon?"

"The Yazdans have brought an extra guest."

"Oh."

"They didn't ask me first."

"Well, I guess maybe in their culture . . ."

Then he all but bumped into Ziba, who was standing just inside the door. "Hello, Ziba," he said, and he accepted her kiss too. As usual, she was packed into a tight T-shirt and tighter jeans, and her heels were so high that she teetered slightly as she stepped away from him. "Happy Arrival Day," she told him. She gestured toward a cavernously thin teenaged boy who stood next to her with his hands clamped in his armpits. "This is Siroos's son, Kurosh," she said.

Dave had no idea who Siroos might be, but he said, "Well, hello. Happy Arrival Day to you," and the boy unclamped one hand to shake his.

"Thank you, sir," he said with no accent. "And many happy returns," which didn't quite suit the occasion if you thought about it long enough.

Brad ambled up, sweating and grinning. "More or less the same weather as the first Arrival Day, right?" he said. He led Dave into the living room, where Mr. and Mrs. Hakimi sat next to one of Ziba's brothers (the oldest one, who could almost have been her father with that bald head and leathery face) and his motherly-looking wife. The four of them formed a decorous row down the length of the couch, the men in suits and the women in good black dresses, and it was probably their general stiffness that made Brad so eager to add Dave to the mix. "You remember Bitsy's dad," he told them. All the Hakimis smiled brightly and made a motion as if to stand, even the women, but then kept their seats—a gesture Dave had grown to expect from earlier occasions.

Sami, who seemed to be in charge of the drinks, was over by the deep windowsill that was serving as a bar. "Hey there, Dave!" he called. "Can I offer you a Scotch? I was just fixing one for Ali."

"Well . . . why not?" Dave said. He was glad to be reminded of the brother's name, although he still couldn't think of the wife's.

"You have seen the pictures?" Mr. Hakimi asked in his booming voice. "Take a look at the pictures! Very nice!"

The pictures lined the mantel and the top of the built-in bookcase beside it—photos from Arrival Parties One and Two, most of them unframed and curling in the middle. Dave turned his face toward them in a perfunctory way, but Mr. Hakimi said, "See the one on the right! You are standing with Jin-Ho!" so that Dave had to walk over there and pull his glasses from his shirt pocket to demonstrate his interest. The photo on the far right showed him lifting Jin-Ho by the waist to light a candle with one of those propane wands meant for lighting stoves. It might have been just the effort of lifting her that caused his face to seem so ropy and strained, but all he could think was, I look like hell! I look ruined! All his adult life he had been a few pounds overweight, large-framed and loose and shambling, but in the photo he had a haggard appearance and the tendons showed in his neck. Connie had been dead just five months when that picture was taken. He saw now that unbeknownst to himself he must have progressed somewhat from those days, because he felt so thankful not to be back there. And he was almost certain he had regained the lost weight.

"See the grandfather-granddaughter!" Mr. Hakimi was saying.

"A toast to the grandfather-granddaughter! Your good health, sir!" And Sami pressed an icy tumbler into Dave's hand.

That Bitsy was bothering with cocktails suggested she was going ahead with her plan to serve a full meal. He supposed she'd had little choice, once she had scheduled the party for a weekday evening. So he resigned himself to a late night, and to seeing very little of Bitsy since she would be occupied with the food. He settled in a rocking chair and listened with what he hoped was an attentive expression as Sami and Brad discussed the Orioles. He didn't follow the Orioles anymore. Once you lost touch with a baseball team—its gossipy human-interest stories, its miniature dramas of heartbreaking personal slumps and miraculous comebacks—it was hard to work up much enthusiasm. And the Hakimis felt even less connected, if you judged by their glazed smiles. Only when Maryam emerged from the kitchen, where she must have been helping out, did they come to life. She was carrying a tray of something, and when she bent over the row of guests on the couch they leaned forward eagerly and there was a murmur of foreign phrases, a quick back-and-forth and a patter of soft laughter that made Dave realize how much went on inside these people's heads that he would never have guessed from their stunted, primitive English.

Wouldn't it feel like a permanent bereavement, to give up your native language?

Maryam wore a deeply V-necked top that revealed her polished collarbones. When she approached him with her tray, she said, "It's good to see you, Dave. Would you care for a canapé?"

"Thank you," he said, taking one. It seemed to be some sort of fish paste.

"Are you pleased you might have a new grandchild?"

"A new . . . ? Oh. Yes, right," he said. "Very pleased," because he supposed that was what was expected of him.

"I wonder if this means that now there'll be *two* Arrival Parties," she said.

"God forbid!" he said before he thought. Maryam laughed.

By the time Abe and Jeannine had shown up with their daughters, everyone had eaten far too many hors d'oeuvres. The sight of the huge banquet waiting when they moved to the dining room made several people groan. "Bitsy, what have you *done*?" Jeannine asked. There were platters of cold chicken, cold salmon, and shrimp, along with half a dozen vegetable dishes and almost as many salads. If this was a competition, Dave dreaded to think what the next year would bring.

The cake at the end of the meal was the usual Stars-and-Stripes sheet cake, and the song was the usual song in spite of all Bitsy's efforts. "I'll know," she began hopefully in a high, sweet voice, but Abe's three boisterous daughters drowned her out. "They'll be coming round the mountain when they come," Bridget led off, and Brad flung open the kitchen door to reveal Jin-Ho and Susan, who stood looking nonplussed as always instead of marching forth as they'd been instructed. "Toot! Toot!" Abe's daughters shrieked. Clearly they enjoyed the sound effects even more than the song itself. "Scratch! Scratch! Whoa, back! Hi, babe!" First Abe and Jeannine joined in and then Sami, then Ziba, and finally Dave, although he hated to seem disloyal. Even the Hakimis mumbled along as best they could, chuckling bashfully each time they came to the toots and sending each other shy peeks.

After cake it was time for the video. *The Arrival of Jin-Ho and Susan,* it began—a whole new title, in italics now rather than copperplate. People paid varying degrees of attention. The Hakimis, for instance, sat erect and kept their eyes fixed respectfully on the screen throughout. At the other extreme, Jin-Ho busied herself with a Tickle Me Elmo doll. Dave, who was standing at the back of the room, watched more closely than he let on because he knew he'd be seeing Connie. He didn't want the others to notice how much this mattered to him. They would worry; they would try to distract him. They would say he was being morbid.

Yes, there she was, smiling beautifully and clasping her hands in front of her chest as if she were praying. GRANDMA, her lapel button read. It was true that she wore a baseball cap—already she was ill—but how full and rosy her face seemed! How sturdily she stood, next to him but not leaning on him! He kept forgetting that this was how she used to look. When he pictured her nowadays, she had the papery white skin and jutting bones of a dying woman.

Then she was gone. Oh, damn. He wondered, as he had the year before, if he could somehow spirit this tape away and take it home to watch in solitude. He would play just the frames with Connie in them over and over and over. He would dwell on the dear slope of flesh beneath her jaw and the cozily embedded look of the wedding ring on her finger.

The infant Jin-Ho arrived in her courier's arms and was surrounded and engulfed. Various Dickinsons and Donaldsons behaved like total fools. Then Susan flashed by—now you see her, now you don't—but Dave barely noticed that part. He knew there wouldn't be any more shots of Connie.

"It was difficult to watch Connie, no?" Maryam asked.

She stood nearby, on his left. The foreign intonation of her "no?" struck him as irritating. He felt so far removed from this random assemblage; he resented being dragged back to it. He kept his eyes fixed stubbornly on the TV screen (the credits rolling by in the original, copperplate font) as he said, "Not difficult at all. I liked seeing her so healthy."

"Ah," Maryam said. "Yes, I can understand that." Then she said, "I used to think that if someone had come to me out of the blue and told me, 'Your husband just died,' when he was in perfect health, I would have found it easier. It was watching him go down, down, down that made it so hard."

He looked over at her. He was often startled by Maryam's smallness—someone so elegant should be statuesque, it seemed to him—and now he had to lower his gaze a few inches to take in her profile, her eyes trained on the other guests and her fingers curved delicately around the handle of a teacup.

"I thought, If only I could mourn the man I first knew!" she said. "But instead there were the more recent versions, the sick one and then the sicker one and then the one who was so cross and hated me for disturbing him with pills and food and fluids, and finally the faraway, sleepy one who in fact was not there at all. I thought, I wish I had been aware of the day he *really* died—the day his real self died. That was the day when I should have grieved most deeply."

"I'd forgotten his was cancer too," Dave said.

She was silent. She watched the others streaming out, the children heading toward the backyard and the grownups to the living room.

"Connie in her final version was . . . very demanding," Dave said. He had started to say something else but changed his mind. Then he went ahead and said it after all. "In a way, she was almost *mean*," he said.

Maryam nodded without surprise and took a sip of tea.

"I guess it was inevitable," he told her. "People when they're sick begin to feel something is owed them. They get sort of imperious. In real life, Connie wasn't like that in the least. I knew that! I should have made allowances, but I didn't. I snapped at her, sometimes. I often lost my patience."

"Well, of course," Maryam said, and she set her cup back in her saucer without a sound. "It was fear," she told him.

"Fear?"

"I remember when I was a child, if my mother showed any sign of weakness—took to bed with a headache, even—I always got so angry with her! I was frightened, was the reason."

He thought that over. He supposed she had a point. Certainly Connie's decline had scared him out of his wits. But somehow he felt unsatisfied with this conversation, as if there were something more that needed to be set straight. He shifted to one side to let Siroos's son edge past him, and then he said, "It isn't only her last days that I regret."

Maryam raised her eyebrows slightly.

"It's her whole life. Our whole life together. Every thoughtless word I ever said, every instance of neglect. Do you ever do that? Think back on those things? I've always been such a concentrator; I mean, driven to concentrate on some project and let everything else go to hell. I remember one time I was wiring our house for a sound system I'd concocted. I wouldn't stop for lunch, wouldn't go with Connie to this movie she wanted to see . . . Now I'm sick about it. I think, What I wouldn't give for lunch with her now, or to be sitting with her at a movie!"

"You folks coming?" Brad asked. "Seconds on cake in the dining room."

"Thanks," Dave told him, but Maryam didn't respond. She took another sip of tea and then looked down into her cup. "Ah, well," she said. "If we had been different, would they have loved us?"

"Pardon?"

"If you were not a man of many interests, enthusiastic about your projects—if you had no interests except for Connie and followed her every footstep—would she have chosen to marry you?"

But she didn't seem to expect an answer, because while he was still considering her words she said, "Jeannine! Hasn't Polly grown up this summer!"

"Yes, alas, she's a teenager now," Jeannine said. "Heaven help us all."

Maryam laughed lightly and turned to accompany her out of the room, and Dave trailed after them. He did think he might want more cake. All at once he felt positively hungry.

⸎

September brought its smell of dry leaves that could so easily be mistaken for the smell of freshly sharpened pencils, and the neighborhood children returned to school with their giant book bags and the college students drove away in their overstuffed cars and the fact of Dave's retirement hit him in the face all over again. Never mind those fond goodbyes last June. Forget the yearbook dedication (*To our beloved Mr. Dickinson, who made physics come alive for three generations of Woodbury girls*) and the plethora of farewell parties yielding their gifts of clocks, mostly, which seemed ironic when you considered that he no longer had much need to know what time it was. This was the moment of truth: autumn, when the rest of the world was beginning anew but Dave himself was just going along, going along the same as in the summer. He had thought he couldn't wait to be done with it all. They had worn him out, those Woodbury girls! But now he found himself missing their shallow, breathy voices that ended every statement with a question mark, and their cataclysmic emotional crises that erupted almost hourly, and even their mysterious fits of giggles although he had often suspected that he was the one they were laughing at. They would already have forgotten him. He didn't kid himself. They were already going gaga over his successor, a debonair young man fresh out of Princeton. It was like walking down a red carpet and then turning to find the attendants rolling it up behind you. He was *gone*. It shook his whole view of himself to discover how much he minded.

Always he'd been a good putterer—a competent repairman, woodworker, seat-of-the-pants inventor—and this was why he'd assumed that retirement would come easy to him. But one day he was down in the basement replacing a three-way lamp socket and he felt all at once that he couldn't stand another minute of the gloomy, dank, earth-smelling air. The scummy little window above his head reminded him of the painted-over panes in derelict factories, and his workbench with its neatly hung tools, each outlined in white and arranged according to function and size, inhabited a chilly cube of fluorescent lighting with the dark pressing in all around even on this sunny afternoon. He imagined he couldn't breathe. He wondered how long he'd be lying here if he happened to have a stroke.

Up in the kitchen (airy and almost too bright), he gulped down a glass of water while he studied the replacement socket he'd unthinkingly brought with him. That was when it occurred to him that he could move his workbench upstairs. Well, maybe not the workbench itself, or the larger of the tools, but certainly the smaller items. He could take over the little room they called the study, which led directly off the kitchen and served as a sort of catchall for Connie's sewing supplies and the unpaid bills and the out-of-date magazines. There was no one to object, after all. He felt a flicker of his old zest bestirring itself. Something to do! He set his glass on the counter and went to the study to investigate.

The house was a rambling Mount Washington place they'd moved into nearly forty years ago when the children were small, and from simple inertia they had allowed the clutter to accumulate. Besides which, Connie had been disorganized by nature. How many times had Dave grumbled about the scissors left on a chair or his best pair of pliers mislaid? One whole corner cupboard was stacked with fabrics, and he knew without looking that some of them were cut up but left unsewn, the tissue patterns still pinned in place; and others had been bought on impulse ten or fifteen years back but never put to use, their folded edges bleached by dust and sunlight. He felt wickedly pleased that finally, finally he could whip this place into shape.

That afternoon and all the next day, he stuffed objects into plastic trash bags for Goodwill. The fabrics and the knitting supplies, a sheaf of Butterick dress patterns, a wicker sewing basket, a half-finished baby afghan that might very well have been started in their oldest grandchild's infancy. A flat tin of watercolor paints dried into shrunken tablets. A sketchbook, perfectly blank, yellowed around the edges. A leather punch he'd been looking for since the previous Christmas. A book on needlepoint dollhouse rugs due back at the Roland Park Library on May 16, 1989. A manual for an electric typewriter they no longer owned. A box of unused thank-you cards. Twenty years of tax returns, some of the years missing.

He did keep the tax returns, on second thought. While he was retrieving them he chanced to notice the sewing basket and he retrieved that as well, because after all he might need to sew on a button from time to time. Then he thought of other things, like the green vinyl case of crochet hooks he'd tossed out at the very start. Crochet hooks made very useful tools for small repair jobs. Which trash bag had he put them in?

By the end of the second day the room was looking much, much worse than when he'd begun. There was hardly any space to walk. The tax returns filled the one armchair and the sofa was heaped with photo albums and fat manila envelopes packed with other photos that he planned to sort through later. He couldn't even sit down. He felt defeated.

He opened the bottom desk drawer, where he was hoping to store the tax returns, and came upon a cache of sickroom supplies.

They dated from the earliest days of Connie's illness, he guessed. In the later days her equipment—like her disease—had spread outward and filled their lives. There'd been a hospital bed in the living room and a wheelchair in the front hall. But the items in the desk drawer were minimal and unobtrusive: a box of alcohol swabs and a digital thermometer and a photocopied information sheet on the side effects of chemo.

Dave himself never called it "chemo." He refused to speak so familiarly about something so horrific. He used the full word: chemotherapy.

Connie had vowed it wouldn't get to her. She'd intended to breeze right through it. Then one morning Dave had wondered why his shower water was ankle deep and he'd looked down to find handfuls of her hair clogging the drain. She hadn't realized yet; it wasn't till that evening that she noticed her matted comb. And he didn't tell her. It was the start of the widening separation between them. Willy-nilly, he remained in the world of the heedlessly healthy and Connie joined an inner circle of fellow sufferers who sought each other out in waiting rooms, comparing symptoms and discussing alternative treatments and trading nuggets of advice on various coping techniques. (Canned peaches, one man swore by.) The caregivers, hollow-eyed and weary, exchanged sympathetic glances but said nothing.

She traveled farther and farther away from him. She swung into battle against each new malady that popped up now here, now there, just when she wasn't looking, just when some test result or consultation had raised their hopes, while Dave dealt alone with the insurance and the medical bills and prescriptions.

Sometimes he thought the side effects of chemotherapy were contagious. He lost his appetite and he felt constantly, faintly nauseated and it seemed to him that when he cut himself shaving his blood took longer to clot. He said as much to Connie and she said,

"Do you have any idea how trivial that sounds to a person in my condition?" The jolt of outrage her question gave him was almost enjoyable. For a moment, it freed him of guilt. But only for a moment.

"All my life," he told Bitsy now on the phone, "I've been so impatient to get to the next stage. I couldn't wait to grow up, to finish school, to get married; couldn't wait for you children to learn to walk and talk. I hurried things along anyhow I could. For what? I ask myself now. But here's the worst: when I think back on your mother's illness I see I reached the point where I couldn't wait for *that* to be over with, either. I'm horrified at myself."

"Well, of course you couldn't wait," Bitsy said in a soothing voice. "You were imagining she'd be well again."

"No, honey, that's not what I mean," he said, although for one moment he considered pretending that it was. "I mean that I was wishing for your mother to go ahead and die."

The silence stretched out long enough for him to regret telling her. Some things were best kept to oneself. Finally she said, "Dad, would you like me and Jin-Ho to come over for a little visit?"

"No!" he said, because he didn't want her to see what had happened to the study.

"Would you like to come here? You could have lunch with us. Only PBJs, but you know we're always glad of your company."

"Thanks, but I've got some chores to finish around the house," he said, and he told her goodbye.

It was wrong to burden her. He would have to endure this alone.

He went to the kitchen and fixed himself a bowl of cold cereal, but he found it too hard to swallow and he gave up after three spoonfuls. He sat dully at the kitchen table and gazed out at the neighbors' backyard, where the tree men were cutting down a huge old gnarly maple. The day before they had lopped off the leafy tip ends and fed them to the chipper, and he could imagine that overnight the maple must have stood there in some botanical version of shock. But only the smallest branches had been removed, after all. A tree so large could adjust to that. This morning, though, the men had moved on to the larger branches, and perhaps that too could have been adjusted to even though the tree had become as stubby and short-armed as a saguaro cactus. But now they were setting their chain saws to work on the trunk itself, and all those earlier adjustments turned out to have been for nothing.

He stood up heavily and carried his bowl to the sink.

At night now he welcomed sleep because his dreams had become so vivid. It was like a whole separate life; the paler his waking life grew, the more colorful his sleeping life. He dreamed, for instance, that he owned a giant tiger with a shaggy, yellowed rug of long white hair beneath its chin. The tiger padded into the room and rose silently to set its front paws on the foot of the bed and survey Dave's sleeping form. Then it appeared to make a decision and leapt up, deeply indenting the mattress, and trod across the blankets to set its nose an inch from Dave's face. Dave could smell its hot, meaty breath and feel the tickle of its whiskers even though they weren't touching him. It was a pleasant, friendly experience, not alarming in the least. But when he awoke the tiger was gone, and he was alone in his bed.

Maybe his dreams had been influenced by the scrabbling of animals in the attic just a few feet overhead—squirrels or raccoons or mice. He should take steps to get rid of them, but there was a companionable intimacy to these nighttime sounds and so he kept putting it off.

If a nonexistent tiger could visit him, why not Connie? Why

couldn't she be watching over him, as nearby as those attic creatures?

She used to believe that her ancestors were taking care of her. She'd been more spiritual than he, if not conventionally religious, and she used to quote a pagan saying, "Gratitude is the root of all virtue," which she interpreted to mean that people should be mindful of those who had gone before. She imagined that her grandparents were cheering her on and guiding her through the hard parts, as well as the great-grandparents she had never known and the great-greats and so forth, all the way back. So why couldn't Connie herself be taking care of Dave? That this was a non sequitur occurred to him only belatedly. Connie wasn't his ancestor. They weren't even related. But he kept forgetting that. He thought of the medical consultation where, briefly and hypothetically, a doctor had mentioned a bone-marrow transplant. "She can have *my* marrow!" Dave had said, and only at the doctor's quizzical glance had he realized his mistake.

He closed his eyes again and willed her, willed her. He summoned up her most concrete details: her long spongy earlobes, the sparrow's-egg speckles on the backs of her hands, the slight croakiness of her voice that always made her sound so appealingly unselfconscious and lacking in vanity. "Do you remember what it was like to have a date on a spring evening?" she asked. It wasn't Dave she was talking to; it was someone on the phone. She was sitting at the kitchen table with a trowel in her lap; evidently the call had interrupted her gardening. "Every year when spring comes, I find myself thinking of that. The boys would come up the front walk in their short-sleeved shirts that still smelled of their mothers' ironing, and we girls would be wearing flowered dresses and ballet slippers and no stockings and there was something so fresh and so . . . free about the first bare legs of the season . . ."

Dave was in the living room with his two sons and someone else. Who? Some neighbor woman, a friend of Connie's who had stopped by for a visit. "Connie's on the phone," Dave told her, "but she ought to be off any second." He cocked his head to listen for a winding-up note in Connie's voice, but she wasn't speaking just then and he realized now that she had been silent for several minutes. Then he understood that the silence was real—the silence in the actual bedroom—and that Connie wouldn't be speaking ever again.

The oldest photo album showed women in rigid dresses and complicated hairdos, men in collars so high that their chins were buried, and stern-faced babies smothered in white lace. These people might have interested him if he had known who they were, but he didn't. The captions inked on the back were frustratingly evasive. *Sunday, September 10, 1893, just before a delicious meal treat,* one read. Or, *With the beautiful amaryllis Mother gave us at Christmas.* It seemed no one had imagined that the day would come when these people would be strangers.

The later albums were more clearly labeled, but even if they had not been he would have recognized his paternal grandparents, sitting on a wide lawn with their firstborn, who grew up to be his Aunt Louise. Poor Aunt Louise: she had lost her only love to TB and died mindless in a nursing home at eighty-eight, but in the photo she was toddling triumphantly toward the camera with both little arms outstretched, and her parents were watching her progress with the proudest, happiest smiles.

In the forties people looked surprisingly glamorous, even his mother in her house dress with the slantwise stripes. In the fifties they took on color, mostly jarring pinks and blues, but they were dowdy now and rumpled and the men's haircuts were too short. Had Connie really consented to be seen in a shiny rose-colored sheath that narrowed at mid-calf so you wondered how she could walk?

After that, life must have grown more rushed, because the later photos weren't mounted. Dave opened each manila envelope to peer inside: Bitsy in her bucktoothed stage, before braces; Abe with a terrier puppy who'd been run over soon after they got him; Abe again, at his college graduation. In the bottom-most, thinnest envelope Jin-Ho and Susan were blowing soap bubbles at each other, but even they seemed long ago, their faces rounder than nowadays and less definite, less specific.

Oh, what was the *point*, what was the *point*, what was the *point*?

He wiped out the corner cupboard (three separate dust rags, that took) and placed the albums and the envelopes on the lowest shelf. He put the tax returns in the desk drawer where the sickroom supplies had been kept. From the basement he brought up his boxed set of miniature tools, his compartmented chest of screws and nails and his repair manuals and his tin of adhesives, and he arranged them on the upper shelves of the cupboard along with the crochet hooks and Connie's sewing basket. He lugged the trash out to the alley, the Goodwill bags to his car trunk. He dusted the desk and the lamp tables. He stuffed his cleaning rags into the hamper. He vacuumed the floor and the sofa, which was littered with specks of paper.

He felt too tired to fix himself supper. Instead he drank two glasses of Scotch and went to bed. His sleep was a drugged sleep, cottony, like a cloth laid over his face. He dreamed he was out in the country, walking through a vast field that he understood to be a furniture graveyard. Abandoned pieces of furniture were grouped by category—an acre of beds, an acre of bureaus, an acre of dining-room tables. Dozens of armchairs sat beneath a mulberry tree, their seats empty except for the weeds growing up through their cushions, and the fact that they were facing each other made them seem all the lonelier. "How can they stand this?" he asked, and somebody off in the distance, some man in faded clothes, caroled, "Ooh, how can they stand this?" in a mocking, cruel voice. He stopped in his tracks, stricken. Then he felt a hand slipping into his, and he turned to see Maryam Yazdan calmly surveying the chairs. "They are thinking of all they have lived through," she told him. "They like to remember that." He found this consoling, for some reason, and so when she said, "Shall we go?" he tightened his hand around hers and followed her out of the field.

He woke up and lay for a long while staring into the dark.

— 6

— By the time Maryam heard about Sami and Ziba's new house, they had already made a down payment and arranged a settlement date. She said, "A new house? I didn't know you were looking!"

"Oh, we hardly knew it ourselves," Sami said, and Ziba said, "We weren't sure we would find what we wanted; so why tell anyone?"

Maryam was not just anyone, though, and it puzzled her that they had been so secretive. They must have pored over real-estate listings, taken numerous tours, debated the merits of one place compared with another. And yet they'd never breathed a word to her!

But she said, "Well, this is wonderful. Congratulations." And she patted Susan on the knee. They were sitting in Maryam's living room, Susan on the sofa beside her with a picture book in her lap. "Are you excited?" Maryam asked her. "Have you seen your new room?"

"It's got a window seat," Susan told her.

"A window seat! Really!"

"You lift up the cushion part and there's space underneath for my toys. Me and Jin-Ho climbed all the way inside it, even."

Jin-Ho had been to the house?

They'd already told the Donaldsons?

Sami cleared his throat and said, "We mentioned this place to Brad and Bitsy because it's in their neighborhood."

"Ah. In Mount Washington," she said.

"I hope you aren't disappointed we're not moving nearer you, Mom. We did *think* about Roland Park, but the general atmosphere of Mount Washington seemed more, I don't know . . ."

The general atmosphere of Mount Washington seemed more Donaldsonian, Maryam thought. Better not say it, though. "Well, still you'll be very close," she said. "Five or ten minutes away! I'm delighted."

Then Sami and Ziba leaned forward at the same moment to pick up their teacups, as if they felt suddenly unburdened. And Maryam picked up her own teacup and smiled at them.

She thought she knew now why they hadn't told her. They were embarrassed to be observed copying the Donaldsons yet again. Oh, those Donaldsons, with their blithe assumption that their way was the only way! Feed your daughter this and not that; let her watch these programs and not those; live here and not there. So American, they were.

But Sami and Ziba thought the Donaldsons were unique, and Maryam didn't feel that she should be the one to set them straight.

The new house was on Pettijohn Street, just three blocks from Brad and Bitsy's. It had a big front porch, lofty old trees, and a spacious backyard. There was only one guest room, though; so Ziba said they would have to buy a foldout couch for the relatives. She invited

Maryam to come along when she went shopping. Of course she knew all the furniture stores because of her work, and she spoke knowledgeably about styles and fabrics and projected delivery times. "Oh, please! Nothing from Murfree-Mainsburgh," she told a salesman. "They take forever with their orders." Maryam was impressed, even though she privately questioned Ziba's taste. Ziba said that her long-range goal was to outfit the house entirely in American Colonial, and she pointed out lace-canopied four-poster beds, velour-lined "life chests" for memorabilia, revolving stools on barley-twist pedestals, and scallop-trimmed entertainment centers, all in a high-gloss, cocoa-colored wood that seemed not quite real. But what did Maryam know?

They moved on a Friday in late April—a nonworking day for Ziba and a working day for Maryam, so that all Maryam had to do was step down the hall to collect Susan from preschool when it was time to go home. She had volunteered to keep Susan till that evening.

Susan was in the Threes class, having turned four only in January. Usually Maryam resisted the urge to look in on her, and when the Threes tramped past the glassed-in office on their way to the playground she tried not to glance up from her desk. It was a pleasure, therefore, to have this excuse to walk straight into the classroom. The children were stowing their art supplies, washing their hands at the knee-high sinks, hanging their smocks in the cubbies labeled with their names. It took Maryam a minute to find Susan because she was sitting at the Reading Table with a book. Had she finished her art project early, or had she never joined the group at all? Maryam always worried, because Susan seemed so reserved next to her rowdier classmates. The teachers kept insisting, though, that she was doing fine. "She's such a little . . . *person*," one had said just recently. Maryam's feeling exactly, and so she had relaxed, for the moment.

"Time to go," she told Susan now. "You're coming home with me today, remember?"

Susan shut her book and filed it neatly away on the shelf, all without saying a word, but as she walked past one of the teachers she said, "I get to sleep in my new room tonight."

"Oh, I *know* you do!" the teacher said. Greta, this was—a spirited type.

"But first I'm going to Mari-june's because Mama's busy setting up my bed."

"Well, aren't you lucky!" Greta said, and she flashed a grin at Maryam. "Have fun, you two!"

Maryam smiled and thanked her, but Susan walked out of the room without responding. And in the car, she refused to discuss her day. You'd think Maryam would have learned by now, but she always found herself asking, "How was school? What did you do?" while Susan gazed out the side window in a silence that seemed not rude but diplomatic, as if she were graciously overlooking Maryam's faux pas. She still rode in a safety seat, because she weighed so little. Jin-Ho had graduated to a booster by now but Susan didn't yet qualify, even though she kept arguing about it.

Just the week before, Maryam had taken in a small stray cat that she'd named Moosh—Farsi for "mouse"—because of his gray coat. Susan was in love with him, and the minute they arrived at the house she had to race through all the rooms calling, "Moosh? Moosh? Mooshi-jon! Where are you, Mooshi-jon?"

"Let him find *you,*" Maryam told her. "Come sit in the kitchen and have your snack. He'll show up by and by."

Which was what happened. Susan had barely started on her milk and cookies when Moosh appeared out of nowhere to twine around the legs of her chair. "Moosh!" she squealed. "Can I feed him something? Can I give him some of my milk?"

"Try these cat treats," Maryam said, and she handed her a box.

Susan slid off her chair and squatted next to Moosh, her sharp bare knees jutting outward. On the wall above her, the phone started ringing, and Maryam reached over to answer it. "Hello?" she said.

"It's Dave Dickinson, Maryam. How are you?"

"Hello, Dave. I'm fine; how are you?"

"I understand you're watching Susan this afternoon."

"Yes, just till the movers are done."

"I was wondering if you might like me to bring Jin-Ho to keep her company."

"Oh, you have Jin-Ho today?" Maryam asked.

"Well, no, but I could go get her."

"That would be very nice. Susan," she said, "would you like for Jin-Ho to come over?"

Susan said, "Yes!" without taking her eyes from the cat, who was cautiously sniffing the treat she held out. So Maryam told Dave, "We'd love to see her. Thank you for thinking of it."

"We'll be there in half an hour," he said.

He made such offers a lot nowadays. He must be missing Connie. And Maryam suspected also that he was having trouble adjusting to retirement. She could tell it from the way he prolonged all conversations, and took forever to say goodbye, and invariably joined in when the Donaldsons and the Yazdans got together for any social event.

This afternoon he stayed on after bringing Jin-Ho even though Maryam told him she'd be happy to watch both girls on her own. "It's not as if I have anything better to do," he said, and then he gave a strange grimace. "I mean," he said, "I *like* sitting here. If I'm not in your way."

"Not in the least," Maryam said. In fact, she had planned on using this time to make a meal to take Sami and Ziba, but she asked, "Could I fix you a cup of tea? Or coffee?"

"Coffee would be good. Oh, but, I'm sorry; you have things to do, don't you? Really, I don't *need* any coffee."

She smiled at his phrasing. Although "need" was, come to think of it, a word that summed Dave up these days. He watched people so expectantly; he kept his eyes fixed on her so steadfastly as she moved around the kitchen. And when she set his coffee in front of him he was so disproportionately grateful. "This is very kind of you," he said. "I really appreciate your going to the bother."

"It was no bother," she told him.

As long as he was just sitting there, she might as well proceed with her cooking. She took a pan from the cupboard almost soundlessly, as if that would keep him from noticing what she was up to. While she was filling the pan with water he said something she didn't catch, and she waited till she'd turned the faucet off before she said, "Excuse me?"

"I was saying, this coffee tastes unusually delicious. Do you get it someplace special?"

"Just the supermarket," she said with a laugh.

"Well, maybe it's because someone besides me made it. I get awfully tired of eating my own cooking."

A streak of gray passed by: Moosh escaping the girls, who followed close behind. He was not so much running as walking very fast, trying to keep his dignity, and the girls managed to corner him between the table and the door. "Mooshi-Moosh," they were saying. "Mooshi-june!"—even Jin-Ho, squatting next to Susan and holding out a cat treat. Like Susan, she wore shorts and a T-shirt, and on her feet were those jelly sandals that all the children favored this year.

"Mooshi? Is that his name?" Dave asked.

"Moosh," Susan told him.

"Well, hi there, Moosh!" Dave said heartily. "Where do you happen to come from?"

Susan turned to Maryam and wrinkled her forehead. She said, "*I* didn't know Moosh could talk."

"He can't," Maryam said, spooning out rice. "You'll have to answer for him."

"Oh." Susan turned back to Dave and said, "Mari-june found him under her porch."

"Lucky Moosh!" he said.

"Guess what," Susan told him. "I get to sleep in my new room tonight."

"So I heard. You have a whole new house."

"The moving truck's moving my bed today."

"Is it a normal house, or is it a magic house?" Dave asked.

"What?"

"Well, for instance, some mornings when I go for my run I see this house two streets over that I really like to look at. It's got a porch swing, and a hammock, and a cupola on the roof. But then other mornings, I *don't* see it."

Susan sat back on her heels and studied him in silence.

"I mean," he told her, "it's not there."

"Where'd it go?"

"Well, I don't know," he said. "Sometimes it's there and sometimes it's not. A lot of things do that—more than we're aware of."

"They do?" She looked at Maryam. "They do?" she asked Maryam.

"'There was one, and there wasn't one,'" Maryam quoted, surprising even herself. "'Except for God, there was no one.'"

Dave said, "What's that?"

"That's how people at home used to begin old stories. It's like 'Once upon a time,' I guess."

"Really!" Dave said. He set down his coffee cup. "That's fascinating! How does it go, again? 'There was one . . .'"

"Oh, well. It's just a loose translation," she said.

"No, really. How does it go?"

She couldn't say why she felt so weary, all at once. She dropped the scoop back into the rice bin. At her feet, Susan was asking, "What's a cupola, Mari-june? Does my new house have a cupola?"

Instead of answering, Maryam told Dave, "You know, it's ridiculous that you should have to stay around here all afternoon just twiddling your thumbs. Why not let me bring Jin-Ho back when I take Susan home?"

"Oh," he said.

She felt a twinge of remorse. "Not that you aren't welcome," she said. "But there's no reason you should tie up your day."

"I don't *have* a day, Maryam."

She pretended not to hear this. "All you'd have to do is switch Jin-Ho's booster seat to my car," she said, "if you don't mind my asking."

So that he was forced to say, "Well, of course, I don't mind at all."

Then he stood up, with his hands hanging loose at his sides in an empty, disconsolate way. But still she didn't relent.

⸎

Susan and Jin-Ho spent the afternoon building Moosh a house out of a cardboard carton. They begged a bath mat from Maryam to pad the floor, and they scrawled windows on the walls with a felt-tip marker. For a bed they lined a shoe box with one of Maryam's scarves, although she warned them that most likely Moosh would refuse to use it. "Cats are too willful to sleep where you tell them to," she said. Jin-Ho said, "Okay, the shoe box can be his bureau, then," but Susan—who was fairly willful herself—said, "No! It's his bed! I want it to be his bed!"

"Well, I guess it won't hurt to try," Maryam told her.

"And we're going to have a cupola, too."

Maryam laughed and went back to her cooking.

Around six o'clock, Ziba called to let her know they were more or less moved in. "At least the furniture's in place," she said. So Maryam wrapped the rice pot in a towel and rounded up the girls and put them in the car. When she dropped Jin-Ho off at the Donaldsons', Bitsy came out with a Styrofoam cooler of food for Sami and Ziba. "This can be for tomorrow," she said, "and then I thought the day after tomorrow I'd invite them for supper at our house. Would you like to join us, Maryam? I could ask Dad to come too."

"Oh, thank you, but I have plans," Maryam said. She didn't want Sami and Ziba to think she was overly involved in their lives.

On the way to the new house, she tried to orient Susan. "See, when you're old enough to walk home from Jin-Ho's on your own you would pass this big house with the trellis, and then you would cross the street—looking both ways first, remember—and then at this next street you would turn right, at the yard with the bird feeder in it . . ."

Susan listened in silence, studying each landmark as if committing it to memory. She had the most beautiful posture. She sat in her seat like a miniature queen, perfectly composed.

Ziba met them at the door in one of Sami's old shirts. Her face was shiny with sweat and there was a smudge on one cheekbone. "Come in!" she told them. "Welcome to your new home, Susie-june!" She swooped Susan up in her arms and showed her the living room. "See how nice it looks? Do you like it? See where we put your rocking horse?" Maryam, holding the rice pot, took a right instead of a left and headed toward the kitchen. She had planned to send Sami out to her car for Bitsy's cooler, but he was nowhere to be seen and Ziba was carrying Susan up the stairs now, chattering in a rather anxious way about how pretty Susan's new bedroom was; so Maryam went back for the cooler herself. She saw when she unpacked it that Bitsy had supplied not just a casserole of some sort and a container of salad, but also a dessert—a homemade pie. She set the pie on the table next to her pot. The pot contained Sami's favorite dish: rice with fish and mixed greens, a meal complete in itself; but now she wished she'd provided something on the side.

Ziba came into the kitchen, holding Susan by the hand, and said, "Will you stay and eat with us?"

Maryam had assumed all along that she would stay, but the fact that the question had been asked made her doubtful, suddenly. She said, "Oh, well, I know you must have work to do."

"You're more than welcome," Ziba said, not denying that she had work.

So Maryam declined again and took her leave.

Slipping back into her car, waving at Ziba and Susan, who stood watching from the porch, she wondered if she had done the wrong thing. Should she have offered to help, to put the meal on the table and share it with them and clean up afterward? Or was Ziba glad to see the last of her? It was so hard to tell. She could understand, sometimes, why Sami lost his patience with these elaborate old-country courtesies that concealed everybody's true feelings.

She cast a final glance at the two on the porch and then pulled away from the curb, feeling unsettled and dissatisfied.

The new house changed their lives, and only for the better. Susan could join in the neighbor children's outdoor games—no more complicated playdate arrangements. It was a ten-minute drive to her preschool, and less than that to the grocery store, and just a short walk to the Donaldsons'. When school let out for the summer and Maryam resumed her Tuesday-Thursday babysitting schedule, she sat on Sami and Ziba's front porch contentedly hulling strawberries while Susan rode her tricycle, or she puttered with Susan and Jin-Ho in the tiny backyard garden they had planted. The first slim carrots were ready in late June, and both girls were beside themselves. They ate them raw for lunch with a dill-and-yogurt dip. Even Susan, who usually spurned all vegetables, polished off three.

Maryam worked at Julia Jessup just one day a week in the summer. She paid a few bills, saw to correspondence, made a couple of telephone calls to order supplies or arrange for routine maintenance. Often the only other person in the building was the janitor, pushing his wide broom down halls that were already gleaming. The school's director, Mrs. Barber, spent her summers in Maine, but she would phone from time to time and ask how things were going. "Oh, fine," Maryam would tell her. "The men are here to resurface that place underneath the jungle gym, remember? And the Windham twins' father has been transferred to Atlanta, so I've written to the next two families on the waiting list." She was aware of sounding busier than she really was, as if trying to demonstrate that she was earning her pay.

Even during the school year this was an undemanding job, carried out at a measured pace among people long familiar to her. She worked in a kind of trance, sitting at an immaculate desk in the center of the so-called "goldfish bowl" that she shared with Mrs. Barber and Mrs. Simms, the assistant director. It soothed her, somehow, to perform the most trivial tasks to perfection. At the end of every day she emptied her computer's recycling bin, and she defragmented her hard drive exactly once a month.

In July she went to Vermont to visit her double first cousin, a daughter of an uncle on her father's side and an aunt on her mother's side. Farah was several years younger than Maryam, and different from her in almost every way. Living in an area where everyone else was a native, married to an ex-hippie she had met while she was studying in Paris, she had chosen to become exaggeratedly Iranian. She met Maryam's plane in an outfit so exotic that even in Tehran, people would have gawked: a maroon satin tunic over tight white leggings, curly-toed sequined slippers straight from a Persian miniature, and a bib of golden chains that all but covered her plump bosom.

"Maryam-jon! Maryam-jon!" she shrieked, jumping up and down. Everyone else at the gate—pale and drab by comparison—turned to stare at her. "*Salaam,* Mari-june!" she cried. For a moment Maryam wanted to pretend she had nothing to do with this woman, but then when they were face-to-face she saw Farah's Karimzadeh eyes, long and narrow with pointed corners, and the Karimzadeh nose as straight as a pin. Unlike Maryam, Farah was letting her hair go gray, and the gray hairs frizzed and corkscrewed up from the black just as their grandmother's used to.

During the drive from the airport (in a dusty beige Chevrolet with a back seat full of machine parts), Farah spoke Farsi in such a rush that it seemed to have been bottled up inside her. She relayed all the news from home, quoting telephone conversations not just word for word but in the appropriate voices—their cousin Sholeh's thin whine, their second cousin Kaveh's bullish bellow. Farah kept in much closer touch with the family than Maryam did. "Oh, a dozen times a week," she said, "one person or another will be wearing me out with complaints, and at my expense, too." Which implied it was she who placed the calls, but why, if she found them so tedious? Some form of survivor guilt, perhaps. "They go on and on about the difficulties of current conditions—their entertainment so limited, almost no films allowed, almost no music, no liquor except what the smugglers deliver in bleach jugs after dark. They imagine my own life is sheer pleasure. They have no idea how hard it is here!"

To look at her, encased in satin and glittering with gold, their relatives might have laughed, but Maryam knew what she meant. It *was* hard, harder than the people back home could possibly imagine, and sometimes she wondered how they both had lasted this long in a country where everything happened so fast and everybody else knew all the rules without asking.

"My sister reads off lists of items she wants me to send," Farah said. "Athletic shoes and cosmetics and bottles of vitamin pills. There are vitamins in Iran! Perfectly good ones, but she believes that the vitamins in America are more powerful. I sent her a bottle of Vigor-Vytes and the first pill she took, she told me, 'Already I feel so much younger! I have so much more energy!'"

Uttering the phrase "Vigor-Vytes" led Farah to change over to English, probably without meaning to. It was a phenomenon Maryam had often observed among Iranians. They'd be rattling along in Farsi and then some word borrowed from America, generally something technical like "television" or "computer," would flip a switch in their brains and they would continue in English until a Farsi word flipped the switch back again.

"I suppose you have less of that because your brothers can ask their children to send things," Farah was saying. "Or Parviz can, at least, with his two up there in Vancouver where all the stores are excellent." (This last sentence flipped back and forth lickety-split, triggered first by "Parviz" and then by "Vancouver.") "And besides, you're so much stronger. You would just say no. *I* should be stronger. I am a, how you say, floormat."

"Doormat," Maryam said.

"Doormat. I am a push-off."

Maryam held her tongue.

They had been traveling through the New England countryside at a speed that was surely illegal, passing small, tidy farms that could have lined the tracks of a toy train set. Now they swerved onto a gravel road, with a clanking of metal from the back seat. A few minutes later they parked in the yard of the Jeffreys' gray clapboard house. "Oh, good," Farah said. "William's home."

He was sitting on the front porch steps—a wiry man in faded jeans. When he saw the car he rose and ambled over, grinning. *"Salaam aleikum,"* he said as Maryam stepped forth, and then, in English, "It's good to see you."

"It's good to see *you,*" she told him, pressing her cheek to his.

William was one of those men who had never quite managed to leave their adolescence behind, in her opinion. His jeans were patched with bits of the American flag, and he wore a wisp of a goatee and a single long braid which, now that he was bald on top, made it seem that his hair had somehow slipped several inches backward on his head. His enthusiasm for all things Iranian struck her as adolescent, too. "Guess what!" he told her now. "I've made *fesenjan* for dinner tonight in your honor."

"Exactly what I'm in the mood for," she said.

William was in full charge of the cooking and the housework. He was also the breadwinner; he taught creative writing at the local college. Maryam couldn't imagine what Farah did with her time. They had no children—hadn't wanted them, evidently—and she had never held a job. When she led Maryam upstairs to the guest room she said, "Now, I *think* the bed's made up . . . oh, yes, good." The wildflowers on the bureau, jammed clumsily into a cruet, were probably William's doing as well.

Once Maryam had unpacked they met for cocktails in the parlor, which had the hollow, barnlike feel of a bare-bones New England farmhouse but was decorated with Persian rugs and Isfahani enamelware and jewel-like paisley fabrics. William talked about his newest invention: he was working on an "executive toy" that he felt sure would make them rich. "It's kind of on the order of a lava lamp," he said. "You remember those. Only this is much classier-looking." He brought it out to show her: an hourglass shape, in clear plastic, filled with a viscous liquid. "See," he said, inverting it, "how the liquid sort of squiggles down, spirals clockwise awhile and then changes to counterclockwise, builds up on the surface in a pyramid shape and then all at once decides to flatten . . . Doesn't it just grab you?"

Maryam nodded. She did find it oddly mesmerizing.

"What gave me the idea was, we were coming to the end of a bottle of McGleam shampoo and so I turned it upside down over a new bottle; you know how you do. Propped it just so in order to get the last few drops out. And I was watching the drip and suddenly I thought, Man! This could be some, like, Zen-like thing that would center people and focus them. We could market it as a device to lower people's blood pressure! So I worked out this design; figured out the most attractive shape . . . only I haven't got the liquid quite right. I mean, it has to be the proper consistency. Thick like McGleam but not too thick, of course, and clear like McGleam because I believe clear is more calming—"

"Why can't you just use McGleam?" Maryam asked.

"Oh. Use McGleam."

"Wouldn't that be the obvious solution?"

"But . . . shampoo? Besides, McGleam's about the most expensive brand in the drugstore." He gazed fondly at Farah. "Nothing but the best for Farah-june," he said.

Farah gave him a languid wave and told Maryam, "What can I say? I have that tanglesome Karimzadeh hair."

Over dinner that evening (a real Iranian meal from start to finish, everything authentic), Farah reminisced about their shared childhood. She had a sunnier vision of the past than Maryam did. All her memories seemed to involve hilarious parties, or wagon rides at the family's summer place in Meigun, or daylong picnics with every single relative on both sides in attendance. Where were the quarrels and the schisms, the uncle who took opium and the uncle who embezzled, the aunts' endless, bitter competition for their father's grudging notice? Did Farah not remember the cousin who killed herself when they forbade her to go to medical school, or the cousin who was refused permission to marry the boy she loved? "Oh, those were happy, happy times," Farah sighed, and William sighed too and shook his head as if he had been there himself. He loved to hear talk about Iran. He would prompt Farah if she skipped a detail. "And the coins!" he said. "Remember them? The brand-new gold coins that they used to give you children every New Year's?" Maryam found this presumptuous of him, although she knew she should feel flattered that he was so interested in their culture.

It must have been the dinner conversation that caused her to dream that night about her mother. She saw her mother as she had looked when Maryam was just a child—pure black hair and unlined skin, the beauty mark on her upper lip accentuated with an eyebrow pencil. She was telling Maryam the story about the nomad tribe she used to spy on as a girl. They had moved into the compound across the street, arriving mysteriously late one night. The women wore gold up to here (and she gestured toward one elbow). The men rode shining horses. One morning she awoke and all of them had vanished. In the dream, as in real life, she told this story in a slow, caressing voice, with a wistful look on her face, and Maryam herself awoke wondering for the first time if her mother might have longed to vanish also. She had never asked her mother a single personal question, at least as far as she could remember; and now it was too late. The thought stirred up a gentle, almost pleasurable melancholy. She still mourned her mother's death, but she had traveled so far from her, into such a different kind of life. It no longer seemed they were related.

The guest room was beginning to grow light, and the window

above her bed showed a square of pale gray sky and a jagged black ridge of fir trees. The scene struck her as no less eerie than a landscape on the moon.

Over the next several days, she fell into the leisurely routine of the women from her childhood. She and Farah sat drinking tea as they leafed through glossy magazines. William was generally tinkering in his workshop or off somewhere cruising hardware stores and junkyards. Then in the afternoon he started cooking, and every evening he served another Iranian dinner. He took great pride in stating the names of the dishes in Farsi. "Have some *khoresh,*" he would say, the *kh* so stressed and labored that it sounded like a cough. As the week wore on, Maryam found this behavior more and more ridiculous. Although really, where was the harm? She knew she was being unreasonable.

On the last evening of her visit he asked, "May I serve you more *polo*?" and she said, "Why don't you just call it rice?"

He said, "Pardon?" and Farah looked up from her plate.

"I mean," Maryam said, backpedaling, "thanks, I'd love more *polo*."

"Am I pronouncing it wrong?" he asked her.

"No, no, I just . . ." She disliked herself, suddenly. She seemed to be turning into a cranky old lady. "I'm sorry," she said to them both. "I guess it's the combination of the different languages. I get confused."

But that wasn't what was bothering her.

Once, a year or two after Kiyan's death, a colleague of his had asked her to a concert. A nice enough man, American, divorced. She hadn't been able to think of a good excuse for declining. In the car she had mentioned that Sami was contemplating tennis camp—she had used that exact word, "contemplating"—and the man had said, "You have an excellent vocabulary, Maryam." And then a few minutes later he had told her he would love to see her sometime in her "native dress." Needless to say, she had not gone out with him again.

And once while she was waiting in her doctor's office a nurse had called, "Do we have a Zahedi here?" and the receptionist had answered, "No, but we have a Yazdan." As if they were interchangeable; as if one foreign patient would do as well as another. And the way she'd pronounced it: *Yaz*-dun. But even if she'd said it properly, Yazdan was an Americanization, shortened from its longer form when Kiyan first came to this country. Besides, in point of fact Maryam was not a Yazdan anyhow. She was a Karimzadeh, and back home she would have stayed Karimzadeh even after marriage. So the person they were referring to didn't even exist. She was an invention of the Americans.

Well. Enough. She straightened in her seat and smiled across the table at William. "I believe this is the best *ghormeh sabzi* I've ever eaten," she said.

He said, "Gosh, *merci,* Maryam."

When she got back to Baltimore, she found that Susan had changed just in that one week. Several freckles as fine as powdered cinnamon were scattered across her nose now, and she had learned how to walk in flip-flops. She strutted through the house with little slapping sounds as the rubber soles hit her heels. Also, Ziba said, she had discovered death. "It's like it all at once dawned on her. I don't know from where. She wakes every night now two or three times and asks if she's going to die. I tell her not till she's old, old, old. I know I shouldn't promise that. But I tell her, '*Children* don't die.'"

"Exactly right," Maryam said firmly.

"Well, but—"

"Children do not die."

"Bitsy told her not to worry about it anyhow, because she'd get to come back again as somebody else."

Maryam raised her eyebrows.

"But Susan said, 'I don't want to be somebody else! I want to be me!'"

"Yes, of course she does," Maryam said. "Tell her Bitsy's crazy."

"Oh, Mari-june."

"People have no business pushing their airy-fairy notions on other people's children."

"She meant well," Ziba said.

Maryam allowed herself a derisive hiss, although she knew that Ziba was right. Bitsy had only been trying to offer reassurance. And she'd been a blessing during Maryam's time in Vermont—keeping Susan not just that Tuesday and Thursday but all of Saturday when Ziba's mother had had to undergo an emergency appendectomy. So on Maryam's first Tuesday back home, she made a point of inviting Jin-Ho over to Susan's for the day. Brad delivered her, along with her bathing suit rolled in a towel, and the girls spent the morning splashing in the inflatable wading pool. After lunch, while they were "napping" together (really just giggling and whispering upstairs in the guest room), Maryam prepared two separate pots of chicken with eggplant, and when it was time for them to walk Jin-Ho home she carried one of the pots with her to give to the Donaldsons.

Bitsy said, "Is that what I think it is?" the minute she opened her door. "Am I smelling what I think I am? You've made my favorite dish!"

"A small token of our thanks," Maryam said. "You were so kind to take care of Susan."

"I was happy to do it. Won't you come in?"

"We should be getting back," Maryam told her.

"I've just finished making a pitcher of iced tea."

"Thank you, but—"

"Right, I forgot," Bitsy said. "When it comes to matters of tea you're such a purist. You must hate when people put ice in it."

Maryam said, "Not at all," although it was true that she had never understood the practice.

For some reason Bitsy seemed to take this as acceptance of her invitation, because she turned to lead the way into the house. The girls scampered after her and Maryam reluctantly followed, wondering how she had ended up agreeing to this. "I didn't leave Ziba a note," she said, placing her pot on the kitchen table. "She'll be wondering where we've gone." But even as she spoke she was settling onto a chair.

"You know what you should do?" Bitsy asked. She opened the fridge and took out a blue pitcher. "You should come help us eat your dish tonight when you've finished watching Susan."

"Oh, I'm sorry; I can't," Maryam told her.

"Dad will be here!"

"I'm having dinner with a friend."

Bitsy went to the cupboard for glasses. Jin-Ho said, "Mama, can me and Susan make popcorn?" but all Bitsy said was, "What a pity. A man friend, or a woman?"

"Pardon? A woman. My friend Kari."

"Mama. Mama. Mom. Can me and Susan—"

"I'm having a conversation, Jin-Ho. So, Maryam, is there ever an occasion when you have dinner with just a man?"

Maryam felt taken aback. She said, "Are you talking about a . . . date? Goodness, no."

"I don't know why not," Bitsy said. "You're a very attractive woman."

"I'm past all that," Maryam said flatly. "It's too much work."

"But you surely don't think my father would be work," Bitsy said.

"Your father?"

"Mama, can me and Susan make popcorn?"

"I am *talking,* Jin-Ho." Bitsy set a glass of iced tea in front of Maryam. She hadn't filled her own glass, but she didn't seem to realize that. She sat down opposite Maryam. "My father thinks you're wonderful," she said.

"Well . . . and I think *he's* very nice."

"Would you ever go out to dinner with him?"

Maryam blinked.

"He doesn't know I'm asking this. He'd be mortified if he knew! But you're so . . . Well, face it, Maryam: you can be fairly daunting. If we waited for him to get up the courage to ask you himself, we'd be waiting forever!"

Maryam said, "Oh, I—"

"He's been mooning over you for months," Bitsy said. She leaned forward, clasping her hands on the table. Her eyes had grown round and shiny. "Don't tell me you haven't noticed," she said.

"You must be mistaken," Maryam said, at the same time realizing that Bitsy was probably right. All those "coincidental" encounters, the way he kept hanging about, the goodbyes that took forever . . . She sighed and sat straighter in her chair. "Let's talk about your new baby," she said. "Ziba says you've heard from the Chinese adoption people."

Bitsy said, "Oh, yes, the . . ." But clearly her mind was not on the adoption people. She stayed frozen in her earnest pose, fingers still interlaced and her gaze fixed on something inward.

"They have a child picked out for you, I understand?"

"Yes, a . . . girl." She appeared to collect her thoughts, finally. "Well, of course a girl," she said. "That's almost always the case. But still we have a long wait. Probably till next spring, can you believe it? Our daughter's going to be ten or twelve months old before we set eyes on her, and meanwhile there she is! All alone in that big orphanage!"

And so on and so forth, all the niggling requirements and rules and regulations. Maryam took a sip of her iced tea. The girls were on the back porch now, playing with a toy that tinkled out a tinny version of "Old MacDonald." The afternoon sun sent a dusty slant of gold across the tiles, and the kitchen seemed safe and peaceful once again.

≠

At dinner that night, Maryam asked Kari, "Do you ever feel exposed because you're not half of a couple?"

Kari said, "Exposed?"

"I mean, oh, not threatened; I don't mean that, but vulnerable? Unprotected? Anyone can walk up to you and just . . . invite you out on a date!"

"Horrors," Kari said, and she laughed. But then immediately she grew serious again, so that Maryam suspected she understood what she had been asked. She must; she was a beautiful, fine-boned woman with hauntingly shadowed eyes. Men surely invited her out all the time, although she had never mentioned it. "I tell them my culture forbids it," she said.

Maryam said, "You don't!" because she'd always felt that Kari was about as liberated as a woman could get.

"I say, 'Pardon? Go out? With a *male* person? Oh, my goodness!' I say, 'It's clear you don't know I'm a widow.' They say, 'Oh. Uh . . .' because of course they do know, but now they're wondering if there's some primitive Turkish taboo that they weren't aware of."

"I should do that," Maryam said, only half joking.

It was probably too late, though. Oh, why had she labored all these years to appear so assimilated, so modern and enlightened?

"Take up wearing a veil," Kari suggested.

But she was laughing again, and so Maryam laughed too and went back to studying her menu.

It was Sami and Ziba's turn to host the Arrival Party. Ziba had grand plans, it emerged. "I'm thinking about a whole roast lamb," she told Maryam after work one day. "Wouldn't that be impressive? You know our Greek friends, Nick and Sofia: they did that for their Easter. Nick dug a hole in their backyard and their auto mechanic made them the spit. We could borrow it, they say. Don't you think?"

"That sounds like a lot of trouble," Maryam said.

"I don't mind the trouble!"

"And a lot of food, too. How many people are coming?"

"Oh, tons of people; you know how it is. Well, only two of my brothers this year, as it happens; but also their wives, and three of their children, and my parents. And all those Dickinsons and Donaldsons—or Mac and Abe, at least, and Bitsy's father . . ."

"Still, a whole lamb!" Maryam said.

But Ziba seemed to be following some other train of thought now. She was gazing at Maryam with a speculative expression. "In fact," she said, "I think her father would come even if you were the only one here." A dimple showed up in one cheek. "*Especially* if you were the only one here."

"It sounds as if you've been listening to Bitsy," Maryam said drily.

"I don't need to hear it from Bitsy! Any idiot can see how he feels."

"Well, this is not a subject that interests me," Maryam told her. She took her handbag from the couch.

Ziba said, "Oh, Mari-june. He's such a kind man, and he always seems so lost. Besides, think how convenient this would be for our two families. Couldn't you just go to dinner with him?"

Maryam stopped digging through her bag for her keys. She said, "For heaven's sake, Ziba! Why would you suggest such a thing?"

"Why wouldn't I suggest it? You're alone; he's alone . . ."

"I'm Iranian; he's American . . ."

"What difference does that make?"

"You should have been at Farah's with me," Maryam told her. "Then you wouldn't ask. Such a point her husband makes about her foreignness! It seems she's not really Farah at all; she's Madame Iran."

"Dave wouldn't do that."

"Oh, no? 'Tell me,'" she said, putting on an earnest tone of voice, "'what are your people's folktales, Maryam? What are your local customs? Tell me your quaint superstitions.'"

"He did *not* say that."

"Well, almost," Maryam said. She had her keys in hand now. She said, "Anyhow, I'm off. Susie-june? Susan? I'm going."

Susan didn't answer. She was singing a song from *Sesame Street* as she rode her rocking horse.

"See you Thursday," Maryam told Ziba.

But this Ziba was so stubborn. Following Maryam to the front hall, she said, "I'm not asking you to marry him."

"Ziba! Enough!"

"Or to have a romantic relationship, even. Why, people go to dinner all the time in this country! It doesn't have to lead anywhere. But you don't understand that, because your own marriage was arranged and you never had the chance just to see a movie with a man or grab a hamburger with him."

There was a great deal that Maryam could have said to this, but she merely waved a hand and stepped out the door. Ordinarily they would have kissed cheeks. Not today. She clicked down the front walk. She could sense Ziba watching after her but she didn't turn around.

What she could have said to Ziba was: her marriage may have been arranged, but it was nothing like what everyone imagined.

She had been the most Westernized of young women, the most freethinking and forward-looking. She attended the University of Tehran but she hardly had time for her classes because of her political activities. This was when the Shah was still very much in power—the Shah and his dreaded secret police. There were terrible, terrible stories. Maryam attended clandestine meetings and carried tightly folded messages from one hiding place to another. She was thinking she might join the Communist Party. Then she was arrested, along with two young men, while the three of them were distributing leaflets around campus. The young men were kept several days but Maryam's Uncle Hassan arranged for her release within the hour. She wasn't sure how he accomplished it. No doubt there was much head-shaking and cluck-clucking and offering of cigarettes from his flat silver cigarette case. Money changed hands too, probably. Or maybe not; Maryam's family had influence.

But not influence enough, they told her—not if she went on behaving like this, endangering herself and all of them as well. Her mother took to her bed and her uncles stormed and shouted. They talked about making her drop out of the university altogether. They considered sending her to Paris, where her second cousin Kaveh was studying science. Maybe she could marry him. She would have to marry *someone*.

Then their neighbor, Mrs. Hamidi, mentioned her friend's son. He was a doctor in America, a pathologist with a good-paying nine-to-five job and no on-calls, and he happened to be home right now for a three-week visit. His mother thought it was time he got married. She had been introducing him to various young women even though he said he wasn't interested.

Mrs. Hamidi came to tea, bringing her friend and the friend's son, Kiyan. He was a tall, stooped, serious man in a dark gray business suit, and to Maryam he had seemed quite old, it amused her now to recall. (He'd been all of twenty-eight.) But she liked his face. He had thick eyebrows and a large, imposing nose, and the corners of his mouth gave away his thoughts, mostly turning downward at the older women's insinuations but once or twice twitching upward when Maryam made some caustic response. She could tell that Kiyan's mother found her impertinent, but what did she care? She was planning to marry for love, perhaps when she was thirty.

The women discussed the weather, which was warming up early this year. Maryam's mother announced that her rosebushes had begun to send out green shoots. Everybody's eyes traveled to Maryam and Kiyan, who had been nudged into adjacent chairs at the start of the visit. "Maryam-jon," her mother said in honeyed tones, "wouldn't you like to show Agha Doctor the roses?"

Maryam sighed audibly and stood up. Kiyan made a grumbling noise but he stood too.

As in every living room that Maryam had ever seen, the dozens of straight-backed chairs lining the walls framed a giant square of empty space, and she and Kiyan had to cross this space in order to leave. When they reached the center, some demon seized her and she stopped short, turned toward all those staring women, and performed a snatch of the Charleston—the part where the hands crisscross saucily over the knees. Not a person moved. Maryam turned and walked on out, followed by Kiyan.

In the courtyard, she gestured toward the scratchy bare shrubs and said, "Notice the roses."

The corners of Kiyan's lips were twitching upward again, she saw.

"Also the fountain, the jasmine, the full moon, and the nightingale," she said.

There was no moon, of course, and no nightingale either, but she flung one arm toward where they might have been.

Kiyan said, "I'm sorry about this."

She turned to look at him more closely.

"It wasn't my idea," he said.

He had the faintest difference in his speech. It was not a real accent, and it was certainly not an affectation. (Unlike the speech of her cousin Amin, who had returned from America pretending such an unfamiliarity with Farsi that he had once referred to a rooster as "the husband of the hen.") But you could tell that Kiyan was out of practice with his native tongue. This made him seem less authoritative, and younger than she had first thought. She found herself warming to him. She said, "It wasn't my idea either."

"Somehow I guessed that," he said, and this time the corners of his mouth lifted into a smile.

They sat down on a stone bench and discussed what had happened to the country since he had been away. "I hear there have been demonstrations against our mighty Shah of Shahs," he said. "My, what bad, rude people," and the two of them dissolved in silent laughter. They exchanged their views about politics, and human rights, and the status of women. On every issue they agreed. They interrupted each other to spill out their tumbles of thoughts. Then after half an hour or so Kiyan cocked his head toward the house, and she followed his eyes and saw three of her aunts clustered at a window. When the aunts realized they had been noticed, they shrank hastily out of sight. Kiyan grinned at Maryam. "We've given them quite a thrill," he said.

Maryam said, "Poor old things."

"Let's go to a movie tomorrow. They'll be in heaven."

She laughed and said, "Why not?"

They went to a movie the next evening, and to a kebab house the day after that—a university holiday—and that evening to a party at the home of one of his friends. This happened to be a period when young women had more freedom than at any other time before or after, in spite of Maryam's complaints, and her family thought nothing of letting her go unchaperoned. Besides, it was understood that Kiyan's intentions were honorable. He and Maryam would almost surely be getting married.

But they had no interest in marrying. They agreed that marriage was limiting and confining, a state that people settled for when they wanted to reproduce.

At night she began to feel his presence in her dreams. He never physically appeared, but she caught a whiff of his nutmeg scent; she felt his looming height beside her as she walked; she was conscious of his particular grave, amused regard.

It was unfortunate that by the time they first met, he had already been in the country for five days of the twenty-one planned. The end of his visit drew closer. The women in Maryam's family became more anxious, their questions more pointed. A hopeful-looking uncle or two began popping into view any time Kiyan paid a call.

Maryam pretended not to notice. She acted breezy and unconcerned.

One day after her English class she was descending a long flight of steps with two friends when she caught sight of Kiyan waiting at the bottom. Spring had backed off somewhat, and he wore a casual brown corduroy jacket with the collar turned up. It made him look very American, all at once; very *other*. He was gazing away from her toward some people boarding a bus. The sight of his strong, pronounced profile sent a knife of longing straight through her.

He turned then and saw her, and he watched without smiling as she approached. When they were face-to-face, he told her, "Maybe we should do what they want."

She said, "All right."

"You would come with me to America?"

She said, "I would come."

They set off walking together, Maryam hugging her books to her chest and Kiyan keeping his hands deep in his jacket pockets.

As it happened, there was no way she could go with him when he left, a mere four days later. They had a long-distance ceremony that June—Kiyan in Baltimore on the phone, Maryam in Tehran in her Western-style floor-length wedding dress with guests from both families surrounding her. The next evening, she left for America. Her mother held a Koran above Maryam's head as Maryam walked out the front door of the family compound, and all the women were crying. You would never guess that they had been praying for this to happen since the day she was arrested.

She had not been one of those Iranians who viewed America as the Promised Land. To her and her university friends, the U.S. was the great disappointer—the democracy that had, to their mystification, worked to shore up the monarchy back when the Shah was in trouble. So she set out for her new country half excited and half resistant. (But underneath, shamefully rejoicing that she would never have to attend another political meeting.) The main thing was, she was joining Kiyan. Not even her closest girlfriends knew how Kiyan had grown to fill every inch of her head. When she stepped into the Baltimore airport and saw him waiting, wearing a short-sleeved shirt that showed his unfamiliar, thin arms, she experienced a moment of shock. Could this be the same person she had daydreamed of all these weeks?

She was nineteen years old and had never cooked a meal, or washed a floor, or driven an automobile. But clearly Kiyan took it for granted that she would somehow manage. Either he lacked the most basic sense of empathy or he had a gratifying respect for her capabilities. Sometimes she thought it was the first and sometimes the second, depending on the day. She had good days and she had bad days—more of the bad, to begin with. Twice she packed to go home. Once she called him selfish and dumped a whole crock of yogurt onto his dinner plate. Couldn't he see how alone she felt, a mere woman, undefended?

Telephoning overseas was not so common back then, and so she wrote her mother letters. She wrote, *I am adjusting very well* and *I have made several friends* and *I am feeling very comfortable here;* and in time, that became true. She enrolled in driver's ed and earned her license; she took evening courses at Towson State; she gave her first dinner party. It began to dawn on her that Kiyan was not as acclimated to American life as she had once supposed. He dressed more formally than his colleagues, and he didn't always get their jokes, and his knowledge of colloquial English was surprisingly scanty. Instead of disenchanting her, this realization made him seem dearer. At night they slept curled together like two cashews. She loved to press her nose into the thick damp curls of hair on the back of his neck.

That part, the most powerful aunts on earth could not have arranged.

Sami said he was dubious about roasting a lamb on a spit. He worried it would disturb the neighbors. So Ziba added more dishes to the menu, and her mother came for a week and helped with the cooking. Afternoons, Maryam joined them. They peeled eggplants and mashed chickpeas and chopped onions until the tears were streaming down their cheeks. Susan was given the task of washing and soaking the rice. It touched Maryam's heart to see her standing on a chair at the sink, no bigger than a minute, wearing an apron that fell to her toes and concentrating importantly on stirring the rice about in its bath of cold water. While she worked she practiced the song that Bitsy was teaching the girls. Evidently Bitsy had given up trying to dissuade the welcomers from their "eternal darned 'Coming Round the Mountain,'" as she put it, and was focusing instead on the arrivers. She had sent away for a CD of Korean children's songs, which to her dismay turned out to have not a single word of English on either the label or the case. "For all we know, these are dirges," she had complained to Ziba. But the song she had selected seemed anything but a dirge, with its jaunty, perky melody and its chorus of Oo-la-la-la-la's. Maryam found it charming, although Susan told her that she and Jin-Ho had preferred another one. She sang no more than a line of the other one—"Po po po," it sounded like—before collapsing in a fit of giggles, for some reason. Maryam smiled at her and shook her head. She was struck by the ease with which Susan had picked up this music, as if her Korean roots ran deeper than anyone had guessed. And yet here she stood, tossing her colander of rice with the efficient, forward-swooping motion employed by every Iranian housewife.

In the intimacy of the kitchen, Mrs. Hakimi timidly ventured to call Maryam by her first name. "Maryam, I don't know, does this have enough mint?" she asked in Farsi. Unfortunately, Maryam couldn't think fast enough to remember Mrs. Hakimi's first name in return, but she compensated by saying, "Oh, you would know far better than I"—using the familiar "you." She wasn't sure why they were still so stiff with each other. By rights they should be as chummy now as sisters. She suspected that the Hakimis considered her too independent. Or too unsocial. Or something.

Ziba was discussing the guest list now. "I wish we had more guests from our side," she said. "I wish Sami had brothers and sisters. There are always so many Donaldsons! Could you invite Farah, maybe?"

"Oh," Maryam said, "well . . ." And she let her voice trail away.

The thing was, Farah would probably accept. And William

would come with her, as long as Mercury was not retrograde or some such New Age prohibition. They would stay with Maryam for a week or more and she would have to involve herself in their many group activities. Farah got along famously with the Hakimis. The last time she was in Baltimore Maryam had had to ferry her to Washington for three separate dinner parties, in addition to giving a dinner herself to pay everybody back.

It was true that she was unsocial.

She went home that afternoon happy to be on her own, grateful for the quietness and neatness of her life. For supper she had a glass of red wine and a slice of cheddar cheese. She watched a television program on the habits of the grizzly bear.

In the middle of the program, Dave Dickinson phoned. He said, "I was thinking about this weekend. Could I offer you a ride to the party?"

"Thank you, but—"

"It seems silly to take two cars."

"But I'll have to be there early," she said, "helping with the preparations."

"Couldn't I help too?"

"No, I don't believe you could," she said. "Besides, you live right there in the neighborhood. It makes no sense for you to drive over here."

He said, "I guess I was just thinking it would be nice to have your company."

"Thanks anyway," she said.

There was a silence.

"Goodbye now!" she said.

She hung up.

The bear shambling through the woods had a matted, rough coat that made her sad, and she pressed the off button on the remote control.

7

The Chinese orphan was ready at last. (Like a muffin, Dave pictured when he heard.) Brad and Bitsy packed baby clothes in three different sizes, gift toys for the orphanage, money in red gift envelopes, disposable diapers, nursing bottles, powdered formula, strained prunes and peaches, zinc ointment, scabies medication, baby Tylenol, a thermometer, antibiotics for both infants and grownups, granola bars, trail mix, vitamin pills, water purification tablets, melatonin, compression kneesocks, electrical adaptors, a dental emergency kit, and pollution-filtering facial masks. Dave was the one who drove them to the airport, and he had some difficulty fitting everything into his car trunk.

He stayed with Jin-Ho at her house rather than his, because her parents felt three weeks was too long for a not-quite-five-year-old to be uprooted from her home. He slept in the master bedroom—an intrusive-feeling arrangement, but Bitsy had insisted. (It was closest to Jin-Ho's room.) Every morning when he awoke, the first thing he saw was a photograph of Brad and Bitsy hugging on a beach somewhere. The second thing was Bitsy's earring tree, hung with big, crude, handcrafted disks of copper and wood and clay.

It was early February, so Jin-Ho had preschool every weekday morning. That was a help. And most evenings they were invited to supper at Mac's or Abe's house, or the Yazdans', or a neighbor's. But the rest of the time it was just the two of them, Dave and Jin-Ho on their own. He told himself that now they could really get to know each other. How many grandfathers were given such a chance? And he did enjoy her company. She was a lively, inquisitive child, full of chatter, fond of board games, crazy about any kind of music. But he never completely lost an underlying sense of nervousness. She wasn't really his, after all. What if something happened? When she went outdoors to play he found himself checking through the window for her every couple of minutes. When they crossed even the narrow, untrafficked street she lived on he made her take his hand in spite of her objections. "My mom lets me cross without holding on," she said, "as long as she's beside me."

"Well, I'm not your mom. I'm a worrywart. Humor me, Jin-Ho."

Sometimes in the evening she would grow the least bit tremulous, once or twice even tearing up. "What do you think they're doing now?" she would ask. Or, "How many more days till they're back?" And occasionally she showed some impatience with his un-Bitsy-like ways. He didn't brush her hair quite right; he didn't cut her toast right. For the most part, though, she adapted very well. She knew her parents would be bringing her a sister—something she very much wanted. She talked about how she planned to feed Xiu-Mei her bottle and push Xiu-Mei in her stroller. Xiu-Mei was pronounced something like "Shao-may," to Dave's imperfect ear. (He'd first heard it as "Charmaine.") He found the sound a bit harsh, but Jin-Ho was more accepting. It was "me and Xiu-Mei" this, "me and Xiu-Mei" that. "Me and Xiu-Mei are going to share the same room as soon as she sleeps through the night," she said.

"What if she gets into your toys? Won't that bother you?" he asked.

"She can play with my toys all she likes! And I'm going to teach her the alphabet."

"You'll be the perfect big sister," he said.

Jin-Ho beamed, two little notches of satisfaction bracketing her mouth.

It amazed him that she had no definite bedtime—no schedule whatsoever, almost. Modern life was so amorphous. He thought of the leashes people walked their dogs with nowadays: huge spools of some sort that played out to allow the dogs to run as far ahead as they liked. Then he chided himself for being an old stick-in-the-mud. He rubbed his eyes as they sat at an endless game of Candyland. "Aren't you sleepy, Jin-Ho?" She didn't even deign to answer; just efficiently skated her gingerbread man four spaces ahead.

While she was in preschool each day he'd go home and check on his house, pick up his mail, collect his telephone messages. He missed his normal routine. The trouble with staying at somebody else's place was that you couldn't putter; you couldn't fuss and tinker. Although he did his best. He bled all of Brad and Bitsy's radiators and he planed the edge of a door that was sticking. He brought some neat's-foot oil from home and spent an evening rubbing it into the scarred leather knapsack that Bitsy used for trips to the farmers' market. "What's that?" Jin-Ho asked him, leaning on his arm, giving off the licorice smell of modeling clay.

"It's neat's-foot oil. It's good for leather."

"What's a neat's foot?"

"You don't know about neats? Ah," he said. "Well, now. There's the shy brown neat, and the bold brown neat. This particular oil comes from . . ." He picked up the can and squinted at it, holding it at arm's length, ". . . comes from the shy brown neat."

It was the kind of tale he used to tell his own children; he was famous for it. They would take on a look of suppressed glee and prod him to go further. But Jin-Ho knitted her brows and said, "Did they kill the shy brown neat?"

"Oh, no. They just squeezed its feet. Neats' feet are very oily, you see."

"Does the squeezing hurt?"

"*No,* no, no. In fact the neats are grateful, because otherwise they would slip and slide all over the place. That's why they don't make good house pets. Their feet would ruin the rugs."

Her expression remained troubled. She stared at him in silence. He was sorry now that he'd started this, but he didn't know how to get out of it. Maybe she was too young to know when someone was pulling her leg. Maybe she lacked a sense of humor. Or maybe—this was it, really—they needed an audience. Another grownup, whose snort would give away the joke. In the old days, that had been Connie. Connie would scold him good-naturedly: "Honestly, Dave. You're terrible." And she would tell the children, "Don't you believe a word of it."

He set down the can of neat's-foot oil. He wished he could fall into bed now.

Maryam telephoned to invite the two of them to supper. "I'll ask Sami and Ziba too," she said, "so Jin-Ho will have someone to play with." But of course, her real reason was that the presence of other people would make the occasion less intimate. He could read her like a book.

She did not have the slightest romantic interest in him. He had come to accept the fact. It helped a bit to know that she didn't seem to have an interest in anyone. At least he couldn't take it personally.

He had begun to look around lately and wonder who else might be out there. On his latest birthday he had turned sixty-seven. He might have a good twenty years left. Surely he wouldn't be forced to spend all those years on his own, would he?

But other women seemed lackluster when he compared them with Maryam. They didn't have her calm dark gaze or her elegant, expressive hands. They didn't convey her sense of stillness and self-containment, standing alone in a crowd.

This evening she wore a vivid silk scarf tied around her chignon, and it streamed down her back in a fluid way as she turned to lead them into the living room. Sami and Ziba were already there, settled on the couch with the cat curled between them. Susan was upstairs; she clattered halfway down in enormous high-heeled pumps and summoned Jin-Ho to play dress-up with her. "Mari-june's piled a whole bunch of clothes in a box for us," she said. "Lace things! Satin! Velvet!" From her shoulders, a full red skirt billowed out like a cloak.

The girls disappeared upstairs, and Dave took a seat and accepted a glass of wine. The subject at first was the news from Brad and Bitsy. Brad had sent out a group e-mail from China. They had collected Xiu-Mei, he reported, and she was perfect. They were traveling now with the other parents to a city with a U.S. consulate, and once they had Xiu-Mei's papers in order they would be on their way home. Everyone had seen this e-mail but Maryam, who didn't own a computer. (Her house was so spare that it took Dave's breath away. No cable or VCR or cordless phone or answering machine; no tangle of electrical wires everywhere you looked.) Sami had printed her a copy, and now she placed a pair of tortoiseshell glasses on her nose and read it aloud. "'Xiu-Mei is tiny and she doesn't sit yet, but every day we put her on our bed and pull her up by the hands just to give her the idea. She thinks it's a game. You should see her laugh.'"

Maryam lowered the letter and looked over her glasses at the others. "Eleven months old and doesn't sit!" she said.

"They lie on their backs all day in the orphanage," Dave explained.

"But isn't it a natural *drive* to sit? Don't babies always struggle to be vertical?"

"Sooner or later they do. It's just that it takes them longer if nobody pays them attention."

Maryam said, "Ah, ah, ah"—a series of brief sighs—and took her glasses off.

Dinner, to Dave's surprise, was entirely American: roast chicken and herb-roasted potatoes and sautéed spinach. He felt oddly discouraged by the competence of it. Did she have to do *everything* well? It pleased him to discover that the potatoes were the slightest bit too crusty on the bottom. Or maybe that was deliberate; these Iranians, with their scorched rice and such . . .

Perhaps he'd been wrong in thinking that he didn't take her lack of interest personally.

Jin-Ho attended dinner in a lady's black silk blouse and a pair of needle-heeled ankle boots. Susan wore a T-shirt as big as a dress with FOREIGNER printed across it. "Foreigner?" Dave said. He assumed the shirt had been Sami's. "You used to be a Foreigner fan?" he asked him.

"Oh, no, that was Mom's."

"*You* were a Foreigner fan?" he said to Maryam.

She laughed. "It's not the singing group," she told him. "It's just the word. Sami had that shirt printed for me as a joke when I got my citizenship. I was so sad to become American, you see."

"Sad!"

"It was hard for me to give up being a citizen of Iran. In fact I kept postponing it. I didn't get my final papers till some time after the Revolution."

"Why, I'd have thought you'd be happy," Dave told her.

"Oh, well, certainly! I was very happy. But still . . . you know. I was sad as well. I went back and forth about it—the usual Immigration Tango."

"I'm sorry," Dave said. He felt like an oaf. He hadn't even known it was usual. He said, "Of course, that must have been difficult. I apologize for sounding like a chauvinist."

"Not at all," Maryam told him, and then she turned to Ziba and offered her more spinach.

He always did this with Maryam—said something clumsy or dropped something, spilled something. In her presence his hands felt too big and his feet seemed to clomp too noisily.

The topic of citizenship led Sami to his cousin Mahmad. "He's a citizen of Canada," he told Dave. "This is the son of Mom's brother, Parviz. He lives in Vancouver now with his twin sister. And last month he was invited to speak at a medical meeting in Chicago. Seems he's some kind of expert on liver regeneration. But just before he boarded the plane, he was stopped by the officials. September eleventh, of course. Ever since September eleventh, every Middle Eastern–looking person is a suspect. They took him away; they searched him; they asked him a million questions . . . Well, end of story: he missed his flight. 'Sorry, sir,' they said. 'You can catch the next flight, if we've finished by then.' All of a sudden, Mahmad starts laughing. 'What?' they ask. He goes on laughing. 'What is it?' they ask. 'I just realized,' he tells them. 'I don't have to go to the States! They're the ones who invited me. I don't have to go, and I don't want to go. I'm heading back home. Goodbye.'"

Maryam said, "Ah, ah, ah," again, although she must have heard this story before.

"That's a damned shame," Dave said. Absurdly, he felt the urge to offer another apology.

"And when Brad and Bitsy land in Baltimore," Sami said, "have you thought about where their friends will meet them? Speaking of September eleventh. When the girls arrived, we were all at the gate, but this time we'll be, I don't know, milling around outside, being shouted at by the police."

Jin-Ho said, "Police! Police are going to shout at us?"

"No, no, of course not," Ziba told her. "Hush, Sami. Talk about something else."

And Maryam jumped in to ask if people were ready for dessert.

They all left immediately after supper, because of Susan's bedtime. (So not every modern-day family had dispensed with regular schedules.) Dave didn't offer to stay behind and help with the cleanup. He knew Maryam would say no, and besides, he didn't even want to stay. The evening had left him feeling off balance. He was dying to get home.

When he thanked Maryam at the door, she said, "If there's anything you and Jin-Ho need, please feel free to call me."

"Oh, I will," he said.

But he knew he wouldn't. Under the glare of the porch light, Maryam seemed stark and severe. Her arms were folded across her chest in a way that struck him as ungenerous, although he knew she was only bracing herself against the cold night air. He recalled the faint look of amusement she often took on around Bitsy, and the time she'd complained that Americans read only American literature, and the time she'd announced that this country didn't understand yogurt. It was just as well he saw no more of her than he did.

As he was settling Jin-Ho in his car, he happened to overhear Sami and Ziba from the car parked just ahead. "Where's Susan's bear?" Ziba was asking. "Did you get her bear?" and Sami said, "It should be in the back. I don't think she brought it inside." The easy companionability of it—the buddy system that was a long-established marriage—made Dave go hollow with longing.

On the evening of Xiu-Mei's arrival, Dave drove Bitsy's car to the airport. It was outfitted now with a second child seat—Jin-Ho's outgrown one, the baby kind. Jin-Ho sat in her booster next to it, wearing a button that said BIG SISTER and holding a giant rectangular box wrapped in pink polka-dot paper. Inside the box was a green plush frog almost as big as she was. Dave had voted for something smaller, but Jin-Ho was adamant. "Xiu-Mei has to *notice* it," she said. So he'd given in.

Bitsy's car was strewn with balled-up tissues and cracker crumbs and parts of plastic toys. It also pulled to the left a bit; he should remember to mention that. He drove more slowly than usual, yielding any time another car edged in front of his. The evening was drippy and misty, not all that cold but dank. He had to keep the defogger on.

Jin-Ho wanted to know if Xiu-Mei would feel homesick. "What if she gets here and decides it's not as nice as China?" she asked.

"Oh, she won't do that. She'll take a look around and say, 'This is great! I like it here!'"

"She doesn't talk yet, Grandpa."

"Right you are. How silly of me."

Jin-Ho was quiet a moment, rhythmically kicking the passenger seat in a way that would have been irritating if anyone had been sitting there. Then she said, "Remember when me and Susan tried to dig a hole to China?"

"I remember it very well," Dave said. "Your dad sprained his ankle stepping into it after dark."

"So the kids in China," Jin-Ho said. "Are they digging to America?"

"Well, I never thought about it, but I guess they might be. Sure; why not?"

"Wouldn't that be cool?"

"Very cool."

"They'd pop up out of the ground one day when me and my friends were playing. They'd say, 'Hey! Where are we?' I'd say, 'Baltimore, Maryland.'"

"Very cool indeed," he said.

He supposed he should point out a few problems with the logistics, but why bother? Besides, he took some pleasure in this uncomplicated, coloring-book version of the world, where children in Mao jackets and children in Levi's understood each other so seamlessly.

In the airport parking garage, he drove past Abe's Volvo as it was pulling into a space. And then on the pedestrian bridge, Jin-Ho called out, "There's Susan! I see Susan!" Susan was walking ahead with her parents, swinging a shopping bag at her side. The three of them turned and waited for Jin-Ho and Dave to catch up. "I'm bringing Xiu-Mei a frog!" Jin-Ho said. She had to crane around her big box to see in front of her, but she'd refused to let Dave carry it for her.

"Well, I'm bringing her a bath towel with a hood for her head and a washcloth and a yellow duck and a bottle of special shampoo," Susan said.

"It was good of you to come," Dave told the Yazdans.

"Oh, we wouldn't miss it," Ziba said. "Jin-Ho, let me read your button. So you're a big sister now!"

There was no sign of Maryam. Dave wasn't sure she'd even been told the arrival time.

Once they were inside the terminal, Dave said goodbye to the Yazdans and led Jin-Ho toward Pier D. The plan was that the two of them would wait immediately outside Security so that they could be the first official greeters. Then they would go down to baggage claim, where the others would be gathered.

Jin-Ho looked very grave and important. She stood beside Dave, hugging her gift, gazing steadily toward the approaching passengers even though the L.A. flight hadn't landed yet. At first Dave tried to entertain her by pointing out the sights ("Can you believe how many people travel with their own bed pillows?"), but Jin-Ho's polite, abstracted responses shut him up, finally. He rocked back on his heels and studied the different faces—all ages and all shades, each one wearing the same dazed expression.

Then at long last, here they came—Brad in front, forging the way, laden with totes and hand luggage, and Bitsy close behind, a bundle of pink quilt on her left shoulder. Bitsy looked exhausted, but when she saw Dave and Jin-Ho she brightened and veered toward them. Brad followed; he had been about to go off in the wrong direction.

"Jin-Ho!" Bitsy said. "We missed you so much!" She knelt and hugged Jin-Ho. Still kneeling, she turned the pink quilt bundle to face outward.

Xiu-Mei had spiky black bangs and sharply tilted eyes that gave her a whimsical air. It was impossible to see her mouth because she was sucking a pacifier.

"Xiu-Mei, this is your big sister," Bitsy told her. "Say, 'Hello, Jin-Ho!' "

Xiu-Mei took a deeper suck on her pacifier, causing it to wiggle. Jin-Ho stared at her in silence. Too late, Dave realized that he should have brought a camera. Downstairs there would be several, but this was the scene they would want to have on record. Not that there was much to show, really. Like most life-altering moments, it was disappointingly lacking in drama.

"Hell of a flight," Brad was telling Dave. "We had turbulence from the Mississippi on, and the takeoff and the landing bothered Xiu-Mei's ears. Everybody swore the pacifier would help, but man, she was screaming her head off."

It was true that a single tear rested on Xiu-Mei's cheek.

"I got her a present," Jin-Ho said.

"Oh, wasn't that nice of you!" Bitsy told her. "What a good sister!" She sent Dave a grateful look and stood up, setting Xiu-Mei against her shoulder again. "Shall we go down and see the others?"

"First she has to open her present," Jin-Ho said.

"Not now, honey. Maybe later."

Dave expected Jin-Ho to insist, but she meekly fell in beside Bitsy. He relieved her of her gift so that she could keep pace. From Brad he took a couple of tote bags, and he followed them toward the down escalator. Jin-Ho looked so big, all at once, that he felt a pang for her. He remembered feeling the same about Bitsy when they brought her new baby brother home. Her hands had looked like giant paws and her knees had seemed so knobby.

Downstairs, a cheer arose. Their welcoming committee was standing at the foot of the escalator—friends and relatives smothered in their winter wraps, bearing gifts and balloons and placards. As soon as Brad reached the ground level, he dropped his bags and grabbed the baby, quilt and all, and held her over his head. "Here she is, folks!" he said. "Ms. Xiu-Mei Dickinson-Donaldson." Cameras flashed, and video cameras followed Xiu-Mei's progress into Brad's mother's arms. "Isn't she precious!" Brad's mother said, hugging her close. "Isn't she a sweetie pie! I'm your Grandma Pat, sweetie pie."

Xiu-Mei stared at her, and the pacifier bobbed.

Now Bitsy could turn to Jin-Ho, thank heaven, and take hold of her hand. Everyone headed for the baggage carousel, where suitcases and knapsacks were just starting to arrive. "You should have seen what they gave us for breakfast every day," Bitsy was telling Jin-Ho. "So many foods we'd never eaten before! You would have loved it." Jin-Ho looked doubtful. Laura's camera flashed in her face. Polly—fifteen years old now and bored to death with family events—adjusted the earphones on her CD player and eyed a boy in a football jersey. People here were wearing a wild assortment of clothing. Some, evidently fresh from the tropics, had on Hawaiian shirts and flip-flops, and some wore puffy ski boots and multiple bobbles of down. A young couple walked by carrying canvas cases the size and shape of ironing boards, mountain passes dangling from their jacket zips, the woman flinging back her streaky dark hair and the man describing a wipeout in an Irish accent that made it sound like "wape-oot"; and right behind them came . . . why, Maryam, strolling up at an unhurried pace with her hands thrust into her coat pockets. She approached Jin-Ho, who was standing to one side now while Bitsy scanned the baggage carousel. "Is your sister here?" Maryam asked her, and Jin-Ho said, "Grandma Pat's got her."

Maryam looked over toward Brad's mother, who was surrounded by various women cooing at Xiu-Mei. "Very cute," she said, without attempting to move closer.

"We're *assuming* she's cute," Dave said, "but we can't be sure till she takes that pacifier out of her mouth."

"Does it bring it all back?" she asked him. "The day Jin-Ho arrived?"

"Oh, yes. My goodness, yes."

But he said this just for Jin-Ho's sake, to make her feel a part of things. In fact, tonight seemed nothing like that evening four and a half years ago. Oh, everyone was making an effort. Lou was walking about with a microphone, recording congratulations. Bridget and Deirdre were harmonizing on "She'll Be Coming Round the Mountain," and one of Bitsy's book-club friends carried a WELCOME, XIU-MEI sign. But the atmosphere was different now that people hadn't been allowed to gather at the gate. The crowd had a mismatched, ragtag feel, and the enthusiasm seemed forced.

Maryam was telling Jin-Ho about Jin-Ho's own arrival. "Your

plane was late," she said, "and we had to stand around for ages. We had shown up early, of course, because we were so eager to meet you. It seemed you were never coming! And not a word of explanation for what was causing the delay."

To hear her, you would think that she herself had been there for Jin-Ho's sake. Dave all but forgot that she hadn't even known them back then.

Susan said, "Our plane was late?" She edged in between Jin-Ho and Maryam. "I didn't know our plane was late! Did you?" she asked Jin-Ho.

Jin-Ho just shrugged and gazed elsewhere. (There were times when Dave wondered if she would prefer not to be reminded of Arrival Day.)

"They never did announce it," Maryam went on. "But a moment came when we understood that something must be happening. They opened the door to the jetway; all of us gathered around . . ."

Brad and several others, meanwhile, were building a mountain of luggage next to the carousel—even more luggage than he and Bitsy had left with. Finally Brad stepped back and started reading aloud from a list. "Duffel bag: check. Garment bag: check. Red suitcase, blue suitcase, smaller blue suitcase . . ." Bitsy had reclaimed Xiu-Mei and was traveling through the crowd inviting all the welcomers to return with them to the house. "Lord only knows what it looks like. Remember I haven't been there myself for the past three weeks," she said (slightly offending Dave, who had cleaned the place top to bottom just that morning). "But we'd love to see you, all of you, and Jeannine is bringing refreshments, bless her heart." A flush had risen in her neck—always a sign of excitement, with Bitsy—and she looked gawky and fervent. Dave felt a stab of love mixed with pity; he couldn't have said quite why.

"Well, I'm an old fool," Lou was saying cheerfully. "I poked my mike at somebody who turned out to be a stranger. I took him for one of the neighbors or some such. But he was mighty nice about it. Said, 'Regretfully, I don't have the pleasure of knowing these people but I certainly wish them the best and I think they're very lucky to have such a beautiful baby.' Of course I could always erase him, but I'm thinking I might leave him in."

"Definitely leave him in!" Bitsy said. "Is he still here? We should invite him back to the house!" She hoisted Xiu-Mei higher on her shoulder and turned to Dave. "Dad, will you be riding with us? Can you fit between the two car seats?"

"I don't see as I'll need to try," he told her. "I'll just hitch a ride with . . ."

He turned to look for Abe or Mac and found himself face-to-face with Maryam. She said, "Certainly. I can take you."

Before he could explain, Bitsy said, "Great! Thanks, Maryam. And thanks for coming to welcome Xiu-Mei."

"I wouldn't have missed it," Maryam said, but in that idle, floating tone that always made Dave wonder if something had struck her as humorous.

Everyone headed for the parking lot carrying pieces of luggage, Dave in front so he could show where he'd left the car. Jin-Ho protested when he tried to stash her present in the trunk. "I have to give that to Xiu-Mei!" she said. "She can open it while we're riding."

"Okay, sweetheart," he said. "See you in a few minutes."

He handed Brad the keys and then set off with Maryam to where she had parked her own car, one more level up. The garage felt colder than outside, bone-chillingly cold, and both of them walked quickly, the sound of their footsteps almost metallic against the concrete floor.

"Isn't it odd," Maryam said. "Just like that, a completely unknown person is a part of their family forever. Well, of course that's true of a birth child, too, but . . . I don't know, this seems more astonishing."

"To me, both are astonishing," Dave said. "I remember before Bitsy was born, I used to worry she might not be compatible with the two of us. I told Connie, 'Look at how long we took deciding whom we'd marry, but this baby's waltzing in out of nowhere, not so much as a background check or a personality quiz. What if it turns out we don't have any shared interests?' "

Maryam laughed and wrapped her coat more closely around her.

They didn't speak again until they were in her car, merging onto the highway with the ticket booth behind them. Then Dave said, "How about Sami and Ziba? Think they'll adopt another?"

"I suspect they feel that one child is all they can afford," Maryam told him. "What with the cost of private schools these days."

"They don't believe in supporting public education?"

She sent him a sideways glance but said nothing; merely drove for several minutes in silence. Her profile, edged in silver by the passing headlights, seemed icy and austere, the long slant of her nose impossibly straight.

"Although I guess that's a very personal decision," he said finally.

She said, "Yes."

He felt a surge of rebelliousness. What right did this woman have to act so superior? He said, "You know, it wouldn't do you any harm to indulge in a little to-and-fro discussion."

She sent him an even briefer glance and went back to watching the road.

"You could tell me, for instance, that the Baltimore public schools are abysmal. I could say, well, yes, but if the parents got involved I still had some hope we could change things. Then you could say you didn't want to sacrifice your granddaughter's future for a mere hope. I could handle that! I wouldn't fall apart!"

Still she didn't speak, but she seemed to be fighting back a smile.

"You act as if you think you're so right that you don't need to bother arguing," he said.

She said, "*I* do?" and now she gave him a full-on stare of surprise.

"It's as if you think, Oh, these cloddish Americans, what do they know about anything?"

"I don't think any such thing!"

"It's harder than you realize, being American," he told her. "Don't suppose we aren't aware how we appear to the rest of the world. Times I used to travel abroad, I'd see those tour groups of my countrymen and flinch, even though I knew I looked pretty much the same. That's the hell of it: we're all lumped in together. We're all on this same big ship, so to speak, and wherever the ship goes I have to go, even if it's behaving like some . . . grade school bully. It's not as if I can just jump overboard, you know!"

"Whereas we Iranians, on the other hand," Maryam said wryly, "are invariably perceived as our unique and separate selves."

He said, "Well." He felt slightly foolish. He knew he had overreacted.

"Did you see how people edged away from Sami and Ziba and me at the airport tonight? No, probably you didn't. You wouldn't even have noticed. But that's what it's been like ever since September eleventh. Oh," she said, "sometimes I get so tired of being foreign I want to lie down and die. It's a lot of work, being foreign."

"Work?"

"A lot of work and effort, and still we never quite manage to fit in. Susan said this past Christmas, she rode home with me after school one day and she said, 'I wish we could celebrate Christmas the way other people do. I don't like being different,' she said. It broke my heart to hear that."

"Well . . . ," Dave said. He spoke cautiously, not wanting to call forth another of Maryam's looks. "Um, maybe you could let her have a little tiny Christmas tree. Would that be a problem?"

"She did have a tree," Maryam said. They were entering the city now and she glanced into her side-view mirror, checking for a chance to switch lanes. "She had a *huge* tree. That much we could do for her."

"Then . . . I don't know, decorations? A wreath, a string of lights?"

"Of course. Also mistletoe."

"Ah. And . . . would it go against your beliefs to give her a few small presents?"

"She received dozens of presents. And gave them."

"She did," he said. He was quiet for a moment. "A stocking, maybe," he said at last. "Did she hang a stocking?"

"Oh, yes."

"And how about the caroling? I mean, not the more religious carols, of course, but maybe 'Jingle Bells' and 'Good King Wenceslas,' and, let's see, 'I Saw Three Ships . . .' "

"She went caroling with the next-door neighbors. They walked up and down her street singing every single carol there is, baby Jesus and all."

"Well, then," he said. "I'm not quite sure—"

"But in the car that day she told me, 'It's not the same. It doesn't feel the same. It's not like a real Christmas.' "

He started laughing.

"Oh, for goodness' sake," he said. "You're talking about every child in this country!"

She braked for a light and looked over at him.

He said, "You don't think that's what all of them say? They say, 'Other families celebrate better; on TV it seems much better; in my mind it was going to be better.' That's just Christmas! That's how it works! They have these idealized expectations."

She did seem to get his point, he saw. Something seemed to clear in her forehead.

"The kid's one hundred percent American," he said.

She smiled and started driving again.

For the rest of the way they rode in a silence that Dave didn't try to break, because she seemed deep in thought. At red lights she tapped a fingernail against the steering wheel as if keeping time with some private dialogue, and as she slowed in front of Brad and Bitsy's house she said, "You're right, of course."

"I am?"

"I am far too sensitive about my foreignness."

"What? Wait. That's not what I said."

But she nodded slowly. "I make too much of it," she said. She had brought the car to a stop now but she left the engine running; so he gathered she would not be coming in. She stayed facing forward, gazing out the windshield. "One could even call it self-pity," she said. "A trait that I despise."

"I would never say that! You don't have an ounce of self-pity."

"No, you see," she said, "you can get in a, what would you call it, a mind-set about these things. You can start to believe that your life is *defined* by your foreignness. You think everything would be different if only you belonged. 'If only I were back home,' you say, and you forget that you wouldn't belong there either, after all these years. It wouldn't be home at all anymore."

Her words struck Dave as profoundly sad, but her voice was cool and her profile remained impassive. A yellow glow kept flickering across her face as guests passed between the car and the front-walkway lamp.

Dave said, "Maryam."

She turned and observed him from a distance, it seemed, her expression friendly but contemplative.

"You belong," he told her. "You belong just as much as I do, or, who, or Bitsy or . . . It's just like Christmas. We *all* think the others belong more."

At least she seemed to be listening to him. She cocked her head and kept her eyes on his. He felt self-conscious, all at once. He hadn't meant to sound so solemn. "Anyhow," he said in a lighter tone. "Aren't you coming inside?"

She said, "Oh . . ."

"Please," he said, and he reached for the ignition key and turned off the engine. She didn't object. "Come in," he told her, and he gave her the key. And then it seemed that the words began to mean something more, and he said, "Come in, Maryam. Come inside," and her fingers closed not just around the key but around his fingers too, and they sat there clasping hands and looking at each other soberly.

— 8

— Well. Ziba didn't know *what* to think. People kept asking her questions—the women, mostly. Her mother and her sisters-in-law and Siroos's wife, Nahid. "Is Maryam . . . is she . . . ? Could there be some special reason she is always with that Bitsy person's father?"

She showed up with him at the Hakimis' New Year's party in March—the real one, the completely Iranian one that Ziba's parents gave every year at a big hotel in Washington. Ordinarily she would not have attended. "Khanom thinks she's too high-class for our simple family gathering," the relatives liked to tell each other, although in fact there was nothing simple about it, which was probably why Maryam had always before sent her regrets. It was very, very dressy, very musical and loud, and it lasted far into the night. But this year, there she was, in a long black silk caftan trimmed with gold embroidery, her chignon of pure black hair pulled back tight and sleek, her face a perfect, stunning oval perfectly made up, and Dave Dickinson stood next to her in a baggy gray suit and blue shirt and striped tie, perhaps the first tie Ziba had seen him in outside of his wife's funeral. He was almost the only American present. Oh, a few of the young male cousins had married blondes—there was no getting past that Iranian thing about blondes—but still the man was noticeable for his pale-skinned, faded appearance. Not that it seemed to bother him. He was looking all around with an expression of open joy, taking in the elaborate decorations and the musicians with their santours and tambours and the dressed-up children running wild among the grownups. When he saw the array of foods, he pressed his huge hands together as if he could barely contain his happiness. This made some of the other guests laugh, and Ziba felt almost sorry for him although he himself seemed unaware.

She had known he would be coming, but only because her parents had told her at the last minute. Maryam herself had said nothing. "Did she say anything to *you*?" Ziba asked Sami, and Sami shook his head. This was before the party began, even, but still it came as a shock to find Dave in the midst of the swirling crowd an hour or so later. He stood beneath a high marble arch, next to a fluted column. There were not two inches of space between him and Maryam. Ziba paid close attention to that. (Everybody did.) All evening he stuck to Maryam like a shadow, although he never actually touched her. Maryam, for her part, seemed merely his acquaintance. She didn't set a hand on his when she spoke to him; she didn't take his arm as they moved toward Sami and Ziba to say hello. It was early in the relationship, then: a first or second date. Or maybe not a date at all; maybe a cultural expedition born of Dave's curiosity. Or a convenience for Maryam, who felt uncomfortable driving at night. (But in that case, why not just ride over with Sami and Ziba?)

Ziba telephoned Bitsy the very first thing the next day. Bitsy said he hadn't breathed a word to her.

In April, at Maryam's own New Year's party that she had put on every spring since the girls' arrival, Dave was already settled in when Sami and Ziba got there. And they got there *early*. As usual, they came to help out ahead of time, not that Maryam ever left the slightest detail unseen-to. It was Dave who offered them drinks, Dave who went to answer when Ziba's parents rang the doorbell. Although again, he and Maryam stayed physically quite separate, and he complimented her food as any casual guest might—wanting to know the name of a spice and appearing to have no previous, inside knowledge of her menu.

Bitsy, when she and Brad showed up, said, "Oh, there you are, Dad! We've been phoning you all morning to see if you'd like a ride."

All morning? Ziba thought. Exactly how long had he been here?

Ziba's mother told her later that she should come right out and ask Maryam what was going on. "She's your mother-in-law!" she said on the phone. "You see her almost daily! Ask, 'Should we be buying our wedding clothes?' "

"Ask *Khanom*?" Ziba said.

As a rule, Ziba objected when her family called Maryam "Khanom" behind her back. "Madame" was all it meant, but in their particular tone it might as well have been "Her Highness." Ziba pretended to disapprove. She never let on how intimidating she had always found Maryam. "Really you just have to get to know her," she often told them, and she hoped with all her heart that someday that would be true. Now, though, she admitted it: "I wouldn't have the nerve to ask her!"

Her mother said, "Well, Sami, then. Surely she would tell Sami."

Sami said he didn't mind asking in the least. But he waited till the next time he saw Maryam in person, Ziba noticed. He didn't just pick up the phone and address the subject head on. (Which Ziba refrained from pointing out. There was a certain delicacy between them, a certain gloved and tentative quality, when it came to discussing his mother.) The next Sunday afternoon, when they stopped by Maryam's house to drop off Susan on their way to a movie, Sami said, "What: no Dave? Seems to me Dave is everywhere I look these days."

"No Dave," Maryam said serenely. "Susan, come look at my garden with me! I need to decide what flowers to plant."

Butter would not have melted in the canary's mouth; wasn't that the saying?

"And if they *are* a couple," Ziba ventured to ask Sami once they were back in the car, "how would you feel about that? Would you feel—"

"I'd feel fine," Sami said.

"Because I know it might seem strange to you, seeing your mother with somebody new."

"I would wish her every happiness. She deserves it, after all. It's not as if my father was an easy man to live with."

"He wasn't?" Ziba said.

"Oh, no." He slowed for an intersection.

"You never told me that."

"Oh, he was very moody. Very up-and-down," Sami said. "You just couldn't predict, with him. When I was a kid I'd check his face every morning to see if it was going to be a good day or a bad day."

"That's not the way your mother talks about him at all!"

"On good days he was quite friendly—asking about my schoolwork, offering to help with my projects. On bad days, he just . . . sank in on himself. He went all morose and dissatisfied; he demanded constant attendance. 'Maryam, where's my this?' and 'Maryam, where's my that?' Had to have his special tea and his English digestive biscuits. Demanding. A very *demanding* man. I always wished Mom would stand up to him more."

Ziba said, "Really."

She wondered how it was that Sami hadn't mentioned this till now. Men! she thought. And then she felt a flood of appreciation for all the ways that he was different from his father. There was nobody steadier, more even-tempered and amiable than Sami, and he was so conscientious about helping with the housework and the child care. The women in her family marveled at that. She moved over as close as her seatbelt allowed and laid her head briefly on his shoulder. "That must have been hard for you, too," she told him.

But he said, "Oh, it wasn't too bad," and then, "What time did you say this movie starts?"

Men.

In May a new contraption appeared in Maryam's kitchen: an electric kettle with a teapot that matched it exactly—both a modernistic brushed steel, the teapot's base the very same circumference as the kettle's top. No longer did she have to balance the one tipsily on the other. "Oh! Where did that come from?" Ziba asked.

"From that import shop in Rockville," Maryam said.

"You went to Rockville by yourself?"

"Bitsy's father drove me."

"Ah."

Ziba waited. Maryam measured out tea leaves.

"I thought you liked your Thousand Faces teapot from Japan," Ziba said finally.

"Well, I did," Maryam said. "But this is nice, too. And besides . . . it was a gift."

"Ah," Ziba said again.

Maryam had her back turned, so Ziba couldn't see her expression.

It was a favorite subject now any time Ziba and Bitsy got together. What was happening? they asked each other. And why bother keeping it secret? Didn't Maryam and Dave realize that everyone in both families would be thrilled to see them dating? They cataloged the few clues they'd gathered: Maryam was less often available for babysitting duty; Dave had been caught playing an LP record of Iranian music sung by a woman named Shusha. "Shusha!" Ziba said. "Maryam's favorite singer! And Maryam is the only person I know who still doesn't own a CD player."

Although she did own an answering machine now. After all the times that Sami and Ziba had urged her to get one! But she didn't seem to know how to work it. Her outgoing announcement kept reverting, for some reason, to the generic greeting provided by the factory—"Please . . . leave . . . a . . . message" in a robot-like male voice without intonation. And then, mysteriously, a new announcement of her own would take its place, even though she had claimed to need Sami's help to record it. He would show up as requested and she would say, vaguely, "Oh, it's back to normal again, I believe. But thanks." As if the new announcement had installed itself by magic, while she was looking elsewhere.

Dave must have done that. Dave must have bought the answering machine in the first place—another gift. She used to say that an answering machine would just complicate her life. "What are you implying: you can't be bothered calling me twice if you don't find me at home?" she would ask. One of those Maryam-isms, those Her Highness–isms, that always made Ziba close her eyes for an instant.

"Oh," Bitsy said, "they're dating, all right."

"But if so, why not admit it?" Ziba asked.

"Maybe Maryam is embarrassed. She told me once she was past all that; maybe she feels sheepish now that she's changed her mind."

"It's hard to imagine Maryam feeling sheepish," Ziba said.

They smiled at each other.

Once upon a time, Ziba had been painfully shy in Bitsy's presence. Bitsy had seemed so much older and more accomplished; she was so creative; she was passionately involved in politics and recycling programs and such and she had very knowledgeable opinions.

But that was before she fell all over herself apologizing for her Americanness and her First Worldness and her "white-breadness," as she called it. She was forever complimenting Ziba's exotic appearance and asking for her viewpoint on various international issues. Not that Ziba *had* much of a viewpoint, or any that was different from what she read in the *Baltimore Sun* if ever she could find the time. But somehow she was granted a kind of authority, even so.

And then lately, she had become Bitsy's moral support—almost her elder—as various difficulties arose with little Xiu-Mei. It seemed Xiu-Mei was having trouble taking root. She was a very sweet child, very warm and loving, but every germ that came along managed to lay her low, and twice since her arrival she had had to be hospitalized. Bitsy had the sagging, sleep-deprived appearance of the mother of a newborn. Sometimes she was still in her bathrobe at ten o'clock in the morning. She snapped at Jin-Ho over trifles and she seemed defeated by her own house. So Ziba ran her errands, and collected Jin-Ho for playdates, and offered what reassurance she could. "Xiu-Mei's so much bigger now than when you brought her home," she said. "And look at how she hangs on to you!"

In the beginning, Xiu-Mei hadn't known how to hang on. It could be that she had never been held. She would arch her back in a stiff, rejecting posture when people tried to pick her up. But now she nestled in Bitsy's lap and clung to a twist of her sleeve, observing the scene narrowly over her pink plastic pacifier. They couldn't get that pacifier out of her mouth. Bitsy said she regretted ever introducing it, although what choice had they really had, with the flight home such a problem? "Now we have a pacifier in every single room," she said, "in case of an emergency, and three or four in her crib and half a dozen in her stroller. When I'm feeding her I have to unplug her mouth, pop in a spoonful of food, and then plug the pacifier back in again; and she objects the whole time. I think that's why she's so thin."

She *was* thin—thin and wispy and small for her age, and at fourteen months she had not yet begun to crawl. But no one could doubt her intelligence. She watched one face and then another so closely she might have been lip-reading, and when Jin-Ho and Susan were playing nearby she grew especially attentive, following every movement with her tip-turned, bright-black eyes.

"If only she would nap," Bitsy said, "I believe I could get on top of things here. But she refuses. I lay her down in her crib and she starts shrieking. Not just crying—shrieking, in this high sharp wailing voice. Sometimes late in the evening I think, There was something I meant to do today. What? What was it I meant to do? And then I remember: comb my hair."

"Which reminds me," Ziba said. "You know the Arrival Party: I think we should have it at our house this year."

"Why? You had it last year."

"Yes, but with Xiu-Mei and all—"

"That party is three months away," Bitsy said. "If life isn't any better by then, I'll be on the psych ward."

"All the more reason to have it at our house," Ziba said, risking a joke. But Bitsy failed to smile.

So Ziba switched the subject, and asked if Bitsy thought the girls might be old enough for day camp this summer. "Oh, I don't know," Bitsy said in a listless voice. "Who can say about such things?"

There was a time when she would have had plenty to say. Ziba missed those days.

One June afternoon Ziba opened her door to find Maryam standing on her porch in a tailored blouse and linen skirt, beige linen pumps, and a bicycle helmet. "What on earth!" Ziba said.

"I'm sorry to arrive unannounced," Maryam said. "May I come

in?" And then she walked on in without waiting for an answer. The helmet was black and orange—the orange a flame shape over each ear—and the chin strap emphasized a pad of flesh beneath her jaw that Ziba had never noticed before. "I was out shopping, as you see," she said, gesturing toward her skirt as if to prove it, "and when I came home I thought I'd try on this helmet I had bought. I wanted to make sure that I knew how to work it."

"You bought a *bicycle* helmet?"

"But clearly I did not know how to work it, because once I had it on I couldn't get it off again."

Ziba had an urge to laugh. She kept a straight face, but still Maryam said, "Yes, I know: don't I make a spectacle! But I thought I would rather ask you than go to one of my neighbors."

"Well, of course," Ziba said soothingly. "Here, let's see, now . . ." She stepped forward to take hold of a plastic buckle at one side. She squeezed it, but nothing happened. She felt for some sort of latch but she didn't find one.

Susan, who had been playing out back, came in just then with a watering can and said, "Ooh, Mari-june! What have you got *on*?"

"Just a bicycling helmet, dearest," Maryam told her. "Any luck?" she asked Ziba.

"No, but give me a minute. I'm sure there must be . . ." Ziba ran her fingers along the edge of the strap. She could smell the faintly bitter cologne Maryam was wearing, and she could feel the heat of her skin. "What was it that you fastened when you put it on?" she asked.

"I believe it was that buckle, but now I don't remember. In the shop the boy who sold it to me undid it in a flash, but now I don't—ouch."

"Sorry," Ziba said. She had attempted to pull the strap up over Maryam's chin, but obviously it was meant to stay put. What did she know about such things? The only sport she'd played as a girl was volleyball—and in a *maghnae* at that, a heavy black fitted headscarf that muffled her ears and covered her chest. "I must be missing something," she said. "Here's the buckle, here's the strap . . ."

"Where's your bike?" Susan asked Maryam.

"I don't have a bike, june-am."

"Then what do you need a helmet for?"

"I had intended to ride a bicycle belonging to a friend."

Susan wrinkled her forehead. Ziba stepped back and said, "Sami will know."

"Sami? Is he home?"

"No, but I expect him any minute. Come in and sit down and we'll wait for him."

"Oh, dear," Maryam said. She went over to the gilt-edged mirror that hung opposite the front door. "Wouldn't you think this plastic piece—" she said, peering at her reflection.

"I tried the plastic piece," Ziba told her. "Come and sit down, Maryam. Let me make you a cup of tea. Or . . . can you drink tea with a helmet on?"

"I don't know," Maryam said. "Oh, I don't want tea! Maybe we should just cut the strap with scissors."

"There's no point in ruining a brand-new helmet. Come in and wait for Sami."

Maryam followed Ziba into the living room, but she didn't look happy about it.

"Does the bike belong to Danielle?" Susan asked, trailing after Maryam.

This made Ziba laugh out loud, finally—the image of Danielle LeFaivre, the most hoity-toity of Maryam's women friends, doggedly pedaling a bicycle in her Carolina Herrera suit and four-hundred-dollar shoes. Maryam sighed and sat down on the sofa. "No," she said, "it was another friend." Then she changed the subject. "What were you watering?" she asked Susan. "Do you already have something growing?"

"No, I was just messing around."

"Yesterday I went to the nursery and bought some catnip plants for Moosh," Maryam told her. "I thought you and I could put them into that patch beneath the kitchen window the next time you come over."

"Is the bicycle Dave's?" Ziba asked abruptly.

Then she was sorry, because Maryam took a long moment before she said, "It was Connie's."

"Oh."

"Dave was planning to take me for a ride in the country this weekend. He still has Connie's bike in his garage, but he thought it would be safer not to rely on her old helmet."

"Oh, he's right!" Ziba said. "It's like children's car seats, I think. You're not supposed to resell them. They have a limited life expectancy."

When Sami opened the front door you would think they had both been rescued; they turned so quickly toward the sound.

Sami wasn't as taken aback as he should have been, in Ziba's opinion. All he said when he walked in was, "Hi, Mom. What's with the helmet?"

"I was wondering if you could help me get it off," she told him.

"Why, sure," he said, and he came over to her, did something to the strap that made a snapping noise, and lifted the helmet from her head.

"Thanks," Maryam said. "And thank you for trying, Ziba." She rose and tucked the helmet under her arm and retrieved her purse from the sofa.

"Have a nice bike ride," Ziba told her.

"Thanks," Maryam said again, already in the front hall.

Sami said, "But, Mom? Will you know how to undo it again?"

She said, "Oh, I'll figure it out. Goodbye."

It seemed she couldn't get away from them fast enough.

In July, Maryam went to Vermont for her annual visit. She boarded Moosh with Sami and Ziba, and Ziba agreed to water her houseplants halfway through the week.

Ziba drove to Maryam's on a Wednesday morning after dropping the girls off at day camp. When she let herself in she felt like a thief; there was something so private and close about the dim little living room. She left the front door open behind her, as if to prove she had nothing to hide, and went directly to the kitchen. A single rinsed cup and saucer sat in the sink, she noticed. She filled the watering can that Maryam had placed on the counter, and then she walked through the house, stopping at each plant and testing the soil with her fingertips. Most of the plants were fine; the week had been mild and humid.

Upstairs she went first to the guest room, where she had often put Susan down for a nap when they were visiting. The double bed with its crocheted white spread, the bureau with its paisley scarf, and the pottery bowl of ferns (these in need of water) held no surprises. And Sami's old room—now a sort of catchall, a combination sewing room and bill-paying room and whatever—had obviously been tidied just before Maryam's departure. The desk was bare, and the twin bed with its boyish plaid blanket had been cleared of the ironing and mending that Maryam often laid out there.

Maryam's room was less familiar, and Ziba couldn't help glancing at the objects on the bureau as she entered. They were the same as last year, though: a painted wooden pen case shaped like a fat cigar, an easel-backed Persian miniature, and a mosaic box. No photos, either recent or old; those would be filed away in the album in the living-room bookcase. It seemed that Maryam had decided long ago exactly how her world should be arranged, and saw no reason to vary it ever after.

As Ziba was watering the ivy plant hanging in the window, she chanced to look out and see Dave Dickinson coming up the front walk. Now, what was *he* doing here? She emptied the watering can of its last few drops and then hurried downstairs. By the time she reached the door, he was peering through the screen with one hand shading his eyes. "Hello?" he said. "Oh, Ziba!"

"I'm watering the plants," she told him.

"Well, of course; I should have realized." He drew back a bit, and she stepped out onto the porch. (She didn't feel she could ask him in without Maryam's knowledge.) He was wearing a chambray shirt and khakis that he might have slept in, and his curly gray head was mussed and damp-looking. "I noticed the door was open as I was driving by," he said, "and I worried something was wrong."

Why he should be "driving by" on a residential street that led nowhere, he didn't explain. And next he asked, "Have you heard from her?" without bothering to say whom he meant.

"No, but we wouldn't usually," Ziba told him. "She's only gone for a week, after all."

"I did talk to her right after she got there," Dave said.

"You did?"

"Just to make sure she'd arrived safely."

He turned and gazed away, out toward the street. He said, in an offhand tone, "I don't suppose *you* knew her husband."

Ziba said, "Me?" The question was so unexpected that she wondered if she had mistranslated it. "Goodness, no," she said. "I wasn't even living in this country yet when he died."

"Yes, I didn't suppose . . ." He followed the progress of a lawn-care truck that was rumbling past. Then he turned back to Ziba. His mussed hair gave him a rattled look, as if he were the one who was surprised by this conversation. "She's still very attached to his memory, I guess," he said. "I'm sure he was a wonderful man."

Ziba debated telling him that Kiyan had been moody and difficult. On second thought, no; better not.

"But anyhow: you may have noticed that I like her," he said.

"Um, yes."

"Or love her, even."

For some reason, Ziba felt herself blushing. "So, does Maryam love you too?" she asked.

"I don't know."

It interested her that he thought it might at least be a possibility. She said, "But you must have an inkling."

"No, I don't," he said. "I don't know what to think!"

These last words seemed torn from him. He stopped short, as if he had shocked himself. Then he said, more quietly, "I don't know what she expects of me. I don't know how to act. I invite her out and we go someplace, dinner or a movie; she seems to enjoy my company, but . . . it's like we have a pane of glass between us. I don't know what she's feeling. I wonder if she still feels, let's say, loyal to her husband's memory. Or maybe *bound* to him, by some Iranian social custom."

"No," Ziba said. "There's no such custom."

"Well, then, something else? Something like, I should ask Sami's permission before I court her?"

A little spurt of a giggle escaped her. Now it was Dave's turn to blush. "Sorry, but what do I know?" he said.

"Well, or me either," she told him. "Maryam belongs to a completely different generation. But I can promise she doesn't think you have to ask Sami's permission."

"Then I'm flummoxed," he said.

She had never heard that word before, but she admired how well it got his point across.

"Look," she told him. "How hard could this be? You like her; she likes you. She *must* like you, because believe me, Maryam would not be putting up with you if she didn't. So what's the problem? I'm sure that sooner or later everything will work out."

"Right," he said.

She could tell she had somehow failed him, though, because the look he gave her was so kind. He said, "Thanks for letting me yammer on." And he patted her shoulder and turned and descended the porch steps.

Bitsy said, "Oh, poor, poor Dad."

Because of course Ziba told her everything, not even waiting till she brought the girls back from camp. She drove straight from Maryam's to the Donaldsons', jabbed the doorbell, and barreled in saying, "Guess what!"

"I just hope he doesn't get hurt," Bitsy said. She was changing Xiu-Mei's diaper on the living-room rug, but she had paused when she heard Ziba's news and she didn't even notice Xiu-Mei reaching for the wipes box.

"Why would he get hurt?" Ziba asked.

"Well, he's so naive, the poor dear. He's so lacking in experience."

"It's not as if Maryam is all that worldly-wise herself," Ziba said.

"No, but—"

"As far as we know, the only man she ever went out with was her husband."

"No, but—well, you're right, of course," Bitsy said. Something still appeared to be troubling her, though.

"I thought you would be glad," Ziba told her.

"Oh, I am! Honestly I am." She recovered the wipes box, finally, and pried a wad of wipes out of Xiu-Mei's fist. "But I would be a lot happier if you told me she was madly pursuing him, calling him at all hours and hanging around his neck."

"Maryam is a dignified woman," Ziba said stiffly. "She's a lady. In our country, ladies don't act that way."

It was probably the first time she had ever used that phrase, "in our country." Always before she had been so eager to say that *this* was her country, and she wasn't sure why now should be any different. Bitsy must have noticed, because instantly she said, "Oh, yes, she's a *lovely* woman, and I am so, so pleased that things seem to be moving ahead with them."

Then they both changed the subject. Wasn't Xiu-Mei the teeniest bit plumper? Ziba wanted to know, and Bitsy said she did seem plumper, now that Ziba mentioned it, and maybe they should weigh her. So they went upstairs to the bathroom, and Bitsy stepped on the scale with Xiu-Mei in her arms and then stepped off and handed Xiu-Mei to Ziba and stepped on the scale again, and they did the math. They were very perky and chattery.

On the wall above the toilet hung a framed black-and-white photo of a much younger Dave and Connie with Bitsy and her brother Abe, all of them in ragged wigs and hideous, hayseed clothes. Dave wore a Groucho Marx mustache-and-glasses set; Connie and Bitsy had enormous artificial buckteeth, and four of Abe's teeth were blacked out. That photo had been taken the summer Mac got engaged, Ziba knew. Connie had mailed a copy to Laura's parents with a note saying that the future in-laws would like to introduce themselves. A joke, of course, but Ziba hadn't laughed quite soon enough when it was explained to her. How could people view themselves so lightly? she had wondered.

And who on earth would hang a family photo above a toilet?

Some things about Americans would forever . . . flummox her.

≠

Maybe being away for a week made Maryam appreciate what Dave meant to her. At any rate, after she got back from Vermont they were seen together more often, and they did appear to be *together*. They chimed in on each other's stories, and reminded each other cozily of shared experiences, and sat side by side and quite close on the couch. When Maryam was speaking, Dave smiled around the room as if inviting the others to join in his admiration. When it was Dave who was speaking, Maryam smiled too but directed her gaze discreetly toward her lap. They acted like teenagers, Sami told Ziba. He said he was glad to see his mother so happy, but it did make him feel sort of funny.

Bitsy said it made her feel old. She couldn't be more delighted, she said, but, "Oh, Lord, how long has it been since you lit up like that when a certain person walked into the room? Be honest, Ziba."

This was at the Arrival Party, which did, after all, take place at the Yazdans' this year instead of at the Donaldsons'. Xiu-Mei had been hospitalized for three days the previous week—some kind of intestinal blockage, now resolved, thank goodness—and so at the very last minute Bitsy had given in. She brought over what she'd already made, a casserole and some home-baked bread, and Ziba and Maryam swung into action and prepared the rest in thirty-six hours.

As fate would have it, the guest list was longer this year than it had been in some time. There was even a rare representative from Maryam's branch of the family: her brother's wife, Roya, who was in the U.S. with her friend Zuzu to visit Zuzu's son in Delaware. Zuzu had been scared to travel alone, was the story. Apparently she could not be left alone at her son's place, either, or else Roya was also scared to travel alone, because Roya brought Zuzu with her when she came to Baltimore, and the two of them stayed at Maryam's. In one way this was helpful: they had been happy to pitch in with the emergency food preparations, and Zuzu, who hailed originally from a town on the Caspian Sea, made an impressive stuffed fish that was the centerpiece of the table. On the other hand, they were your traditional sharp-eyed, sharp-nosed Iranian women, and not ten minutes into the party they began to focus very closely on Dave Dickinson. They watched every move he made and were not above whispering to each other after his most inconsequential remark. Of course they might just have been working out a translation (neither of them spoke much English), but Ziba suspected they were gossiping. She was interested to see that they appeared to have no prior knowledge of him; they had been at Maryam's for three days but required an introduction when he arrived at the party, and from their first, dismissive reaction it was clear they didn't know that he had any special importance. Then he said, "Aha! *Salade olivieh!*" and rubbed his hands together. He started walking around the table surveying the dishes, which had already been laid out in two long rows. *"Fesenjun!"* he said, putting a *u* in the last syllable—less formal and more intimate-sounding than *"fesenjan."* "Is it yours?" he asked Maryam, and she nodded, smiling at him with her lips sweetly closed, and that was when the two women grew extremely, extremely alert.

"Doogh!" he said. "I adore *doogh,*" he told the two women, and he said it with some pride, evidently knowing that most Americans were disgusted by the very notion of a carbonated yogurt drink. He pronounced the *gh* sound with a conscious, laughable effort, practically gargling in his attempt to speak far enough back in his throat; and in fact the women did laugh—or tittered, at least, each raising a

hand to her mouth and exchanging a glance with the other. He laughed too. He must have thought he was connecting with them beautifully. And Maryam may have thought the same, for she went on smiling from the other side of the table. It was Ziba who moved forward, at last, and took him by the elbow. "Wait till you see the baklava," she told him. "My mother brought it over this morning."

But this only caused the women to exchange another glance. ("See how Maryam's daughter-in-law treats him so familiarly!") Dave said, "Your mother brought her baklava? I *crave* her baklava." He told the women, "She makes her filo dough from scratch. You wouldn't believe how good it is."

They pursed their lips, as if assessing something. They looked thoughtfully toward Maryam.

The baklava was serving as the Arrival Cake, in fact. Ziba had spiked it all over with tiny American flags and set it on the sideboard at the end of the meal. She omitted the candles, and she didn't bother sending the girls out of the room. Instead she plunged straight into "She'll Be Coming Round the Mountain," and the others joined her—even the girls themselves. If Bitsy was disappointed, she didn't show it. She might have been too tired to care. Xiu-Mei was asleep on her shoulder, head lolling and pacifier halfway out of her parted lips, and Bitsy swayed with her in time to the song. "Toot, toot!" the girls were shouting. "Hi, babe!" They sang louder than anyone else, as if they'd been waiting all these years just for the opportunity.

And later the videotape ran almost unobserved; most people knew it so well. Jin-Ho went off in a corner to play Old Maid with two cousins. Linwood and his girlfriend grew all whispery and nuzzly. Several of the women started cleaning up while the other guests stood about in small groups, merely glancing toward the screen from time to time and remarking on how small the girls used to be, or how much more hair Brad used to have, before returning to their conversations. When Ziba crossed in front of the TV with a stack of dishes, she had to say "Excuse me" only to Susan and Bitsy. Susan was watching the video from her seat on the rug. Bitsy, in the rocker with Xiu-Mei, seemed on the verge of sleep. But then Bitsy asked, out of the blue, "Remember how we used to tell each other we wouldn't want to go back to that day for anything on earth?"

"I remember," Ziba said.

"But now I think that in some ways, I *would* want to go back. I hadn't made any mistakes yet. I was still the perfect mother and Jin-Ho was still the perfect daughter. Oh, not that I'm saying . . . I don't mean to say—"

"I know what you're saying," Ziba told her, and she would have given Bitsy a hug if she hadn't had her hands full of cake plates.

"What do you suppose their lives were like before they came to us?" Bitsy asked, not for the first time. "They've had all those months of experiences that we will never know about. I'm sure they must have been treated well, but, oh, it kills me, it just kills me that I wasn't there to hold Jin-Ho when she first opened her eyes on the day that she was born."

On the day that Susan was born, Ziba was on the other side of the world wondering if she'd be able to love a total stranger's baby. And she had cried for half of one night some weeks after Susan's arrival, not knowing what she was crying about till all at once she had thought, What happened to my *own* baby?

Two things she would never say aloud to anyone—not Bitsy, not even Sami.

She told Bitsy, "Oh, well, just look at her. She turned out fine anyhow, didn't she?" For Jin-Ho was chortling gleefully while Deirdre, studying the card she'd just picked, was pantomiming despair.

In the kitchen, Ziba found her mother scraping plates. Roya and Zuzu were spooning leftovers into refrigerator containers, and Maryam was knotting the drawstring on a plastic bag of garbage.

Dave said, "Oh, Maryam-june! Don't lift that! Let me!" and he stepped forward to wrest the bag from her. Maryam straightened, brushing a strand of hair off her face. Roya set down a salad bowl and sent a long look toward Zuzu.

Susan started kindergarten that September. She'd been accepted at a private school out in Baltimore County. Every morning Sami drove her there, since he worked in that area anyway, and on Mondays, Wednesdays, and Fridays Ziba picked her up. But the kindergarten program ended at noon, which meant that on Tuesdays and Thursdays Maryam had to be the one who fetched her. Maryam brought Susan back home with her, gave her lunch, and kept her until Ziba arrived several hours later. Ziba told Maryam that she worried this was an imposition now that Maryam was leading such a busy social life; but Maryam said, "What do you mean, busy?" Ziba didn't answer that.

Often when Ziba got to Maryam's she would find Dave there before her. He would be sitting in the kitchen while Maryam prepared supper and Susan played with the cat. (Later, Ziba would ask Susan, "Did Dave eat lunch with you?" and most days Susan said, "Mmhmm." No telling if he'd been around even longer. All morning? All the previous night?)

Touchingly, Dave made a point of rising when Ziba walked in. "Well, hello! Good to see you," he'd say, running a hand through his pelt of gray curls. A mug of coffee would be sitting on the table in front of him—he drank coffee around the clock—and a jumbled pile of newspapers. He liked to read aloud from the papers and make comments to Maryam. As soon as Ziba turned to greet Susan, he would sit back down and resume where he had left off. "Listen to this," he told Maryam. "Here's a man arrested for road rage as a *jogger*, for mercy's sake." Maryam smiled and topped off his coffee with the pot that she kept going for him. "Oh, thank you!" he said. He never failed to show his gratitude—another touching quality. Although Ziba thought the newspaper-reading could get a little tiresome. "'Area residents complained that the club's exotic dancers performed with denuded breasts,'" he read from another page. "'Denuded'! Don't you love it?" Maryam laughed gently as she rinsed out her Thousand Faces teapot. Where was her new electric contraption? Ah: shoved toward the back of a counter, half hidden by a package of pita.

Susan said a boy named Henry had called her a poop-faced poop-head. "Oh, that's just boys," Maryam told her, and Dave announced, with some urgency, "Now, here is a bunch of parents protesting the multiplication tables." Ziba was reminded of how a child will tug at his mother's sleeve when she is on the phone, requiring cookies, milk, juice, complaining of a stomachache, desperate to reclaim her attention. "They feel that rote memorization dampens the students' love of learning," Dave said. "And they don't see why anyone should have to diagram sentences. That's old-fashioned, they say." He lowered the paper to frown at Susan over his reading glasses. "You *need* to diagram sentences, young lady. Don't let anyone tell you otherwise."

Susan said, "Okay."

"If a certain TV anchorman could diagram a sentence, he would not have reported on the national news that as the father of two young children, chicken pox was sweeping the country."

"Huh?"

Maryam lit the flame beneath her kettle. "Was today your day with the leopard-skin lady?" she asked Ziba.

"Yes, and you'll never guess now what. Now she wants tiger-striped curtains in the master bedroom. I said, 'But the wallpaper there is zebra-striped!' She said, 'Of course. It's a theme room.'"

Maryam leaned back against the counter and folded her arms. She was wearing a long white apron over her black slacks; she looked crisp and almost too thin. "Last night I had the most upsetting dream," she said. "You've just reminded me. The zebra stripes reminded me. I was driving in a strange city, trying to get to the zoo, and I couldn't find a parking space. So finally I parked on a side street. And then I told the ticket lady, 'Oh! I forgot where I parked!' I said, 'Wait a minute; I just need to make sure I can get back to my car.' So I turned and I went down this street, went down that street . . . but I couldn't find my car again. All the streets looked the same."

"Maryam, sweetheart?" Dave said, lowering his newspaper. "Are you feeling particularly anxious these days?"

"Why, no, not that I—"

"Because I would call that an anxiety dream. Don't you think so, Ziba?"

Ziba said, "Well . . ."

"I do have to drive to Danielle's tomorrow night," Maryam said. "And you know how far out of town she lives."

"Aha, that's it," Dave told her. "You hate driving at night! You don't have any night vision. You always end up getting lost."

"Not always."

"I will drive you."

"No, no . . ."

"I will drive! I will be at your beck and call! I will drive you there and come back for you at some appointed time."

"That's just silly," Maryam told him.

"Oh, let him, Mari-june," Ziba said.

"Yes, let me, Mari-june. Besides," Dave said. He winked at Ziba. "This way I might finally get to meet the famous Danielle."

"You haven't met Danielle?" Ziba asked.

"I haven't met any of her friends."

"Why, Maryam! You ought to introduce him," Ziba said. "Invite him in when he comes to bring you home."

Ordinarily she would not have been so forward, but all at once she felt a kind of impatience that amounted almost to anger. Wouldn't you think Maryam could show a little more warmth? Clearly she loved the man; why was she so stiff-necked, so obstinate, so *frustrating*?

But Maryam said, "I will drive my own self, thank you," and turned back to her kettle.

Then Susan complained that Moosh had snagged her hair, and Ziba said what did she expect if she swung her braids in his face, and Dave said, "Look at this! Now churches are projecting the words to hymns on overhead screens with little bouncing balls like Lawrence Welk. They say it's too much trouble for people to read down the staves in the hymnbooks. For God's sake! Too much trouble!"

Maryam clicked her tongue. Ziba told Susan to collect her things because they had to be going.

When the Donaldsons gave their leaf-raking party in October, Maryam attended. She hadn't in the past, not after the very first one. ("I have my own leaves to rake," she always said, although her own leaves were oak and barely beginning to turn by then.) But here she came, emerging from the passenger side of Dave's car and waving to the others. She went into the house first to drop off her purse and a bottle of wine, and then she joined Dave, who'd already started raking a section near the front. The girls were helping too this year, each wielding a child-sized rake and competing to see who could make a bigger pile. Xiu-Mei was sitting on a tarpaulin that Brad had spread nearby, reaching for the shiny brass grommets. You could tell she had not had much practice operating her hands. They moved as waveringly and unpredictably as those scooping-claw games on boardwalks.

It was a perfect day for this—a breezy, bright Saturday afternoon, warm enough so that bit by bit, people shucked their sweaters off. Brad's mother, who as usual was just standing about decoratively, gathered the sweaters and put them in a heap beside Xiu-Mei. Bitsy stopped work for a minute to go inside and check on dinner. Brad's father started a boring real-estate discussion with Sami, and Dave dropped his rake in order to walk over and confer with the girls about something. Ziba couldn't hear what he was saying. All she heard was Sami telling Lou how difficult the insurance companies were making home-buying these days.

Bitsy came back out of the house with a pitcher and a stack of tumblers. "Who's for lemonade?" she called, and the girls said, "I am! I am!" Ziba laid aside her rake and went to help, but the men continued working. So did Maryam, till Dave said, "Maryam? Want to stop for lemonade?"

"Oh," she said, "maybe later." She was raking alongside the driveway with languid, leisurely strokes. She didn't like sweet drinks, Ziba knew—not that she would ever be so rude as to say so.

Dave went over to Bitsy and accepted a glass of lemonade from her. Then he bent and whispered to the girls. Jin-Ho said, "Oh," and handed her tumbler back to Bitsy. Susan said, "Here, Mama," and shoved her own tumbler at Ziba. They followed Dave across the lawn toward Maryam. Bitsy raised her eyebrows at Ziba, but Ziba had no idea.

"Maryam?" Dave was saying. "Won't you sit down? I brought you a glass of lemonade."

"Oh, thank you, but—"

"Sit down, Mari-june! Sit down!" Susan said, and Jin-Ho said, "Please, *please* sit down." They were tugging at her arms and giggling. Maryam seemed puzzled, and no wonder; the only place to sit was directly on the ground. But she did allow herself to be dragged down, finally, until she was seated tailor-fashion on a stretch of mossy grass already cleared of leaves. Then Dave handed her the lemonade.

In the distance, Sami was telling Lou, "It's like the insurance companies have completely forgotten that gambling is their job description. They won't insure a house if it has ever in its life had a leak; never mind that the leak has long ago been—"

Dave called, "Sami?"

Sami broke off and looked over at him.

"Girls," Dave said.

Still giggling, the girls dug something out of their pockets. They pressed closer to Maryam and started working busily just above her head. Maryam said, "What—?" She tried to bat their hands away but they were all over her, four insistent little fists making brisk, bustling motions. "It's sugar!" Susan cried. "We're grinding sugar!"

"What on—?"

"Maryam," Dave said. "Will you marry me?"

Maryam stopped swiping at her hair and stared at him. The girls were still working away, but Dave said, "Okay, kids, that's enough now." Reluctantly, they stepped back.

Maryam said, "What?"

"This is a formal proposal," he said, and he dropped to his knees beside her. "Will you be my wife?"

Instead of answering, she looked at the girls. Sure enough, their hands were full of sugar cubes—the uniform white rectangles that came in the yellow Domino box.

The sugar should have been cone-shaped. That was what they used in Iran: rough white cones of sugar some six or eight inches tall. And the people grinding it should have been grown women known for their happy marriages, and they should have worked over a veil so that the crystals would not be speckling Maryam's hair like a very bad case of dandruff. And it was never ground at proposals. That happened only at weddings.

Either Dave had been gravely misinformed or else he had decided to redesign the whole tradition. Switch it around and embellish it. Americanize it, you might say.

Maryam looked past the girls to the others: Bitsy smiling above her pitcher, Pat clasping her hands as if praying, Sami and Lou gaping, and Ziba herself . . . what? Probably clench-jawed with tension, because it would be so sad if Maryam said no to this poor, sweet, foolish man.

Maryam looked at Dave again. She said, "Yes."

Everybody cheered.

On Sunday Ziba woke with a headache from way too much champagne. It had been a rowdy celebration, extending so late that finally Maryam herself had been the one to break it up. By that time both girls were sound asleep on the couch, which Ziba would have noticed earlier if she hadn't been so tipsy. Sami had to carry Susan out to the car. (He practically had to carry Ziba.) He'd drunk very little himself because he was driving, and this morning he was cheerfully—smugly, even—putting on his socks while Ziba said, "Oh, oh, my head," and squinted toward the alarm clock. Nine-fifteen. "Oh, God," she said. "Where's Susan?"

"Downstairs watching TV."

"I feel as if I've got a bowling ball in my head. I turn this way—wham! Turn the other way—wham!"

"Want some aspirin?"

"I'm afraid I might throw it up."

"I warned you," Sami told her.

"Sami, don't even start. Okay?"

He rose and padded in his stocking feet to the bathroom. She heard the medicine-cabinet door slide open. "One, or two?" he called back.

"Four," she said.

She heard water running.

"I hope Maryam doesn't feel this bad," she said.

"She didn't drink all that much that I noticed."

"Oh, great, was I the only one?"

"Well, Brad was putting away quite a bit, and it seemed to me that Pat and Lou were fairly—"

Downstairs, the doorbell rang.

Sami stepped out of the bathroom and sent her a questioning look.

"Don't answer it," Ziba told him.

But a moment later Susan called, "Mama? Mari-june's here."

Ziba said, "Oh, God," and fell back on her pillow.

"I'll go," Sami said. He set two aspirin on the nightstand, along with a paper cup of water, and left the room. After a pause, Ziba heard his chipper "Hi, Mom!" and then murmur, murmur—normal morning voices that made Ziba feel even worse.

Well, no getting around it; she would have to show herself. She sat up to swallow the aspirin. Then she hauled herself out of bed and went to the closet for her bathrobe.

By the time she arrived downstairs, Maryam was seated at the kitchen table watching Sami fill the kettle. Whether or not Maryam had drunk much champagne, she had the drawn, unhealthy look of someone who had stayed up too late. Her black blazer turned her skin almost yellow, and she wasn't wearing lipstick.

"Morning, Mari-june!" Ziba said. She tried to sound fresh and energetic.

Maryam said, "Good morning, Ziba." Then she said, "I was just telling Sami that I feel horrible."

"Oh, do you really? Me too. I don't know what I could have been—"

"This is the worst mistake of my life."

"Excuse me?" Ziba said.

She looked over at Sami. He was standing to one side of the stove now, waiting for the kettle to heat. "Mom didn't mean to say yes," he told her.

"Didn't mean . . . ?"

Maryam said, "I was trying to be . . ." She let out a little breath of a laugh, although her expression stayed grim. "I was trying to be polite," she said.

"Polite!" Ziba echoed.

"Well, what would *you* have done? If someone put you in a spot like that, asked you in front of everyone? Funny," Maryam said. "I've always wondered about those very public proposals. The men who propose on billboards or hire a plane to fly a banner past. What if the women have no wish to get married? But there they are, trapped. On public view, and so what can they say but yes?"

Ziba was speechless. After a moment, Sami cleared his throat and said, "Well, ah, but it's always been my assumption that those couples have arrived at some understanding beforehand, so that the men feel fairly sure of their answer. Are you saying that you and Dave never discussed the subject?"

"Never," Maryam said. Then she hesitated. "Or never in so many words, at least."

Sami cocked his head.

"It's true we have been . . . a couple for some time," she said. "I admit that he means a great deal to me. And my first reaction yesterday was 'yes'; I won't deny it. But not two minutes later I thought, My Lord, what have I done?"

She looked at Ziba when she said this. Instead of responding, Ziba sank onto the chair across from her. She didn't know whether the hollow in her stomach came from her hangover or from dismay.

"He is so American," Maryam said, and she hugged herself as if she felt cold. "He takes up so much space. He seems to be unable to let a room stay as it is; always he has to alter it, to turn on the fan or raise the thermostat or play a record or open the curtains. He has cluttered my life with cell phones and answering machines and a fancy-shmancy teapot that makes my tea taste like metal."

"But, Mari-june," Ziba dared to say. "That's not American; it's just . . . male." Then she shot a quick glance at Sami, but he was too focused on his mother to take offense.

"No, it's American," Maryam said. "I can't explain why, but it is. Americans are all larger than life. You think that if you keep company with them you will be larger too, but then you see that they're making you shrink; they're expanding and edging you out. I could feel myself slipping away. I was thinking so for a while now! And then before I could say that, he did this thing in public."

She was speaking in an unusually stilted manner, Ziba noticed, and with more of an accent, perhaps to prove that she herself was not American in the least—that she was the opposite of American. And her huddled posture, so unlike her, did make her seem to have shrunk.

"All his fuss about our traditions," she said. "Our food, our songs, our holidays. As if he's stealing them!"

"Oh, well, but, Mom," Sami said. "That's a *good* trait, his interest in our culture."

"He's taking us over," she said, unhearing. "Moving in on us. He's making me feel I don't have my own separate self. What was that sugar ceremony but stealing? Because he borrowed it and then he changed it, switched it about to suit his purposes."

Even though she had had nearly the same thought herself, Ziba said, "Oh, Maryam, he just wanted to show he respects our way of doing things." She was suddenly filled with sympathy for him, remembering Dave on his knees and his eager, open face. "You can't object to his Americanness and then fault him for trying to act Iranian. It's not logical."

"It may not be logical, but it's how I feel," Maryam said.

The kettle was boiling now, and Sami turned to lift it off the stove. Ziba didn't know how he could take this so calmly. She asked Maryam, "Couldn't you give it a little more time? Maybe it's just a case of, what do they call it. Wet feet."

"I *have* given it time," Maryam said. "Otherwise I would have told him last night. But no, all I said last night was that it was late and I was tired; he should drop me off at my house and I would see him in the morning. And then this morning I came to you two first to explain the situation, because I know everyone will be angry at me. All of you, and I don't blame you. It will cause an awkwardness in your friendship with Brad and Bitsy."

"Oh, don't worry about that," Sami said, although Ziba herself was worrying about exactly that. Here they'd been just about to join ranks, become one big happy family! Would the four of them stop being friends now? And what would they tell the girls?

But Sami was saying, "If you can't marry him, you can't. No two ways about it."

"Thank you, Sami-jon," Maryam said.

She looked next at Ziba, but Ziba said nothing.

Then Maryam told them she had to go—"I want to get this over with," she said—and she refused a cup of tea and collected her purse. "Goodbye, Susan," she called as she passed the living room. Sami followed, but because he had no shoes on he didn't see her out to her car. He stopped at the front door, with Ziba some distance behind. "Drive carefully," he said. Ziba kept quiet. She couldn't fight down her sense of outrage. None of this should have happened, she wanted to say. She wanted to shout it. This was all so unnecessary, and so cruel, and there was no excuse for any part of Maryam's behavior from start to finish.

Maryam was descending the steps, walking toward the street with her purse clutched tight against her. She seemed much smaller than usual. In her black blazer and slim black pants, she was a single, narrow figure, straight-backed and slight and entirely alone.

9

Jin-Ho's little sister had a pacifier in her mouth about a hundred hours a day. The only time it came out was when she was eating, but she didn't really like to eat so that didn't take very long. On account of her not eating she was itty bitty, teeny-tiny. She was two and a half years old but Jin-Ho could still lift her up. So Jin-Ho's mother said they would have to get rid of the pacifier. Maybe then Xiu-Mei would take more interest in food.

Except it didn't work. "Binky! Binky!" Xiu-Mei howled. (That was what she called pacifiers, because that was what Grandma Pat called them.) Jin-Ho's mother said, "The binky is all gone, sweetheart," but Xiu-Mei wouldn't hush. She screamed and screamed, and Jin-Ho's mother went upstairs with a headache and closed her bedroom door. Then Jin-Ho's father carried Xiu-Mei around the house and sang her a song called "Big Girls Don't Cry," but still she went on screaming. Finally he said a bad word and put her down on the couch not very gently and went into the kitchen. Jin-Ho went too because the screaming hurt her ears. She colored in her workbook while her father unloaded the dishwasher. He made a lot of noise, enough to drown out Xiu-Mei's noise, and every now and then he would absentmindedly sing another piece of his song. "'Bi-ig girls . . . don't . . . *cry*-y-y,'" he sang in a high thin girly voice. Usually when Jin-Ho's parents sang it made her crazy because they didn't land on the notes quite right. This time it was okay, though, because he was just clowning. "'*Do*-on't cry-y,'" he sang, and the "don't" went so low that he had to tuck in his chin to get down there.

Then Xiu-Mei stopped screaming. Jin-Ho's father turned from the dishwasher and gave Jin-Ho a look. It was very, very quiet. He tiptoed back to the living room, and Jin-Ho slid off her chair and tiptoed after him.

Xiu-Mei sat on the couch reading her favorite board book, busily sucking a pacifier she must have found between the cushions.

Because she didn't have just one pacifier; she had dozens. She might have had a thousand. She had about ten in every room, and more in her stroller and more in her crib and more in both the cars so she would never be caught short. Jin-Ho's mother had gathered up handfuls of them earlier in the morning, but no way could she get hold of every single one.

So that afternoon during Xiu-Mei's nap, Jin-Ho's mother announced a new plan. They were going to throw a party. As soon as Xiu-Mei woke they all told her, "Guess what, Xiu-Mei! Next Saturday we'll have a huge party and the Binky Fairy will fly in to take away all your binkies and leave you a wonderful present instead." Even Jin-Ho told her that. (Her mother said she should talk it up.) "Only six more days till she comes, Xiu-Mei!" Xiu-Mei just looked at them and made a winching sound on her pacifier. She seldom said very much, because her mouth was usually full.

"What's her present?" Jin-Ho asked, but her mother said, "Oh, that's a secret," which probably meant she didn't know. Jin-Ho wasn't stupid. If the Binky Fairy could fly, she must be bringing something that mortals couldn't even imagine.

"Did the Binky Fairy bring *me* a present?" she asked her mother.

Her mother said, "Well, no, actually, because you never used a pacifier. That was so impressive to the Binky Fairy! She really, really admired you for it."

"I'd rather she'd brought me a present," Jin-Ho said.

Her mother laughed as if Jin-Ho had made a joke, although she hadn't.

"And how does she know when to come?" Jin-Ho asked.

"Well, she's magical, of course."

"Then why didn't she come this morning, so you wouldn't need to take away the binkies on your own?"

"Oh, that was just a . . . miscommunication," her mother said.

"So what if on Saturday you have a miscommunication again and—"

"It's going to work out, okay?" her mother said. "Trust me. Take my word for it."

"But if it didn't work out this morning—"

"Jin-Ho," her mother said. "Enough! We'll send the Fairy a letter. Will that satisfy you?"

"I think it would be safer," Jin-Ho said.

So her mother got on the computer and printed out a special card showing a stork carrying a baby because she couldn't find a picture of a pacifier. On the inside she wrote in block letters that Jin-Ho could read for herself: *SATURDAY, SEPTEMBER 20, 2003, AT 3 P.M., PLEASE COME FOR XIU-MEI'S BINKIES.* She put the card in a bank-deposit envelope, and that evening when they were barbecuing chicken out on the patio she set the envelope on the grill and they watched it go up in smoke. Jin-Ho's father said, "Jeepers, Bitsy," and moved a drumstick away from the black papery bits with his tongs. Jin-Ho's mother said, "I know! I know! You don't have to tell me!" Then she plopped onto a chaise longue. "How did I get myself into this?" she asked him.

But after that she cheered up. "Come sit with me, sweetheart," she said to Xiu-Mei, and Xiu-Mei toddled over and climbed into her lap. Her pacifier this evening was yellow, shaped like a sideways 8. "Once upon a time," Jin-Ho's mother told her, "there was a tiny, sparkly fairy who was known as the Binky Fairy."

"I sure hope we don't regret this," Jin-Ho's father said.

Whom to invite? Anyone who would come, Jin-Ho's father said. They discussed it over supper. He said, "Invite the damn mailman, if you want. Invite the garbage guys."

"Yes! Alphonse!" Jin-Ho said.

"Who's Alphonse?"

"He's one of the garbage guys."

"We'll ask my dad, of course," Jin-Ho's mother said. "And your parents. And my brothers and their families. Well, it's an excuse for a get-together! The pacifier issue is incidental, really. And the Copelands, because little Lucy will be company for Xiu-Mei. And maybe . . . what do you think? The Yazdans? Or not."

She was looking at Jin-Ho's father, but Jin-Ho was the one who answered. She said, "We always have the Yazdans! I always have to play with that bossy Susan."

"We do not always have them, in fact," her father told her. "We haven't seen them in nearly a month. We don't want things to get uncomfortable, Bitsy. I think we ought to invite them."

"Well, it's no fault of mine we don't see them," Jin-Ho's mother said. She handed Xiu-Mei a chicken wing. Xiu-Mei was no longer allowed to suck her pacifier at the table, but even so she just turned the wing this way, turned the wing that way, and then set it down on her plate. "You know, somehow Ziba's acted differently toward me ever since the breakup," Jin-Ho's mother said. "She's seemed . . . I don't know. Strained."

"She feels anxious; that's all it is. She worries you hold it against her."

"Well, that's absurd. She knows I'm a fair-minded person. Why would I blame *her* for something her mother-in-law did?"

Maryam, she meant. Susan's grandma. Who was once about to marry Jin-Ho's grandpa; and if she had, then she would have been Jin-Ho's grandma as well. (Jin-Ho's father had pointed out that also, Jin-Ho's mother would have been Jin-Ho's aunt. "You could start calling your mom 'Aunt Bitsy,'" he'd said. Jin-Ho had said, "Huh? I don't get it.") But Maryam had changed her mind, and now they didn't see her anymore. She didn't give her New Year's dinner in the spring and she was out of town during this year's Arrival Party. "Conveniently" out of town, Jin-Ho's mother had said. Jin-Ho wished *she* could have been out of town. She hated Arrival Parties.

"Here's a thought," Jin-Ho's father said. He was talking to Jin-Ho now. "We do invite the Yazdans, but we invite a friend from your school besides so you'll have someone not bossy to play with."

"Oh! Brad?" Jin-Ho's mother said. "Why go complicating my guest list? That's just one more complication!"

"Now, hon, you remember what it was like when you were a kid—your parents always pushing their friends' kids on you, even if the friends' kids were dorks."

"Susan Yazdan is not a dork!"

"What I meant was—"

"I would invite Athena," Jin-Ho said in a definite voice.

Jin-Ho's mother said, "Oh."

Athena was African-American, which Jin-Ho's mother approved of.

"Well, all right," she told Jin-Ho. "But promise me that you won't make Susan feel left out. She's a guest. You promise?"

"Sure."

Anyhow, it was the other way around. Susan was the one who could make a person feel left out.

Jin-Ho's mother said, "Someday, sweetie, you're going to value that friendship. I know you don't think so now, but you will. Someday you might even travel to Korea together and look up your biological mothers."

"Why would we want to do that?" Jin-Ho asked.

"You could do it! We wouldn't mind! We would support you and encourage you!"

"Well, getting back to the subject—" Jin-Ho's father said.

Jin-Ho was not about to travel to Korea. She didn't even like the food from Korea. She didn't like wearing those costumes with the stiff, sharp seams inside, and she never, ever, even once in her life had watched that stupid videotape.

Jin-Ho's grandpa said he thought they should do this more gradually. "It's like giving up cigarettes," he said. "You can't expect Xiu-Mei to go cold turkey all in a single day."

"Well, I see your point," Jin-Ho's mother said. "Maybe you're right."

They were in the TV room. It was Monday afternoon, and she was folding laundry while they waited for Xiu-Mei to finish her nap. "So," she said, "let me see how we could work this. Maybe today I could tell her no binkies in the car anymore. Only when we're home, I'll say; not when we're out and about."

"You'd better get rid of all the binkies in the back seat, then," Jin-Ho told her.

"Yes, yes, I know . . . They're everywhere! I can't believe I actually went out and *bought* those infernal things!"

She shook a pillowcase with a snapping sound and folded it in half. "Then tomorrow," she said, "I'll say no binkies in the yard, either. You know how she loves the swing set. She'll have to do without her binky if she's planning to use the swing set, I'll say. And Wednesday she can't have her binkies anywhere except her crib. And not at nap time next, on Thursday; and then Friday will be her last binky at night before the party on Saturday."

"I had in mind more like a month or two," Jin-Ho's grandpa said. "What exactly is your hurry?"

"I can't wait a month! I can't stand it anymore! Those damn things are driving me crazy!"

Jin-Ho and her grandpa looked at each other. Sometimes Jin-Ho's mother did get sort of crazy.

"In school today we talked about planets," Jin-Ho said.

"Did you!" her grandpa said in a brighter-than-usual voice. "And which planet do you like best, Jin-Ho?"

"Pluto, because it looks kind of lonesome."

"I could put up with it if she ate better," Jin-Ho's mother said. "But I think she finds her pacifier so satisfying that she doesn't feel the need for food. It's discouraging to have a child who won't eat! Here I make such healthful meals, whole-grain and free-range and organic, and she just . . . spurns me!"

Jin-Ho's grandpa was bending over to get his rain hat from under his chair. It had been sprinkling when he arrived, although now it seemed to have stopped. As he stood up he said, "I'll just leave you with one thought, Bitsy. Have you ever seen a teenager who still has a pacifier? Think about it."

"Yes! Yes!" Jin-Ho said. "*I* have!"

"You have?"

"Those girls from Western High," she said. "Sometimes they wear gold pacifiers on a chain around their necks."

"Well, thanks a lot for bringing that to our attention," her grandpa told her. "But you see what I'm saying, Bitsy. Sooner or later, Xiu-Mei will give it up on her own."

Then he left in a rush, as if he didn't want to hear what Jin-Ho's mother would answer.

≠

Jin-Ho's grandpa didn't use to visit so often, but after Maryam changed her mind he got to dropping by almost every day and talking, talking, talking to Jin-Ho's mother. He would start out discussing politics or his volunteer tutoring job or a TV program he'd watched, but before you knew it he would have moved on to Maryam. "Sometimes I'm walking toward my house," he would say, "coming back home from your house or the mailbox or whatever, and just before I turn onto my block I think, What if I find her waiting there for me? She could be waiting on my porch, planning to say she was sorry and she didn't know what had come over her and begging me to forgive her. I don't look up as I'm rounding the corner because I don't want her to think I'm expecting her. I feel a little self-conscious knowing she might be watching me. I have a sense that my posture doesn't seem entirely natural. I want to act nonchalant but not, you know, *too* nonchalant. She shouldn't think that I'm carefree; she shouldn't think she hasn't harmed me."

When he talked like this, Jin-Ho's mother would first pat his hand or make a low murmuring sound but in a sort of hurried way, as if she couldn't wait to get past that part. Then she would start in on Maryam. "Why you give her a thought, Dad . . . why you *ever* gave her a thought, I honestly can't imagine. She's not worth it! She was wicked! Oh, not that I'd have blamed her if she'd simply said,

'No, thank you.' It's true that you'd been dating for just a few months. And besides, a lot of women that age feel they simply *can't* remarry because of their late husbands' health insurance or pension payments or some such. Plus you didn't show the best judgment in springing it on her; admit it. With no warning like that; out in public. But she should have made herself clear right away—dismissed the subject tactfully, brushed it off, made light of it. Instead, she told you, 'Yes.' And we all celebrated! We offered all those toasts! Jin-Ho and Susan started figuring out how they would be related! Then, bam. Just . . . bam. She tells you to get lost."

"Well, not exactly to get—"

"Why couldn't she have kept seeing you, at least? You could still have gone on dating, you know. It didn't have to be all or nothing."

"Ah. Well, in point of fact," Jin-Ho's grandpa said, "I believe that was more my decision than—"

"From the start I felt she was a very cold person. I can say that now that it's over. Very cold and aloof," Jin-Ho's mother said.

"She's just a woman with boundaries, hon."

"If she's so fond of her boundaries, what did she ever immigrate for?"

"Bitsy, for goodness' sake! Next you'll be telling me she ought to love this country or leave it!"

"I'm not talking about countries; I'm talking about a basic . . . character flaw."

Jin-Ho always worried that her mother might be hurting her grandpa's feelings when she criticized Maryam. But he kept coming back to visit; so it must have been all right.

When Xiu-Mei got up from her nap, their mother took the two of them grocery-shopping without any pacifiers. Xiu-Mei cried the whole way there. She cried in the store, too, but Jin-Ho's mother gave her a banana and that helped a little bit. She went on snuffling, but she did eat part of the banana. On the way home, when she started crying again, Jin-Ho's mother pretended not to notice and talked right over her, discussing the party. "I've bought colored sugar, and chocolate sprinkles, and those little silver BBs . . . I think cupcakes will be better than a single big cake, don't you agree?"

Jin-Ho said, "Mmhmm," with her fingers stuck in her ears.

As soon as they reached home, Xiu-Mei got herself a pacifier from under the hall radiator and went off to sulk in the TV room.

On Tuesday, when Jin-Ho's car pool dropped her off after school, she found her mother sitting on the front steps in her big thick Irish sweater. "What are you doing *here*?" Jin-Ho asked, and her mother said, "Waiting for you, of course." But she wouldn't have been waiting there ordinarily. And then she said, "I thought maybe we could have our snack on the patio today," which was odd because it was real fall weather—sunny, but cool enough that Jin-Ho was wearing a jacket. It all made sense, though, once her mother had the tray ready to take outside. "Coming, Xiu-Mei?" she asked. Xiu-Mei was pushing her kangaroo mama and baby around the kitchen in her purple toy shopping cart. "But you'll have to leave your binky in the house," her mother said, and Xiu-Mei stopped short and said, "No!" which caused her binky to fall to the floor. She bent to pick it up, jammed it back in her mouth, and started pushing her cart again. They had to go on outside without her.

Over their snack, which was peanut butter cookies and apple juice, Jin-Ho's mother talked some more about the party. She didn't like the sound of the weather forecast; a hurricane was heading up the coast. "This is one time the weather matters," she said, "because I've thought of a really good solution for the binkies. We're going to tie them to helium balloons and let them fly up in the sky. Won't that be beautiful? Then we'll go into the house, and we'll find the present the Fairy has left."

"Could a hurricane blow us away?" Jin-Ho asked. (She'd just seen *The Wizard of Oz* on TV.)

"Not this far inland it couldn't, but it could bring a lot of rain. We'll just have to hope it's over by then. They're predicting it for Thursday, which would give us two days to recover, but since when has the Weather Bureau known what it was talking about?"

Then she turned toward the house and called, "Xiu-Mei? Have you changed your mind? Yummy peanut butter cookies, honey!"

They'd left the back door cracked open, so Xiu-Mei had to have heard her. But she didn't say a thing. The only sound was the squeak-squeak of her shopping cart. Jin-Ho's mother sighed and reached for her apple juice. She pulled her sweater sleeve over her hand like a mitten before she took hold of her glass.

Wednesday was No Binkies Outside of the Crib Day. Jin-Ho's father said all *he* could say was, he was mighty glad he had a job to go to. Then he left for work half an hour early. And Jin-Ho was glad she had school to go to, because already she could see how things were shaping up. By the time the car pool honked out front, Xiu-Mei had thoroughly searched the house and found not a single pacifier. They were all in a liquor-store carton on top of the refrigerator, but she didn't know that. She curled into a ball underneath the kitchen table and started crying very loudly. Jin-Ho's mother was in the bathroom with the door closed. Jin-Ho called, "Bye, Mama," and after a moment her mother called back, "Bye, sweetie. Have a nice day." From the sound of her voice, it seemed she might be crying too.

So Jin-Ho sort of dreaded coming home again. But when she walked in, the house was quiet—a cheerful, humming quiet, not a sulking quiet. She found her mother stirring cocoa on the stove, and her grandpa sitting at the table with the newspapers, and Xiu-Mei in her booster seat sucking a pacifier.

"Well, hey there, Ms. Dickinson-Donaldson," her grandpa said, and Jin-Ho said, "Hi, Grandpa," carefully not looking in Xiu-Mei's direction, because maybe the grownups had failed to notice the pacifier and she was not about to point it out.

But then her mother said, "As you can see, we've changed the rules a bit."

Jin-Ho said, "Mmhmm," and climbed onto a chair.

"I was telling your mom," her grandpa said, "if the Binky Party is the big renunciation scene, why put Xiu-Mei through all this misery ahead of time? Right, Xiu-Mei?"

Xiu-Mei busily sucked her pacifier.

"We should just wait for the actual moment," he said. "I know earlier I suggested a tapering-off approach, but I've reconsidered." Then he nudged Jin-Ho with his elbow and said, "'Consistency is the hobgoblin of little minds.'"

Jin-Ho said, "Okay . . ."

"Ralph Waldo Emerson."

"However," Jin-Ho's mother said, turning from the stove, "Saturday is still Binky Day! Remember that, Xiu-Mei! Saturday is still the day the Binky Fairy comes; you know that, don't you?"

"Oh, hon, give it a rest," Jin-Ho's grandpa said.

"I just don't want her assuming—"

But he said, "So! Jin-Ho! What did you do in school today?" and that was the end of that.

Snack was cocoa and alphabet cookies. Jin-Ho picked different cookies out of the tin and set them in front of Xiu-Mei. "See?

An A," she said, and Xiu-Mei removed her pacifier long enough to say, "A."

"Right," Jin-Ho said. She felt happy and relieved, as if Xiu-Mei had just come back from a very long trip. "And here's a B. And another A. And a C. And an A again." They seemed to be all A, B, Cs. She rummaged through the tin, hunting up an X to show Xiu-Mei her initial.

Jin-Ho's grandpa was telling her mother that he had been a fool. "Maybe it was just too long since I'd been part of the courtship scene," he said. "I mean, what was I thinking? I picture how I must have looked, stashing that champagne in your fridge ahead of time like a total idiot, so cocksure, so all-fired sure that she would say yes—"

"Well, and she did say yes," Jin-Ho's mother said. "You weren't an idiot in the least! She said, 'Yes,' in plain English, and we *drank* that champagne. It was only later that—"

"You know, her English seems to be a lot better than it is," Jin-Ho's grandpa said. "Did you ever notice that? She wrote me a letter once when she was away in Vermont, and that was the first time I realized that she often doesn't put article adjectives where she's supposed to. 'I am having very nice time,' she wrote, and 'Tomorrow we go to antique shop.' I guess that's understandable, when you've grown up speaking a language that doesn't use 'a' or 'the,' but it implies some, I don't know, resistance. Some reluctance to leave her own culture. I suspect that that's what went wrong between the two of us. The language was a symptom, and I should have paid more attention to it."

She also didn't put her *s*'s on some things, Jin-Ho had noticed. "Too many cracker will spoil your dinner," she would say. Jin-Ho didn't mention that, though, because she loved Maryam and she wanted her grandpa to love her too.

"It's nothing to do with language," Jin-Ho's mother said. "It's her. She has this attitude that she knows better than us. I wouldn't be the least bit surprised if she claimed there wasn't *supposed* to be an article in those sentences."

"She might," Jin-Ho's grandpa agreed. "When you think about it—the way she observed the Iranian New Year but never ours; and calling everyone 'june' and 'jon'; and that harem in the kitchen cooking rice for every occasion . . . Well, sometimes it seems to me that most of the adapting in this country is done by Americans. Do you ever feel that way?"

"But that's not really what I have against her," Jin-Ho's mother said. "What I have against her is, she's elusive. Oh, I hate it that the world finds elusiveness so attractive! Elusive people are maddening! Why doesn't anyone realize?"

"Did she suppose I didn't have my own doubts from time to time?" Jin-Ho's grandpa asked. "I had recently lost my wife—a lot more recently than she had lost her husband. I was working very hard to start over. It wasn't always easy, believe me."

"You're well out of it," Jin-Ho's mother told him. "Never mind, Dad. Someone else will come along."

"I don't want anyone else," he said.

Then he must have thought he had left the wrong impression, because he said, "Anyone, I mean. I don't want anyone, period."

Jin-Ho's mother patted his hand.

≠

Everybody would be coming to the party except Grandpa Lou and Grandma Pat. They had accepted another invitation and they refused to change their plans. Jin-Ho's mother said she couldn't understand that. "Where are their *priorities*?" she asked. "Between some random couple and their own granddaughter—"

"It's not a random couple; it's their closest friends," Jin-Ho's father said. "And their friends are celebrating a golden anniversary, while their granddaughter is merely giving up her pacifier."

"Well, I don't know why I care, anyhow. I'm beginning to think this whole event is doomed, from the way they're talking on the radio. After Hurricane Isabel hits, we'll be floating in the Inner Harbor."

"You said we couldn't blow away!" Jin-Ho told her mother. "You said we were too far inland!"

"No, no, of course we can't blow away. We don't have a thing to worry about. I was exaggerating," Jin-Ho's mother said.

But that evening, she and Jin-Ho's father dragged all the patio furniture into the garage just to be on the safe side.

Maybe the radio announcer was exaggerating too, because he said they'd be hit on Thursday and on Thursday the weather was fine. Jin-Ho went to school the same as usual, came home as usual, had her snack. The sky was getting darker, though, by late afternoon, and there was a bit of wind and a smattering of rain. When Jin-Ho's father got home from work he said, "It's picking up out there." Jin-Ho began to feel prickly-skinned and excited, the way she did on Christmas Eve. During supper she kept twisting around in her chair to look out the kitchen window. The air was a weird shade of lavender and the trees were flipping their leaves wrong side to. "Keep your fingers crossed for our elms," her father told her. "As much money as I've spent on those things, I might as well be putting them through college." Jin-Ho giggled, picturing that.

Then the lights went out.

Xiu-Mei began to cry.

Jin-Ho's mother said, "We're all right! No reason to panic!" and she got up and fetched the candles from the dining-room buffet. Jin-Ho's father lit them with the pistol thing they lit the bad burner on the stove with—two candles on the table and two more on the kitchen counter. Everybody's face looked flickery and different. Xiu-Mei kept waving one hand, and at first they didn't know why but then they saw she was experimenting with the shadows on the wall.

"Isn't this fun?" Jin-Ho's mother said. "It's just like camping out! And it won't be for very long. Pretty soon BG and E will have it fixed."

But all evening, they stayed in the dark. They read picture books by candlelight, and at bedtime they climbed the stairs with the flashlight from the kitchen utility drawer. They left the flashlight lit and standing on Xiu-Mei's bureau so she wouldn't be scared, but she cried anyhow and Jin-Ho was a little bit worried herself. So they both ended up sleeping with their parents. The four of them lay in a row on the bed, which luckily was king-size. Outside the wind was roaring and the trees were making crackly sounds and every now and then a handful of rain flung itself against the windowpanes. Jin-Ho's mother had left one window propped open an inch because she'd read somewhere that otherwise, the house might implode. Jin-Ho's father said no, that was tornados, and they argued about it awhile until Jin-Ho's mother went to sleep. Not long afterward, Jin-Ho heard her father get out of bed and tiptoe over to the window to shut it. Then he came back and went to sleep too. Xiu-Mei was already asleep, although still from time to time she took a faint suck on her pacifier. Outside the wind went on and on till Jin-Ho started feeling mad at it. Several times she heard sirens. She wondered if their house was floating in the harbor yet. So far it felt pretty solid, though.

Then it was morning and she was the only one there. The window nearest her was matted over with leaves, which gave the room a greenish tinge although the weather seemed sunny. She climbed out of bed and went to look more closely, but she couldn't see; so she went to the other window and looked through that. The front yard was a mass of tree limbs. A huge old oak from across the street was lying on its side, extending into their yard and almost completely hiding her father's station wagon. He had parked it out front last night because the patio furniture was using up his half of the garage. Only a patch or two of the station wagon's gray roof showed from beneath the branches.

Downstairs, Jin-Ho's mother was making toast by holding a slice of bread over the stove with a pair of kitchen tongs. Xiu-Mei was stirring a bowl of Cheerios around, and her father was on the phone. "Well, good," he was saying. "You're luckier than we are, then! It looks like it could be days before we get our power back." He listened a minute and then he said, "Thanks, Mom. But even assuming we could make it over there, one of our cars is smushed and the other's trapped in the garage with an elm across the driveway. We'll just have to leave things where they are and not open the freezer door, I guess."

He was wearing his pajamas and the red plaid bathrobe he ordinarily saved for weekends. When he got off the phone, Jin-Ho asked him, "Aren't you going to work?" and he said, "Oh, I doubt any of my students will be showing up today, hon."

"Do I have school?"

"I don't imagine it's open. In any case, how would you get there?"

Jin-Ho's mother came to the table with the piece of toast, which was streaked with black and smelled nasty. "I don't want it," Jin-Ho said, and her mother said, "Fine, because I'd prefer you eat some kind of cereal. We need to use up the milk before it goes bad."

"When is BG and E going to fix our electricity?" Jin-Ho asked.

"I don't know, honey. There are thousands and thousands of people all in the same boat, according to your daddy's little radio."

"Aren't you glad now I bought that?" Jin-Ho's father asked her mother. "I told you it might come in handy!"

He was a sucker for gadgets. It was the cause of a lot of arguments between the two of them.

From breakfast time till lunch time, the whole family worked at cleaning up the yard. Of course they couldn't do anything about the Cromwells' oak tree, which crossed the street completely and blocked all traffic, or the elm that lay in front of the garage. But they collected the smaller branches, and the sprays of leaves still green and wet and healthy-looking, and they stuffed them into garbage bags and lugged them to the alley. Jin-Ho found a bird's nest. There weren't any birds in it, though. She was in charge of the little tiny twigs, which she put in a plastic bucket that her father emptied from time to time. On either side of them their neighbors were cleaning up too, and people called back and forth to each other in a friendly sort of way. Mrs. Sansom said one house down the block still had electricity. They were letting their neighbors run long, long extension cords to power their refrigerators. "If BG and E doesn't get things fixed by tonight," she said, "I vote we combine all our perishables and have a great big neighborhood cookout on our grills." Jin-Ho thought that sounded much better than using up the foods at home. She hoped BG and E *wouldn't* get things fixed. The weather was cool and breezy and pleasant, with a fresh smell to the air, and she had never seen so many of the neighbors out in their yards at one time.

For lunch they had an omelet to finish off the eggs. Then Xiu-Mei went down for her nap, and Jin-Ho watched from her parents' bedroom window as the tree men worked on the oak tree in the street. Their saws were angry-sounding, like hornets. They cut a passageway for cars through the middle of the trunk, but they left the base in the Cromwells' yard with its roots clawing the air and the top in the Donaldsons' yard all leafy and bushy, still hiding their station wagon. Jin-Ho's father said they would have to see to that later, when it wasn't a state of emergency. He took Jin-Ho out to count the tree rings after the men had left. Mr. Sansom was counting too. It wasn't as easy as you might expect, though, because one ring sometimes blended into another and they kept losing track. The trunk had a strong, sharp, sour smell that caused Jin-Ho's mouth to water.

Now her mother was fretting seriously about her frozen foods. She had casseroles stashed in the freezer that she had spent a lot of time preparing, she said. Jin-Ho said, "That's okay; we'll bring them to the cookout and grill them," but her mother said, "You can't grill spinach lasagna, Jin-Ho." She wasn't talking anymore about what fun this was, and she had stopped saying, "Think of the poor Iraqis," which was a good thing, in Jin-Ho's opinion.

In the end, there wasn't a cookout after all. Mrs. Sansom must have forgotten she'd suggested it. As twilight fell the neighbors disappeared indoors, and all that Jin-Ho could see of them was the glimmer of a candle here and there in a window.

Jin-Ho's mother carried the flashlight down to the basement and came back with a casserole. "I just whipped the freezer door open and whipped it shut again," she said. "I don't think I raised the temperature all that much, do you?" She put it straight into the oven, but since it hadn't been thawed it took forever to cook. They were waiting, waiting, waiting, and reading books by candles again because there was nothing else to do. Right after supper, which didn't happen till nearly eight, they all went to bed in the king-size bed. Jin-Ho's mother didn't even wash the dishes. "I'll do that tomorrow morning, when I can see," she said.

"This is how people *used* to live, I guess," Jin-Ho's father said. "Arranging their lives by the sunrise and sunset."

Jin-Ho's mother said, "Whatever."

They didn't have their baths, either, although it had been two days now. That was something else that would have to wait till morning.

And why bother getting up early when they couldn't see to do anything? They slept so late that Jin-Ho's grandpa had to wake them by banging on the front door. "Hello? Hello?" he was shouting, because the doorbell didn't work. Jin-Ho's mother went to let him in while the others got dressed. Nobody mentioned baths. By the time Jin-Ho came downstairs, her grandpa was sitting in the kitchen watching her mother burn the toast. "Jin-jin!" he said. "How do you like roughing it?"

"It's getting boring," she told him.

"You just have to pretend you're in Colonial times, honey. That's what *I'm* pretending."

Beside him on the table was a pack of disposable diapers. Jin-Ho's mother didn't believe in disposable diapers, but she was running out of the cloth ones. He had also brought three cardboard cups of store-bought coffee, and a quart of Xiu-Mei's special milk, and a rocket-looking silver object taller than Jin-Ho that stood just inside the back door. "What's that?" she asked him.

"Helium."

"Helium?"

"For the balloons we're tying the binkies to."

"The binkies?" she said. "The binky party!" She'd forgotten all about it.

"You know your mom," he told her. "She is one determined lady."

"I said today was the day she would give her binkies up, and today it's going to be," Jin-Ho's mother said without turning from the stove. "We don't want Xiu-Mei thinking I'm inconsistent."

"'Consistency is the hobgoblin of—'"

"Dad, I don't want to hear it."

"Okay! Okay!" He held up both his hands.

"Sami and Ziba are bringing cold drinks, and everything else is room temperature anyhow—cupcakes, cookies . . . I'm scrapping the ice cream. What more do we need?"

"Well, there is the little matter of getting here. Half the city's streets are blocked by fallen trees, or downed power lines shooting sparks, or both. Hundreds of traffic lights are out. The police are advising people to stay off the roads unless it's a life-or-death emergency."

"All our guests think they can make it, though, except for Mac. That little bridge is gone that runs across the bottom of Mac's driveway. But I told him he should try fording the stream in his car, because it isn't really that deep."

Jin-Ho's grandpa started laughing. It was just a whiskery sound at first, but gradually it took him over until he was gasping for breath and wiping his eyes with his sweater cuff. "What," Jin-Ho's mother said. She had turned from the stove to look at him, still holding the toast with her tongs. "What is it? What's so funny?"

But instead of waiting for an answer, she turned next to Jin-Ho and said, "Where in heaven's name is your *father*?" as if Jin-Ho were the one she was cross with.

"He's dressing Xiu-Mei," Jin-Ho said.

"Well, tell him we have coffee down here and he'd better hurry up if he doesn't want it to get cold."

When Jin-Ho left the kitchen, her grandpa was blowing his nose on his big white cloth handkerchief.

Filling helium balloons was hard work. Jin-Ho's father and her grandpa did that, and it made them very crabby because every so often a balloon would escape from the nozzle and go zooming around the kitchen and scare everyone half to death. "Bitsy, could you please get these kids *out* of here?" Jin-Ho's father finally said, although it wasn't their fault. In fact Jin-Ho was being a help. She and her mother were tying binkies to the strings of the balloons after they were filled. But her mother said, "Okay, girls, let's go have your baths." As they left, Jin-Ho heard her father say, "Other people would just order a dozen filled balloons from a balloon place; but not us. *Oh,* no, no. *We* have to rent our own helium canister and fill the balloons ourselves."

"If it were a matter of merely a dozen balloons, that's what I would do," Jin-Ho's mother told her as they climbed the stairs. She seemed to think Jin-Ho was the one who had objected. "But we have forty-seven binkies to fly! No, forty-eight, because Xiu-Mei's still using one. Brad?" she called down. "It's not forty-seven balloons we need; it's forty-eight."

"Unthinkable that we could fly just one or two token binkies, and bury the rest in the garbage," Jin-Ho's father told her grandpa.

Her mother rolled her eyes. Jin-Ho rolled hers too, because one or two binkies would be boring. Forty-eight would be something to see. They would cover the whole sky.

"So here's what's going to happen, Xiu-Mei," her mother said in a storytelling tone of voice. "Everyone at the party will take a couple of balloons and go outside. Let's see: with nineteen people . . . or seventeen, at least . . . Well, some of us will take more than a couple. You, for instance, because you're the guest of honor. You could take three balloons."

"Four," Xiu-Mei said.

"Four, then. You can take—"

"Five. Six," Xiu-Mei said. Apparently she was just practicing her numbers. But six was as high as she knew them; so that was the end of that. She held up her arms for her mother to pull her shirt off. Water was running into the tub and the mirror was steaming over.

"Then we'll say, 'Ready, set, go!' and we'll all let loose of our balloons at exactly the same moment and the binkies will fly up, up, up . . . far, far away, and the Binky Fairy will look over the edge of a cloud and say, 'Oh, my, someone's outgrown her binky! I can see I will have to—' "

"I am not outgrown my binky," Xiu-Mei said. She took the binky out of her mouth so she could speak extra clearly, but then she popped it back in again.

" 'I'll have to come down there and bring that someone a wonderful present,' the Binky Fairy will say. And she'll go into her treasure room—"

"I am not outgrown my binky."

"Get into the tub, Xiu-Mei."

"It's too hot," Xiu-Mei said.

"It is not too hot! You haven't even felt it yet! You're just being contrary! Oh, Lord . . . Jin-Ho, get in the tub, please."

Jin-Ho was still undressing, but she finished in a hurry. Her mother lowered Xiu-Mei into the water. As soon as she was settled Xiu-Mei put her binky in the soap dish, because she always cried when her hair was washed and it was difficult to cry and suck on a binky at the same time. Jin-Ho climbed in after her, holding on to her mother's shoulder for balance. "Mom," she said, with her mouth very close to her mother's ear.

"What is it, honey?"

"What do you think her present is?"

"Well, we'll just have to wait and see, won't we?"

"Do you think it might be an American Girl doll complete with all assessories?"

" 'Accessories,' you mean; not that that's a word you should have any use for at your age. And no, I do not think that's what it is. I think the Binky Fairy's too smart to fall for a toy that encourages blatant consumerism."

"But *Ziba's* smart, and she bought Susan one."

Her mother let out a breath that puffed the hair over her forehead. Then she said, "In my opinion, Jin-Ho, the doll Susan has that's nicest is her little Kurdish doll. You know that doll on her bureau, the one with the long red veil?"

"But the Kurdish doll doesn't have any ack-sessories," Jin-Ho said.

"Don't forget to wash behind your ears," her mother told her. Then she stood up and went over to flick the light switch. She'd been doing that all day. Nothing happened, though.

While they were toweling off, Jin-Ho's mother talked some more about the party. She said, "The present will be on the hearth, Xiu-Mei, because the Binky Fairy comes down the chimney just like Santa Claus. And everybody will gather around to watch you open it. Grandpa, Uncle Abe, Uncle Mac perhaps, the Yazdans . . . and Lucy is coming, too! Your friend Lucy will be here!"

"Is Lucy have her binky?" Xiu-Mei asked.

Her mother said, "Oh." Then she said, "Well, *maybe* she will. But that's because Lucy's younger than you. She's a whole month younger! Practically a baby still! I bet when she sees your present she'll say, 'I'm going to give up *my* binky, too.'"

Xiu-Mei set her front teeth together hard. Her binky made a sound like a door squeaking.

By the time they came downstairs again, all the balloons were filled and floating up under the living-room ceiling with their long tails hanging straight down and pink, blue, and yellow binkies tied to their ends. Xiu-Mei must have thought it was a dream come true, because she started running around the room with both hands reaching up for them. Some she could touch and set swinging, but most she wasn't quite tall enough for. Her mother said, "Won't they look pretty going up in the sky?" Xiu-Mei didn't answer.

While Jin-Ho's mother frosted cupcakes in the kitchen, Jin-Ho and her grandpa went out in his car to fetch lunch from the deli. Somehow Jin-Ho had managed to forget about the hurricane, and it was a shock to see all that had happened—the torn-off branches everywhere, ragged white shreddy wood showing on the tree trunks, and here and there a sheet of blue plastic covering a broken roof. Twice they had to go a different way because a street was closed. Almost none of the traffic signals worked; so they drove through intersections extra slowly, her grandpa looking both ways and whistling no particular tune the way he always did when he was concentrating on something. The dead lights reminded Jin-Ho of a doll's poked-out eyes—just that hollow and blank-looking. It was almost as hot as summer, and the men sawing the trees were sweating through their shirts.

"Your mother has really, really creative ideas, doesn't she," her grandpa said. "I know sometimes it might seem she goes a little too far, but at least she's . . . invested. Interested. You have to admit she cares deeply, right?"

Jin-Ho said, "Mmhmm." She was looking at a tree that had fallen over in perfect shape, as if someone had just laid it gently on its side. She wondered if it could be planted back in its hole the way Brian at school had his tooth planted back after he knocked it out jumping off the jungle gym. His mother had put the tooth in milk and brought it with them to the dentist. How did mothers know these things?

By the time they got home again, everything was ready in the dining room—a flowered tablecloth on the table and platters of cupcakes and cookies and bowls of mints the same pale colors as the binkies. They had their lunch in the kitchen. Jin-Ho's mother barely ate because she was worried about the weather forecast. It was supposed to start raining again. She kept looking out at the sky, which was a pure, bright blue, and asking everybody how they could expect to send up balloons in a downpour. Jin-Ho's father told her not to trouble trouble till trouble troubled her. It was one of his favorite sayings.

After lunch Xiu-Mei took her nap, and Jin-Ho and her mother got dressed for the party. Jin-Ho put on a red T-shirt and her new embroidered jeans and then she walked into her mother's room and checked her mother's face. She knew that embroidered jeans weren't very Korean. But her mother just said, "You look nice, sweetheart," with no sign of disappointment. And she dressed Xiu-Mei in jeans, too, when Xiu-Mei woke up; so it must have been all right.

Xiu-Mei didn't sleep nearly long enough. Maybe she was excited about the party. Or else upset. And she wouldn't take her after-nap sippy cup of juice but sat in a bundle on a kitchen chair, looking squinty and cross, and sucked her pacifier.

The first guests were the Yazdans. That was because they were in charge of the drinks. Sami and Ziba were lugging a Styrofoam cooler between them, and everyone went down to the street so that Jin-Ho's father could take Ziba's end away from her. "This morning our lights flickered," Ziba said, "and I thought, Oh, no! What if *our* fridge dies? But it was only for a moment."

She was wearing bellbottom jeans and a black knit top that showed part of her stomach. She looked very beautiful. Her ponytail stuck out straight behind her head like an enormous bunch of grapes, that same kind of purplish black.

Suppose the adoption people discovered they'd made a mistake. They'd handed the babies out to the wrong mothers. They would say they were very sorry but the girls would have to be switched back. Jin-Ho would get Ziba, and Susan would get Bitsy in her sleeveless sack dress and her sandals that showed the knobs on her toes.

Wouldn't it be terrible if mothers could read people's minds.

Jin-Ho had hoped Susan would bring her American Girl doll, but she didn't. Susan didn't seem to like dolls, actually. What a waste. Instead she whipped a yo-yo out of her pocket—that must be what they played with at private school—and spun it snappily up and down as she walked. Meanwhile, Jin-Ho's mother was telling Ziba about her frozen foods. "It's like the stages of mourning," she said. "Denial the first day: maybe the power will come back on before any damage is done. And then grief the second day. You sink into a slough of despair and mentally say goodbye to all your casseroles."

"*I* have a friend coming," Jin-Ho told Susan.

Susan said, "So?"

"Her name is Athena, and me and her play on the sliding board every recess."

But Jin-Ho's mother jumped in to say, "She's not as old a friend as you are, though, Susan! You and Jin-Ho go *way* back!"

She had this knack for listening to two conversations at once.

"Why, maybe even your mothers go back!" she said. "Maybe your biological mothers were best girlfriends in Korea."

Jin-Ho was very careful not to let her eyes meet Susan's.

Wouldn't you know it, when Athena arrived—stepping from her parents' car just as the rest of them were heading into the house—she turned out to be the type that lost her voice around grownups. She stopped short when she saw them all and she stuck a finger in her mouth. Jin-Ho called, "Athena! Hey!" but Athena only stood there, wearing a frilly white dress and holding a wrapped gift.

"Go and welcome her," Jin-Ho's mother whispered.

So Jin-Ho went down the front steps calling, "*Come* on! *Come* on!" in an encouraging way, and Athena started toward her inch by inch. When they were even with each other she pushed the gift into Jin-Ho's hands. It was some kind of book, Jin-Ho could tell through the wrapping. She said, "Thanks," but Athena said, "It's for your sister," which made Jin-Ho feel stupid. She said, "I knew that." Then she led Athena toward the others.

Jin-Ho's mother did the introducing. She bounced Xiu-Mei on her hip and said, "Athena, this is Jin-Ho's oldest friend, Susan Yazdan. And Susan's parents, Sami and Ziba, and Jin-Ho's grandpa, Dave . . ."

Athena put her finger back in her mouth. She wore eentsy colored beads threaded on braids all over her head and another bead in each ear, gold. Jin-Ho had been wanting pierced ears for ages, but her mother was making her wait until she was sixteen.

It was awkward sitting in the living room because of the balloons. Somehow no one had thought of that. With all those strings hanging down, the ceiling seemed to be raining. The grownups had to duck their heads in order to talk to each other across the room, which made them have poor posture. Then Uncle Abe walked in without knocking and said, "Whoa, what is this: a jungle?" and Jin-Ho's mother said, "Oh, all right, let's move to the dining room. Athena, these are Jin-Ho's cousins, Deirdre, Bridget, Polly . . ."

In the dining room it was awkward too, though, because once the grownups had found chairs, why, there they were, sitting at the table like people expecting a meal, but the only things on the table were the platters of desserts that were meant to be passed around later. "Maybe I should bring out some plates," Jin-Ho's mother said. "Or . . . wait! The drinks! Where'd we put the drinks?" Then she got the giggles. She did that sometimes. She told Ziba, "Inventing a new tradition is not as easy as you might think."

Ziba said, "I'll get the drinks. You sit still." Because Jin-Ho's mother had Xiu-Mei on her lap.

"Thank you, Ziba," Jin-Ho's mother said, and then she turned to Aunt Jeannine. "Someone is a little C-L-I-N-G-Y today," she said. "But I guess that's to be expected."

Aunt Jeannine said, "Xiu-Mei, what's that in your *mouth*? Is that a binky I see?"

"It's the one last holdout," Jin-Ho's mother explained. "When everybody gets here we're going to tie it to the last balloon and send it up, up, up . . ." She seemed to be talking now to Xiu-Mei, but Xiu-Mei only frowned and chomped down on her binky.

"Give her the present," Athena told Jin-Ho. They had managed to sit on the window seat next to Polly, who wore almost-black lipstick and six earrings in each ear, not a one of them matching any of the others. Jin-Ho slid to the floor and walked over to hand Athena's present to Xiu-Mei, and while Xiu-Mei was ripping gift paper the Copelands walked in. Mercy Copeland said, "Sorry! But it doesn't seem your doorbell works." She was carrying Lucy, who of course the grownups had to make a fuss about. Lucy was so cute that Jin-Ho just wanted to bite her. Her cheeks were round and soft and her eyes were as blue as flowers and her hair was full of a million yellow curls that made people say, "What an *angel* child!" In fact she was a whole lot cuter than Xiu-Mei, who had straight black hair and slit eyes. Also, even though Lucy had brought her binky it was just dangling from her neck on a ribbon—a clear plastic binky with colored polka dots inside the plastic, a really fancy kind that Jin-Ho hadn't seen before. So Lucy's mouth wasn't all plugged up the way Xiu-Mei's was. She had a cute, pink, pursy mouth, very small. She was holding a square box wrapped in striped paper, and as soon as her mother put her down she toddled over and set the box in Xiu-Mei's lap. "Aww," everybody said, but Xiu-Mei seemed more interested in the polka-dot binky. She leaned forward and reached for it but Lucy was already heading back to her mother. "Why, thank you, Lucy," Jin-Ho's mother said, and then, "Thank you, Ziba," because Ziba was setting the Yazdans' present on the table in front of her. (The Yazdans always, always brought presents, for every possible occasion. It was one of the best things about them.)

"Does everybody know each other?" Jin-Ho's mother asked, and when no one spoke she said, "Wonderful. Now, I think we should do the balloons first thing, don't you all agree? And get it over with."

"Sort of like ripping off a Band-Aid," Jin-Ho's grandpa said.

"Right. So you bring that last balloon, Brad, and Xiu-Mei, you give me your binky . . ."

She didn't wait for Xiu-Mei to give it to her, though. She just plucked it out of Xiu-Mei's mouth. Xiu-Mei's mouth stayed in a damp, surprised O shape and she looked around the room as if she wondered what had just happened. "*Here* we go," her mother said, tying the binky to the balloon. It was a red balloon with white stars on it. "The last, last one," her mother said in a sort of singsong. "Ready, everybody? Everybody get some balloons from the living room, two or three apiece, and we'll go outdoors and let them fly off."

She stood up, setting Xiu-Mei on her hip again, and led the way to the living room. Xiu-Mei's mouth was still in an O shape. Jin-Ho kept expecting her to let out a howl but it seemed she was too surprised.

"We *fly* the balloons?" Athena asked Jin-Ho.

Jin-Ho said, "Yup."

"I want to bring mine home with me."

"You can't," Susan said from her other side. "You've got to let them go."

"Other parties, you're allowed to bring them home."

"Not when they have binkies on them, silly," Susan said.

Athena blinked.

They went into the living room and chose three balloons apiece. Susan said, "I'm taking all pink," which Jin-Ho didn't understand at first because the balloons were either red or white or blue, some with stars or stripes or with both, as if they might have been left over from the Fourth of July. Then she saw that Susan was talking about the color of the binkies. Jin-Ho herself had two blue binkies and one yellow. The yellow happened to be the binky that looked like a sideways 8, and that made her sad, a little, because she had a very clear picture in her head of Xiu-Mei sucking on it.

They all went back through the dining room, through the kitchen, out the back door, and down the porch steps. Mercy Copeland said, "Oh! What a shame!" She was looking toward the elm that had fallen across the garage front.

"Yes, it broke our hearts," Jin-Ho's mother said. "Not to mention we can't get my car out, or the patio furniture."

She was holding just one balloon, the last one with the white stars. Xiu-Mei wasn't holding any. Didn't she say she'd have six? She was sitting astride her mother's hip with her lower lip kind of pooched.

"All right, everybody!" Jin-Ho's mother called. "Ready, set, go!"

All the balloons floated upward. They went at different speeds, though, and some didn't go very far. One of Jin-Ho's balloons snagged on the fallen elm. One of Susan's landed in the Sansoms' hedge. But a lot of the others made it, and in a minute you couldn't see the binkies anymore but just the balloons they were strung to, like little red, white, and blue thumbtacks stuck to the perfect sky. Jin-Ho's mother had been right: they did look pretty.

Then Mrs. Sansom called, "Bitsy?"

She was standing on the other side of the hedge, holding Susan's balloon.

"Bitsy, it seems there are infants' pacifiers everywhere in our yard," she said.

Jin-Ho's mother said, "Oh, dear."

"There are pacifiers in our rosebushes and our gutters and our dogwood tree."

"I'm sorry, Dottie—"

"That TV cable that's hanging down from the electric pole in the alley? There are pacifiers all over it."

"We'll clean them up, I promise," Jin-Ho's mother said. "Oh, dear, I never thought—"

"Say there! Xiu-Mei!" Jin-Ho's father called.

Jin-Ho's mother turned toward him as if she were glad to hear from him.

He was standing on the back porch, although Jin-Ho had assumed till now that he was in the yard with everybody else. "Wonder if the Binky Fairy's left you something!" he called.

"Ooh!" people said, and "Xiu-Mei! Let's go look!"

Xiu-Mei turned from face to face, still poochy-lipped, as her mother carried her up the steps to see what she had gotten.

Well, it wasn't an American Girl doll. But it was a fairly good present, even so: a little tiny stroller she could push instead of her grocery cart. It sat in front of the fireplace with a red bow tied to the handle. "Won't your kangaroos just love this?" her mother asked. Xiu-Mei didn't answer, but when her mother set her down she went over to her grocery cart and hauled out her kangaroo mama and baby and piled them into the stroller. Then she started pushing them around the living room. She looked a little naked without a binky in her mouth. She was so short that even though the stroller was toy-sized, she had to reach up to hold the handle. Everybody said, "Aww," again. Lucy came toddling over and grabbed hold of the handle too, and the two of them pushed the stroller together while Jin-Ho's father and Lucy's father snapped about a million photographs.

In the dining room, Ziba was handing out soft drinks from the cooler she'd set on the table. Jin-Ho wasn't allowed to have soft drinks. She accepted one and walked off toward the window seat where Athena and Polly had settled again. "Did the holes at the tops of your ears hurt more than the holes at the bottoms?" Athena was asking. "I want to get more holes too but my mom believes that's trashy."

Polly said, "Trashy! Well, that's just because she's a grownup." And the two of them smiled at each other as if they were oldest, best friends. Neither one of them paid any heed to Jin-Ho.

Deirdre was talking on her cell phone over in the corner, facing the wall and keeping her voice low. She had a boyfriend, Jin-Ho knew, although she was only thirteen, which was way, way too young for a boyfriend according to Jin-Ho's mother. And Bridget was telling Mercy Copeland where she went to school and what grade she was in and so on and so forth, poor Bridget, while Mercy nodded very seriously and took a sip of her soft drink.

Jin-Ho's soft drink tasted like tin, but maybe it was supposed to.

Now her father was photographing Uncle Abe and Aunt Jeannine. They had their arms linked like a movie-star couple and they were smiling with all their teeth and Uncle Abe was saying, "Cheddar! Roquefort! Monterey Jack!" which was his way of being funny. But Lucy's father had stopped taking pictures and was talking with Sami in the living room. "You want three megapixels at the very least," he was saying. Jin-Ho drifted on past them, keeping her drink can down by her side in case she ran into her mother.

But where *was* her mother? Oh, yes, there: standing on the front-porch steps with Jin-Ho's grandpa. Jin-Ho could see them through the screen door. They had their backs to her and they didn't even notice when she came up and set her nose against the screen.

Her grandpa was telling her mother that anyhow, he had work to do. He still had branches on his lawn as big around as his arm. "And why I own an electric chain saw instead of gasoline, *I* don't know," he said. "You might have thought it would occur to me that if I needed to cut any trees up, perhaps it would be due to a storm that had interfered with my power. So I'm having to use a hand saw, and I've still got a good, oh, eight or ten—"

"I understand, Dad," Jin-Ho's mother said, "and I'm not trying to stop you, honest. But if you're leaving for some other reason—if you're leaving because of Sami and Ziba . . . well, that's just silly. They love to see you! They don't feel the least bit strange!"

"No, I know that," Jin-Ho's grandpa said. "Goodness! It's nothing to do with them. It's only that my yard, you see . . ." Then he trailed off, and when he started speaking again he'd switched to a whole new subject. He said, "I keep going over and over it, trying to figure it out. I say, 'She seemed so happy; she never gave me the slightest indication; why did she let me imagine she loved me?' I remember how she'd bring me something to eat and then sit down across from me and watch my face to see if I liked it. No one will ever do that again. I don't kid myself! Nobody else is going to care about me that way again at my age."

Jin-Ho was expecting her mother to argue. Of course, they all cared, she should say. What on earth was he thinking? But she didn't. She said, "Oh, Dad. It wasn't just that she seemed happy; she *was* happy. You both were. And she did love you, I swear it. She deeply, truly loved you; anyone could see that, and I am so, so sorry you're not together anymore."

Behind Jin-Ho, her father said, "Psst."

She turned and looked up at him.

"Do me a favor," he whispered. "Inch the door open. I want to get a picture of the two of them."

She pushed the screen door as silently as possible. Sometimes the spring made a twanging sound but not today, luckily. Her father stuck his camera through the opening and pressed the button. "Thanks," he whispered. "Got it. I can tell it'll be a good one. Doesn't your mom look great?"

She did, really. Her face was turned toward Jin-Ho's grandpa and the sky beyond lit her smooth skin and the sweet, full curve of her mouth.

Jin-Ho closed the screen door and followed her father back to the living room.

Once again he was aiming his camera at Xiu-Mei and Lucy. They were still in front of the fireplace, but the stroller was off to one side now and they both faced Susan, who was leading them in some kind of game. She stood with her hands on her hips, as bossy as a schoolteacher, and said, "Okay, repeat after me: Wah, wah, wah, we always cry at bedtime."

Dutifully, they echoed, "Wah, wah—"

"No! Wrong! Did I say, 'Susan says'? Repeat: Wah, wah, wah, we always cry at lunchtime."

"Wah, wah—"

"What is the *matter* with you guys? Now. *Susan says:* Wah, wah, wah, we always cry at swimming-lesson time."

"Wah, wah, wah . . ."

Lucy spoke very clearly for her age, but Xiu-Mei was harder to understand because she had a polka-dot binky in her mouth.

10

Maryam was picking up Susan at the Tiny Toes School of Ballet and Modern Dance. Unfortunately she was early, because she'd never been there before and she'd allowed too much time for the drive. She was filling in for Ziba, who had a dental appointment.

It was a sunny day in late June, and she could feel the heat rising from the sidewalk as she stood in front of the school, which was an ordinary brown shingle-board house set back a bit from the street. Another woman was waiting also, but she was busy chasing her toddler and so they merely exchanged smiles, which suited Maryam just fine.

Then a man said, "Maryam?" and she turned and found Dave Dickinson standing next to her.

"Hi," he said.

"Oh," she said. "Hello."

This wasn't the first time they had run into each other. Once shortly after their breakup she had met him when he was dropping Jin-Ho off at Sami and Ziba's, and once again a few weeks later when she was standing in line at the post office. But that had been over a year ago, and on both occasions he had been so curt—almost not speaking, really—that she was uncertain how to behave now. She lifted her chin and braced herself for whatever might come next.

He had that strong, tanned, leathery skin that was so attractive in aging men and so unattractive in women. He was in need of a haircut, and if she had reached up to touch his curls they would have encircled her fingers completely.

"Is Susan taking lessons here?" he asked.

"Yes. Beginning ballet."

"So's Jin-Ho."

Well, of course: that would be how Ziba had come up with the idea. Maryam should have known. She said, "I guess it's that summer panic. What to do with them once school is out."

"Yes, for sure it's not because of any God-given talent," Dave said. "Or not in Jin-Ho's case, at least. How about Susan? Is she at all graceful?"

Maryam shrugged. In fact she considered Susan to be very graceful, but she didn't want to say this to the grandparent of a child as clunky as Jin-Ho. "I believe they just want to introduce her to all the possibilities," she said. "Last year it was art camp."

"Oh, yes, Jin-Ho went to that."

They both smiled.

Then Dave said, "Bitsy's sick."

It was the suddenness of his remark that told her he meant something more than the usual. She waited, fixing her eyes on his. He said, "That's where they are at this moment, she and Brad: consulting with the oncologist. Last week they removed a lump from her breast and now they're discussing options."

"Oh, Dave. I'm so sorry," Maryam said. "I know this must bring it all back to you."

"Well, naturally I'm worried."

"But every year they find new treatments," she said. "And they caught it early, I assume."

"Yes, the doctors have been very encouraging. It's just that it's kind of a shock to all of us."

"Of course it is," she said. She shaded her eyes with one hand; the sun had moved directly above him. "I hope she'll let me know if there's anything I can do," she said. "I'd be happy to pick up the children, bring food . . ."

"I'll tell her that. Thanks," he said. "I know she means to talk to Ziba as soon as they're sure what the plan is."

Another woman approached, pushing a baby in a stroller. Now that they had an audience, Dave changed the subject. "Anyhow!" he said. "Will you be going to the Arrival Party this year? Oh. Of course you will. It's your turn."

"Well, not *my* turn; Sami and Ziba's. And I may be in New York then."

"New York?"

"Kari and Danielle and I have been talking about seeing some plays."

"But you could do that anytime," he said.

"One of the plays may close soon, though. And besides. You know. Really that's a young people's party. I'm getting too old for such things."

"Old!" he said, so sharply that the woman with the stroller sent Maryam a curious glance.

"And also there's a chance that my cousin Farah will be here," Maryam said.

"It's both the time when you're away *and* the time you have a guest?"

"Well, not on the exact same date . . ."

She gave up. She stopped speaking.

Dave said, "Look. Maryam. It's absurd to think we can't both attend the same social event."

This from the man who had told her straight out, "No, we can *not* go on seeing each other."

But she said, "Well, you're right, of course."

"You didn't come last year either. You missed a good party."

"Yes, so I heard. Ziba told me."

"Jin-Ho accidentally dropped the videotape in the punch bowl, but we fished it out before any damage was done. And 'Coming Round the Mountain' got so raucous that when the cousins shouted, 'Hi, babe!' you'd swear they must be hanging out the windows of a brothel. Other than that, though . . ."

Maryam laughed. (She had always loved his particular way of wording things.)

"Think about it," he said.

She said, "All right."

Then the children started trickling forth from the school—their own two in front, blocky-haired Jin-Ho and Susan with her long braids swinging—and they went their separate ways.

During the next few days, she found herself haunted by a lingering sorrow. Partly, of course, this was due to the news about Bitsy. Maryam assumed—she fervently hoped—that the cancer had been caught in time, but still she hated to think of what the Donaldsons must be going through. And then another part of her grieved once again for Dave. Seeing him had reminded her of how he'd stood on his porch that morning watching her drive away, his frayed, patched gardening pants buckling at the knees in an elderly manner. She missed him very much. She tried never to allow herself to know how much.

She wrote Bitsy a note, expressing her concern and offering any help that was needed. *I am sending you my best thoughts,* she wrote, wishing for the thousandth time that she were religious and could volunteer her prayers. *I hope you will not hesitate to call on me.* She debated a moment before she signed it. *Sincerely? Yours very truly?* In the end she settled on *Affectionately,* because Bitsy might have her faults but at least they were well-meaning faults. She was a good-hearted, generous woman, and Maryam felt the same sympathy for her that she would feel for an old friend.

Her world had become very peaceful since the breakup. Well, it had been peaceful before, too, but somehow her brief venture into a livelier, more engaged way of life made her appreciate the blessed orderliness of her daily routine. She awoke before dawn, when the sky was still a pearly white and the birds were barely stirring. One of the cardinals on her block had a habit of omitting the second note of his call and repeating just the first in a flinty, bright staccato. "*Vite! Vite! Vite!*" he seemed to be saying, like an overeager Frenchman. A jet plane crossed the highest windowpanes perfectly level, perfectly silent, and sometimes a wan, translucent moon still hung behind the neighbors' maple tree.

She lay gathering her thoughts, absently stroking the cat, who always slept in the crook of her arm, until the young doctor down the street started his noisy car and set off for morning rounds. That was the signal for her to get up. How creaky she was becoming! Every joint had to learn to bend all over again each morning, it seemed.

By the time she came back from her shower, the sun had risen and more of the neighborhood was awake. The new puppy exploded from the house next door, yapping excitedly. A baby started crying. Several cars swished past. You could tell what time it was on this street just by counting the cars and hearing how fast they were going.

She dressed with care, eyeliner and all; she was not a bathrobe kind of woman. She made her bed and collected her water tumbler and the book she had fallen asleep with, and only then did she head downstairs, trailed by the cat, who liked to twine between her feet.

Tea. Toasted pita bread. A slice of feta cheese. While the tea was steeping she arranged her silver on a woven-straw place mat. She refilled Moosh's water bowl and checked his supply of kibble. She went out front for the newspaper, barely glancing at the headlines before laying it aside and sitting down to breakfast. (She preferred to concentrate on one thing at a time.) The tea was fresh and hot and bracing. The feta was Bulgarian, creamy and not too salty. Her chair was placed to catch the sunshine, which gilded the skin on her arms and felt like warm varnish on her head.

What a small, small life she lived! She had one grown son, one daughter-in-law, one grandchild, and three close friends. Her work was pleasantly predictable. Her house hadn't changed in decades. Next January she would be sixty-five years old—not ancient, but even so, she couldn't hope for her world to grow anything but narrower from now on. She found this thought comforting rather than distressing.

Last week she'd noticed an obituary for a seventy-eight-year-old woman in Lutherville. *Mrs. Cotton enjoyed gardening and sewing,* she had read. *Family members say she hardly ever wore the same outfit twice.*

No doubt as a girl Mrs. Cotton had envisioned something more dramatic, but still, it didn't sound like such a bad existence to Maryam.

If it was a Wednesday—the one day she worked, in the summer—she would set off for Julia Jessup shortly after nine, when the rush-hour traffic had finished. She would greet the janitor, open the mail, see to the small bit of paperwork. The smell of waxed floors made her feel virtuous, as if she were the one who had waxed them, and she drew a sense of accomplishment from discarding the past week's calendar pages. The school without its children—their "Hi, Mrs. Yaz! Morning, Mrs. Yaz!"—gave her a gentle twinge of nostalgia. On the bulletin board, an unclaimed mitten from last winter seemed to be shouting with life.

If it was not a Wednesday, she would take the newspaper into the sun porch after clearing away her breakfast things. She read desultorily—bad news, more bad news, more to shake her head at and turn the page. Then she placed the paper in the recycling bag underneath the sink and went to weed her flowerbeds, or paid some bills at the desk in Sami's old room, or busied herself with some household task. Very rarely did she go out in public during the morning. Going out was work. It required conversation. It raised the possibility of mistakes.

She had noticed that as she grew older, speaking English took more effort. She might ask for "es-stamps" instead of stamps, or mix up her "he's" and "she's," realizing it only when she saw a look of confusion cross someone's face. And then she would feel exhausted. Oh, what *difference* did it make? she would wonder. So unnecessary, for a language to specify the sexes! Why should she have to bother with this?

She was lonelier in public than she was at home, to be honest.

Before lunch she generally took a long walk, traveling the same route every day and smiling at the same neighbors and dogs and babies, noticing a new sapling here, a change of house color there. Summer was the time to call in the painters and the nursery crews. Workmen swarmed over the neighborhood as industriously as ants. She encountered her favorite plumber clanking through the tools in his panel truck.

It was hot now, but she liked being hot. She felt she moved more smoothly in heat. The glaze of sweat on her face took her back to airless nights in Tehran, when she and her family slept on mattresses dragged up to the rooftop and you could look across the city and see all the other families arranging their mattresses on *their* rooftops, as if every house had split open to show the lives going on inside. And then at dawn the call to prayer would float them all up from their sleep.

It wasn't that she wished to be back there, exactly (so much about that unprivate way of life had gone against her grain, even then), but she wouldn't have minded hearing once more that distant cry from the minaret.

She went home and rinsed her face in cool water and fixed herself a light lunch. Made a few phone calls. Looked at her mail. Sometimes Ziba stopped by with Susan. Or sometimes she just left Susan off while she ran errands; Maryam liked those days best. You could amuse a child more easily if no grownups were around. She would let Susan play with her jewelry box, sifting gold chains and clusters of turquoises through her fingers. She would show her the photo albums. "This is my maternal great-uncle, Amir Ahmad. The baby on his knee is his seventh son. It was unusual in those days for a man to be seen holding a baby. He must have been an interesting person." She studied his face—stern and square-bearded, topped by a heavy black turban, giving nothing away. She had only the faintest memory of him. "And this is my father, Sadredin. He died when I was four. He would be your great-grandpa." But would he? The words sounded untruthful the instant they slipped from her mouth. Close though she felt to Susan—as close as any grandmother could possibly feel—she had trouble imagining the slightest link between the relatives back home and this little Asian fairy child with her straight black hair, her exotic black eyes, her skin as pale and opaque and textureless as bone.

On several occasions Jin-Ho came along, and twice Xiu-Mei too. Ziba looked after them quite a bit during the month of July, because Bitsy's chemotherapy made her want to nap all the time. But she was doing very well, Ziba reported. She said, "Are you sure you don't mind, Mari-june? I promise I won't be gone long." Maryam said, "Of course I don't mind," and meant it. For one thing, this was a way of helping Bitsy. And then two or three children could entertain each other. All Maryam did was serve them refreshments at some point during the visit—homemade cookies or brownies and apple-juice "tea" in tiny enamelware cups.

Jin-Ho was now a head and a half taller than Susan, and she had asked to be called "Jo," although none of them could remember to do it. Xiu-Mei was still small and frail but feisty, with a mind of her own. She wore hand-me-downs from both Jin-Ho and Susan; it was strange to see Susan's faded playsuits resurrected, coupled with Jin-Ho's old sandals and a pacifier strung on a length of elastic around her neck.

In the late afternoon, on her own again, Maryam might finally venture forth for whatever shopping she needed to do. Then she would fix a complete and serious dinner, even if she was the only one eating it. Often, though, her friends would come over. Or else she would go to one of their houses. The four of them were all excellent cooks. Each had a different cuisine: Turkish, Greek, French, and Maryam's own Iranian. It was no wonder they ate less and less frequently at restaurants.

Dressing for an evening with her friends, Maryam felt none of the anxiety she used to feel dressing for social events in the old days. Back then she might change outfits several times before deciding what to wear, and she used to prepare a mental list of conversational gambits. It wasn't just age that made the difference (although that helped, no doubt); it was more that she had winnowed out the people she wasn't at ease with. No longer did she accept invitations to those meaningless, superficial parties she and Kiyan had endured. Her friends occasionally questioned this. Or Danielle did, at least. Danielle was forever seeking new acquaintances and new experiences. But Maryam said, "Why should I bother? This is one good thing about getting old: I know what I like and what I don't like."

Whenever Danielle heard the word "old," she would wrinkle her nose in distaste. But the other two women nodded. They knew what Maryam meant.

They talked often about aging. They talked about where the world was headed; they talked about books and movies and plays and (in Danielle's case) men. Surprisingly little was said about children or grandchildren, unless they happened to be dealing with some specific crisis. But almost always the subject of Americans came up, in an amused and marveling tone. They never tired of discussing Americans.

Whether Maryam spent her evening in or out, she was in bed by ten as a rule. She read until her eyelids grew heavy—two or three hours, sometimes—and then she turned off her lamp and slid further under the covers and curled one arm around Moosh. Outside her window the neighborhood mockingbird sang alone in the sycamore, and she would fall asleep feeling thankful for the tallness of her trees, which let birdsong fall from such a great height and were wonderful too during summer rains, when they gave off a steady murmur that sounded to her like "Aah. Aah."

One morning she answered her phone and a woman said, "Maryam?"

It was only from her pronunciation that Maryam knew it was Bitsy. (Bitsy always broadened both the *a*'s in Maryam's name to a comical degree, evidently believing that foreign *a*'s couldn't be flat.) Her voice was faint and slightly hoarse, as if she were getting over a cough. In fact she did cough, just then.

Maryam said, "Bitsy? How are you?"

"I'm fine," Bitsy told her. "The treatments have been no fun, but I'm finished with them now and the doctors are very pleased." Then she coughed again and said, "Sorry, a little side effect. Nothing that worries them. Anyhow: thanks for your note. I should have written back long ago."

"No, you should *not* have written back. Or only if you had thought of something for me to do."

"But just to thank you for getting in touch, I mean. I was so happy to hear from you! I've really missed you; all of us have. We're looking forward to seeing you at Sami and Ziba's party."

Maryam said, "Oh, the . . . Arrival Party."

"Dad mentioned you might be coming."

"Well, I did say I'd think about it," Maryam said. "But this summer is so complicated; I'm not quite sure if—"

"It would be like old times!" Bitsy said, so forcefully that she coughed again. "It didn't feel the same last year. Even Xiu-Mei noticed. She said, 'Where's Mari-june?' I hate to think that you might not be in our lives anymore."

Maryam said, "Why, thank you, Bitsy."

The excuses she'd been about to offer—New York, Farah's visit—suddenly seemed transparent. Instead, she told the truth. "I'm afraid it might be awkward, though."

"Awkward! Nonsense. We're all grownups."

This argument came as a disappointment; Maryam wasn't sure why. What had she wanted Bitsy to say? A pinch of injury tightened her chest. She said, "I know your father feels I didn't handle things very well."

"Now, is that in any way relevant to this discussion? We're talking about a simple little, normal little family get-together," Bitsy said. "Shoot, we should just shanghai you."

Shanghai. As a verb, it was unfamiliar. Maybe it meant something like "lynch." Maryam said, "Yes, perhaps you should," in a tone that must have sounded more bitter than she had intended, because Bitsy said, "Well, forgive me, Maryam. I'm a meddlesome person; I realize that."

Which she was, in fact. But Maryam said, "Oh, no, Bitsy, you're very kind. You were very sweet to call." And then, trying to match Bitsy's energy, "But you haven't told me what I can do for you! Please, give me a task."

"Not a thing, thanks," Bitsy said. "I'm getting stronger every day. You'd be amazed. Wait till you see me at the Arrival Party."

That was Bitsy for you. She always had to have the last word, Maryam thought as she hung up.

"How will you tell your family?" he'd asked her. "They were so happy for us. How will you explain throwing everything away?"

She said, "I've already told them. I've just come from there."

The look on his face made her wish she'd kept this to herself. "You told them before you told me?" he said.

"Well, yes."

"How could you *do* that, Maryam?"

"I don't know," she said flatly. She no longer had the strength to defend herself. "I just did, that's all," she said. "It's done."

Now, though, it crossed her mind to wonder the same thing. Why *had* she told them first? What an odd way to proceed!

Had some tiny part of her hoped that Sami and Ziba would talk her out of it?

And, oh, if only, only she hadn't admitted that she'd told them, would he perhaps have agreed that they could go on seeing each other?

She had fallen in love with him while she was looking the other way, you might say. It had come as a total surprise. First he was just another hapless man desperate for a helpmate—a likable man, but what was that to her? Even after they had started spending time together, she didn't feel, oh, related to him, as she'd felt related to Kiyan. "Really, Dave," she had told him once, "we have nothing in common. We have no common ground. Why, I can't begin to imagine what your childhood might have been like."

"Childhood?" he'd said. "Where did *that* come from? What difference does my childhood make? It's what we've boiled down to in the end that really matters—when we're left with just the dregs and the essence."

Yes, he could be persuasive, all right. When he said such things, she could see his point. But only while he was saying them.

She had left for Vermont that summer with a sense that she was escaping. Somehow, against her better instincts, she had started seeing too much of him, and here was her chance to regain some distance. She had greeted Farah with such a flood of Farsi that Farah had laughed at her. "Maryam! Slow down! I can't understand you! Maryam, are you speaking with an accent?"

Was she speaking with an accent? In her own language? What was her own language, anyhow? Did she even have one, at this point?

She had slowed down. She had settled once again into Farah's molasses-like tempo. Lolling on a recliner in the pine-shaded backyard, she had cast a sideways glance at William and wondered how Farah had ever adjusted to someone so outlandish. That summer he'd been perfecting a pet-stain-removal product that he felt sure would make him millions. "This started life as an extra-fast-drying correction fluid for typists," he had confided to Maryam. "I thought it up a few years back. D'elite, I was going to call it—D apostrophe elite; get it? But then just my luck, typewriters went kaboom; so I've invented this new use for it. And here's the best part: without even a name change! D'elite! Don't you love it? Plus, people who don't know any better could go on and say 'Delight' with no real harm done."

And meanwhile Farah, reclining next to her, was murmuring away in Farsi as if William hadn't spoken. "Why is it that older women in this country cut their hair to resemble monks? Why do the women of the upper classes here never wear enough makeup?"

Like two small children, they had competed for Maryam's attention; and Maryam, to her own surprise, found herself favoring William—his enthusiasm, his innocence, his endearing optimism. There was a world-weariness to Farah that could be dampening, at times. Maryam smiled at William and thought suddenly of Dave. Dave in fact was nothing like William, certainly not so extreme or eccentric; but even so . . .

"I don't know why truly good people always make me sad," Kiyan had told her once. She understood now what he had meant.

She had written Dave during that Vermont trip to tell him that she missed him. Well, she had put it more subtly than that. *(I am having a very nice time here, but I think of you constantly and wonder what you are doing.)* Still, she knew the effect it would have. Slipping the letter through the mailbox slot, she had held on to it for a long, indecisive moment before she let it fall. And then she'd thought, What have I done? and half wished for some way to retrieve it.

When Dave met her return plane, though, he had behaved no differently. Clearly he was pleased to see her, but he didn't refer to her letter or act as if things had changed. "Enjoy your visit?" he had asked. "Catch up on all the family gossip?" She had been mortified. How conceited of her to believe that what she had written would matter to him! She had treated him coolly, and sent him home early. She had tossed and turned all night mourning what she had seen to be her very last chance at love. Forever after she would be one of those resolutely cheerful widows carrying on alone.

Oh, the agonizing back-and-forth of romance! The advances and retreats, the secret wounds, the strategic withdrawals!

Wasn't the real culture clash the one between the two sexes?

The next day he had arrived on her doorstep in the middle of her lunch. "I got your letter," he'd told her.

"My letter?"

"They delivered it just ten minutes ago. You beat it home."

"Oh!"

"Maryam, you thought about me constantly? You missed me?"

Then even before she could answer he had gathered her up and covered her with kisses. "You missed me!" he kept saying. "You love me!" and she was laughing and returning his kisses and fighting for breath all at once.

It was nothing like her marriage. This time around, she proceeded knowing that people died; that everything had an end; that even though she and Dave were spending every day together and every night, the moment would come when she would say, "Tomorrow it will be two years since I last set eyes on him." Or else he would say it of her. They were letting themselves in for more than any young couple could possibly envision, and both of them were conscious of that.

This made them less likely to quarrel or take umbrage. They wasted little time on petty irritations. She was tolerant of his clutter and his insistence on reading the paper aloud. ("Listen to this: '"I have a three-million-dollar home," the boxer boasted to one interviewer, "and sheets with a ten-thousand thread count."' Ten thousand threads! Is that possible?") He, for his part, learned that she could be revived by a bowl of plain white rice when she was feeling fluey or tired; and once when Moosh disappeared for two days he had printed up dozens of posters reading LOST and REWARD and CHILD GRIEVING. "Child grieving?" she had asked. "What are you talking about? There's no child here."

But he had said, "*You* are. You are the child." And he'd taken her face between his hands and kissed the top of her head.

And he'd been right.

⸎

She used to fantasize about traveling on a time machine to eras long, long ago. To prehistory, for instance, where she could witness how language had developed. Or to Jesus's time; what had *that* all been about? Now, though, she would choose a much more recent period. She would like to board a BOAC plane again to visit her mother, crossing the tarmac on clicking heels because in those days, women always did wear heels for plane trips, and settling in one of the two-by-two seats and smiling at the stewardesses in their aerodynamic-looking uniforms. She would like to dine with Kiyan in Johnny Unitas's old Golden Arm Restaurant on York Road. (She would order the famous shrimp salad and the crusty fried eggplant slices, and the waitress would be singing "Strangers in the Night" to herself as she served them.)

Then she remembered how whenever she and Kiyan ate out, Kiyan would study the menu too long before he finally made his selection, and after their food arrived he would look at his meal, look at hers, look at his again and say, "Poor me!" She always seethed when he did that.

Or that time she'd dumped the crock of yogurt on his plate: she'd spent all afternoon making his favorite meal, *baghali polo*, with the lima beans whose skins she'd had to pop off one by one till her fingertips grew puckered and waterlogged; and when she'd set the platter before him he had said, "No yogurt to put on top, I see."

A forgivable remark, but the wrong one for the moment, and that was why the crock of yogurt had ended up where it did.

She saw her past self as grudging, miserly. She should have told him, "Here, take my shrimp salad if you like it better." She should have said, "Yogurt? Of course. I'll fetch it." But at the time she had resented his never-ending neediness. It hadn't yet occurred to her that a life where no one needed her would be a weak, dim, pathetic life.

Wasn't that what had drawn her to Dave? It had been so clear that she could make him happy. All it took was a "yes"; how long since she'd had that power? *Seduced by Need,* she thought, picturing it as the flame-edged title on a lurid romance comic book. In the end, that had been her downfall: the wish to feel needed.

Fool.

For the sake of feeling needed she had linked herself to a man so inappropriate that she might as well have fished his name out of a hat. An *American* man, naive and complacent and oblivious, convinced that his way was the only way and that he had every right to rearrange her life. She had melted the instant he said, "Come in," even though she knew full well that inclusion was only a myth. And why? Because she had believed that she could make a difference in his life.

"How could you *do* that, Maryam?" he had asked. And, "How will you explain throwing everything away?"

Sometimes lately she felt as if she had emigrated all over again. Once more she had left her past self behind, moved to an alien land, and lost any hope of returning.

The reason Farah was visiting Maryam this year, instead of Maryam's visiting her, was that William had a plan to refinish all their floors and he said it would be easier if Farah was out of the way. But her visit didn't really coincide with the Arrival Party; that had just been an alibi. She arrived on a Friday afternoon at the end of July, bringing so many clothes that you would think she was staying a month rather than a weekend. Her hostess gift was a painted tin box filled with saffron. (Living in rural Vermont, she had no inkling that saffron could be found nowadays in most supermarkets.) "I ordered it off the Internet," she said. "I have become an Internet wizard! You should see me with my mouse, click-click!" She had also brought an assortment of little cardboard squares streaked to resemble wood in different shades of brown or yellow. "What do you think, Mari-june? Which finish should we choose for our floors? I say this one; William says that one."

To Maryam there was little difference, but she said, "Yours is nice."

"I knew you would agree! I'll call William tonight and tell him." Then she said, "Oh, Maryam, American men can do anything. Unstop a toilet, replace a light switch . . . Well. But *you* know that." She looked flustered, suddenly, and Maryam couldn't think why until Farah asked, "Do you ever hear from him?"

"From . . . ? Oh. From Dave," Maryam said. "No."

"Well, you must have had your reasons," Farah told her forbearingly. "Remember back home: Aunt Nava? How everybody urged her to marry the man her father chose for her? And she said no, no, no, and her parents were at their wits' end, but of course they couldn't force her. So one night she's lying in bed; her father knocks on her door; 'Nava-june. Are you awake? Nava, june-am,' he says . . ."

Oh, those old, old stories, repeated with all the proper inflections, lowered tones, dramatic pauses! Maryam found herself relaxing and drifting as if to music.

But the visit was not relaxing in general. It never was, in Maryam's experience, because Farah was so intent on catching up with all her acquaintances. First they had to fix a dinner for Sami and Ziba and Susan, and Farah had to make a big fuss over Susan and display the many gifts she had brought her. This was fine with Maryam; her own family wasn't work, after all. But next they had to drive to Washington to visit Ziba's parents, who adored Farah (so much more fun than Maryam, they no doubt felt) and never failed to throw a party for her when she came. A *huge* party, overflowing with caviar and iced vodka, at which Farah held forth like a queen. She sparkled and she trilled her jeweled fingers and she laughed with her head flung back. Graciously, she tried to make Maryam feel a part of things. "You all know Maryam, yes? My favorite cousin! We were girls together." Maryam would move forward, smiling stiffly, offering her hand; but she was not a member here. As soon as possible she retreated to a quiet corner, where she found Sami reading Susan a coffee-table book about Persepolis. (He was not a member either, although Ziba was happily circulating among the younger guests down in the rec room.)

"If we lived in Iran," Maryam told Sami, "every night would be like this."

Sami glanced up at her and said, "Even now?"

Maryam said, "Well . . ." She wasn't sure, as a matter of fact. She said, "When I was a girl, how I hated it all! At any of the family parties, I'd be sitting where you are this minute."

She wondered if there was a gene for that—for holding oneself back, resisting the communal merriment. It had never before occurred to her that she had passed this trait on to Sami.

On Farah's last day, a Sunday, they went shopping at a giant mall and Farah fell in love with a discount store that catered to teenage girls. She bought a multitude of billowy rayon pants that looked extravagant and sophisticated when she tried them on—not discount at all, not teenage. Then they had lunch in the food court. "And what did *you* buy? Nothing," Farah said in a fond, scolding tone. "I tell you, Maryam-jon: There are two kinds of people in this world. One kind goes out shopping and comes back with way too much and says, 'Oh-oh, I overbought.' And the other comes back with empty hands and says, 'Oh, dear, I wish I'd bought such-and-such.'"

Maryam had to laugh at that. It was true that she often saw something she wanted but the transaction seemed too complex; it required too much energy, and so she passed it up and then later she was sorry.

In the afternoon they cooked together, preparing several of the Iranian dishes that had proved most successful with foreigners, and that evening Maryam's three women friends came to dinner. They knew Farah from past visits; so it was a comfortable occasion. Maryam traveled between kitchen and dining room while Farah kept the others amused with a description of the Hakimis' party. "Really it was two parties, the old people's and the young people's," she said. Maryam instantly understood what she meant, although she hadn't considered it at the time. "The old ones dressed up and the young ones wore jeans. The old ones listened to Googoosh on the sound system upstairs while the young ones danced to something bang-bang-bang playing downstairs in the rec room."

Then she said, "They're losing their culture, the young ones. I see this everywhere. They pay their traditional New Year's visits but they're not sure what they're supposed to be doing once they get there. They go through all the motions but they keep looking at everyone else to see if they've got it right. They *try* to join in but they don't know how. Isn't that true, Maryam? Don't you agree?"

Maryam's guests turned to her, waiting for her to answer. And although she could have simply said, "Yes," and let the moment pass, she had a sudden guilty feeling, as if she were an impostor. What right did she have to speak? She was outside the culture herself. She had always been outside it. Somehow, for no reason she could name, she had never felt at home in her own country or anywhere else, which was probably why her three best friends were foreigners. Kari, Danielle, and Calista: outsiders every one, born that way themselves.

"Don't you agree, Mari-june?" Farah was asking again, and Maryam stood in the kitchen doorway with a salad bowl in her hands and wondered if every decision she had ever made had been geared toward preserving her outsiderness.

Ziba told Maryam that for this year's Arrival Party, she wanted to serve something different. "All those Iranian dishes are getting a little old," she said. "I was thinking maybe sushi."

"Sushi?" Maryam repeated. For a moment, she thought she had heard wrong.

"I could order it from that place in Towson that delivers."

Maryam said, "Ah. Well, but—"

"For my parents and my brothers I'd get California rolls. You can be sure they won't eat raw fish."

"But California rolls have crabmeat," Maryam said.

"Oh, nobody observes those old restrictions anymore. Last Christmas, Hassan's wife served lobster."

And the Donaldsons? Maryam wanted to ask. The Donaldsons would be devastated! No authentic Middle Eastern cuisine!

But all she said to Ziba was, "Let me know what I can bring."

"A bottle of sake would be nice," Ziba said.

Maryam laughed, but Ziba didn't. Evidently she was serious.

Maryam did plan to attend this year. She had given herself a talking-to. It was cowardly of her, she realized, not to have gone to last year's party. Apparently she still cared too much about other people's opinions. At this age, she should be able to say, "Oh, so *what* if things would be awkward?"

She chose ahead what to wear, perhaps giving too much thought to it, and she consulted the man at the liquor store about which brand of sake to buy. The night before the party, she slept poorly. In fact she would have said that she didn't sleep at all, except that at one point she had a dream and so she must have drifted off at least for a moment. She dreamed she was back in primary school and her class was singing the chicken song. *"Jig, jig, jujehayam,"* they sang, in cute little ducklike voices; and Dave was looking on and reproachfully shaking his head, Dave the same age he was now, with his gray curls and his drooping eyelids. "Child grieving, Maryam," he said, and she woke annoyed with herself for dreaming a dream so obvious. Her clock radio read 3:46. After she'd lain there watching it change to four, four-thirty, and five, she got up.

Probably her restless night was the reason she passed the morning in such a fog. It was a Sunday, unusually cool and pleasant for August, and she should have worked in her garden but instead she lingered over the newspapers. After that she finished reading a novel she had started the evening before, even though she had trouble remembering the beginning and she wasn't all that interested in the end. Then all at once it seemed to be twelve-thirty. How had that happened? The Arrival Party was scheduled for one o'clock. She rose and collected her newspapers and went upstairs to change.

Ziba would be setting out the sushi trays now and the chopsticks she had bought. Her brothers would be stealing pistachios from the sheet of baklava bristling with American flags, and she would shoo them away and call for her sisters-in-law to come take charge of their husbands. Everyone would be milling about, jabbering half in English and half in Farsi, sometimes confusing the two, so that they would accidentally address Susan in the wrong language.

Such a noisy bunch, Iranians could be! More than once Dave

had pointed out that they were a whole lot noisier than the Donaldsons. Maryam would have to concede his point, but still it seemed to her that the Donaldsons were . . . oh, more self-vaunting, self-advertising. They seemed to feel that *their* occasions—their anniversaries, birthdays, even their leaf-rakings—had such cataclysmic importance that naturally the entire world was longing to celebrate with them. Yes, that was what she objected to: their assumption that they had the right to an unfair share of the universe.

"Remember the night the girls arrived?" she had once asked Dave. "Your family filled the whole airport! Ours was squeezed into a corner." She had taken care to speak lightly. This was an amicable discussion, after all—a theoretical discussion; not a quarrel. And yet underneath she had been aware of a little flare of resentment. "And when Xiu-Mei came: the same thing again. That time, our two families met the plane together, but I felt as if we were . . . borrowing your festivity. Clinging to the edges of it."

He hadn't understood. She could see that. He really hadn't understood what she was talking about.

She went to the closet for the dress she had chosen—a sleeveless black linen, very plain. Instead of putting it on, though, she draped it over the back of a chair. Then she slipped off her shoes and stretched out on her bed, laying one arm across her eyes, which felt hot and tired and achy.

The Donaldsons would be dressing their daughters in something ethnic. Or they would be dressing Xiu-Mei, at least. Jin-Ho ("Jo") might resist. Bitsy would be complaining about "She'll Be Coming Round the Mountain," although probably she had given up trying to find an alternative. "Aw, hon," Brad would be saying, "don't get in such a swivet. Let the kids have their song."

Last week in Tuxedo Pharmacy, Maryam had noticed a couple cruising the greeting-card aisle and she had wondered why they seemed so familiar. Then she thought, Oh! It was the tall young man who'd stepped off the jetway the night of the girls' arrival, and the young woman who had been waiting for him. Only now they had two children—a handsome little brown-eyed boy was shepherding his ponytailed sister down the aisle ahead of them—and the young woman carried one of those motherly knapsacks bulging with diapers and sippy cups. They would never guess they had been captured on a videotape that was shown to a crowd of strangers every August in perpetuity.

Something was ringing. Maryam thought first it was her doorbell and next she thought it was her oven timer; that was how deeply asleep she was. She actually reached for the knob on her stove before she caught her mistake. She opened her eyes and rose up on one elbow to look at the clock: 1:35.

The Arrival Party.

It was her telephone that was ringing. She lifted the receiver. "Hello?" she said, trying to sound wide awake.

"Mom?"

"Oh, Sami, I'm so—has the party already begun? I'm so sorry! I must have fallen asleep!"

"Yes, well," he said drily, "the coast is clear now, you might care to know."

"What?"

"The Donaldsons have left. You're free to come over now if you like."

"They've left?" she said. She looked again at the clock. "They've already left the party? What happened?"

"Beats me," Sami said. Now she could detect a note of injury in his voice, or perhaps she was imagining it. "They were out in the living room with the others," he said. "Zee was in the dining room doing something last-minute; I was getting ice in the kitchen. Then Zee comes into the kitchen and says, 'Where have the Donaldsons got to? They're gone,' she says, 'every last one of them! I went to call people to the table and it was only *my* family; not theirs. I asked where they were and everyone said, "Oh! Aren't they out there with you?" But they're not anywhere,' she tells me. 'They're gone!' "

"Well, did . . . Could someone have said something that offended them, do you think?"

"Not that anyone knows of. And what would that have been, anyhow?" Sami asked.

Maryam felt her lips start to twitch. "Maybe they got upset when they heard you were serving sushi," she said.

"This is not funny, Mom," Sami said. "Do you suppose they felt it was too big a crowd? There's an awful lot of Hakimis here this year, I have to admit."

It was only then Maryam noticed the babble of Farsi in the background. She said, "Well, I can't believe a little thing like that would faze the Donaldsons. Oh, I hope it wasn't some issue with Bitsy—that she started feeling ill."

"Ziba's in a state, as you might imagine," he said. "She telephoned them right away, but there was no answer. They may be *refusing* to answer; that's what worries her. Although if it was Bitsy; if she had to go to the emergency room . . . But anyhow, Mom, you can come over now. It's just us and the Hakimis. Ziba felt really bad when she saw you weren't going to show up."

"Oh, Sami, I never meant not to show up! I'm on my way right now. I'll see you in a few minutes."

She replaced the receiver, but the party sounds seemed to hang on in her ears—the clink of glasses and the Hakimi men's booming voices, the beautiful roundness of vowels in Farsi.

She rose and took off her blouse and her slacks, lifted the black linen dress from the chair and drew it over her head. Still zipping the side zipper, she stepped into her shoes. She went to the bureau for her hairbrush, passing the open window, where she happened to notice Brad Donaldson down on her front walk.

He was holding Xiu-Mei in his arms, and he wore his usual summer outfit of stretched-out T-shirt and enormous, wrinkled Bermudas, his knees sweetly round like a toddler's. He was facing the house but just standing there. From the direction of his gaze, Maryam gathered that he must be looking toward someone on her porch. "Don't ring yet," he said clearly. "Wait for the rest of them." He sounded so close that Maryam took a reflexive step backward, although she was fairly certain she couldn't be seen.

Then a car pulled up, Dave's car, and parked behind the Donaldsons' car directly in front of her house. Two more cars slid into place behind his. The first belonged to Abe—his red Volvo. The second, a gray sedan, was so generic that not until Laura emerged from the passenger side could Maryam be sure it was Mac's. "Is she there?" Laura called.

"I'm waiting till everyone gets here," Bitsy answered in a low voice, and that was how Maryam knew it was Bitsy on her front porch.

The two cars parked behind Dave's spilled forth grownups and teenagers. Maryam had a blurred impression of sun-bleached hair and gauzy summer dresses and the glint of bangle bracelets. Jeannine was telling one of her girls—it was hard to say which—to spit out that gum this instant. Xiu-Mei was asking Brad to put her down but he wasn't listening. He had turned now to look at Dave's car, and gradually all of them turned, one by one, as they arrived next to Brad.

Brad called, "Dave?"

And Mac called, "Coming, Dad?"

Dave's car door opened slowly and he climbed out by degrees. He shut the door with a loose and inconclusive click. He bent to brush something from one trouser leg. He straightened and looked at the others.

"Okay, I'm ringing," Bitsy said, and Maryam heard her doorbell ring.

But she just stood there.

The doorbell rang again. A second later, the brass knocker clattered.

Bitsy called, "Maryam?"

Dave was trudging up the walk now, and the group in front of the house parted to let him pass through. From this angle, he seemed older. A patch of thinning hair could be seen on the top of his head.

"Call her name, Dad," Bitsy said.

He stopped and squared his shoulders. He said, "Maryam."

Maryam didn't answer.

Downstairs, the doorknob rattled loudly. For a moment it seemed that Bitsy had somehow managed to break in.

"It's us!" Bitsy called. "It's all of us! Maryam, are you there? Please open up. We've come to collect you for the party. We can't have the party without you. We need you! Let us in, Maryam."

In the silence that followed, the *"Vite! Vite!"* of the overeager cardinal chipped the air above their heads.

"She's not home," a small voice said sadly—Maryam's first indication that Jin-Ho must be standing on the porch with her mother.

The others were murmuring and debating. "Maybe . . . ," one said.

And, "See if . . ."

Then either Mac or Abe said something decisive that Maryam couldn't make out, and she bent closer to the window and saw a kind of shuffling motion in the group below—first one person and then another turning away, hesitating, then peeling off to leave. Brad was no longer holding Xiu-Mei, who was headed now for Dave. When she reached him she took his hand, and he looked down at her for a second as if trying to remember who she was before he, too, turned and began walking toward the street. Polly and Bridget had Jin-Ho between them. Deirdre twirled a little purse by its pink ribbon strap as she followed.

And then at long last here came Bitsy, catching up with Brad and taking hold of his arm. So frail, she seemed! In fact, she was leaning on him for support, and her tightly wrapped headscarf gave her skull a shrunken look.

Maryam thought of Bitsy's hopefulness, her wholeheartedness, her manufactured "traditions" that seemed brave now rather than silly. The sudden wrench to her heart made her wonder if it might be Bitsy she loved. Or maybe it was all of them.

She spun away from the window. She left the bedroom. She crossed the hall. By the time she reached the stairs, she was running. She ran down the stairs; she ran to the door. She burst out of the house crying, "Stop!"

"Wait!" she called. "Don't go!"

"Wait for me!" she called.

They stopped. They turned. They looked up at her and they started smiling, and they waited for her to join them.

A NOTE ABOUT THE AUTHOR

Anne Tyler was born in Minneapolis, Minnesota, in 1941 and grew up in Raleigh, North Carolina. She graduated at nineteen from Duke University, and went on to do graduate work in Russian studies at Columbia University. This is Anne Tyler's seventeenth novel; her eleventh, *Breathing Lessons,* was awarded the Pulitzer Prize in 1988. She is a member of the American Academy of Arts and Letters. She lives in Baltimore, Maryland.

A NOTE ON THE TYPE

This book was set in Caledonia, originally a Linotype face designed by W. A. Dwiggins (1880–1956). It belongs to the family of printing types called "modern face" by printers—a term used to mark the change in style of the type letters that occurred around 1800. Caledonia borders on the general design of Scotch Roman but it is more freely drawn than that letter.

Composed by Stratford Publishing Services,
Brattleboro, Vermont
Printed and bound by Berryville Graphics,
Berryville, Virginia
Designed by Anthea Lingeman